Literacies Across Media

Young people today are learning about reading, viewing and interacting with technology in times of rapid transformation. *Literacies Across Media* presents a longitudinal study of sixteen children and adolescents, aged between 10 and 14, and explores their reactions to changing media technologies over a period of eighteen months.

The study reported in this book, conducted just as the century turned and first published in 2002, offers insights into the behaviours of articulate young people as they encounter a range of text formats, including novels, a picture book, video and DVD, a CD-ROM picture book and a CD-ROM encyclopedia, computer games, and an electronic book. This new edition:

- Re-visits many theoretical insights in terms of continuing developments in technological uptake among young people
- Includes an afterword at the end of each chapter addressing historical and national variations in media use
- Illustrates the conclusions about the significance of play with a new case study of media change in particular local circumstances.

Literacies Across Media has much to offer to teachers, librarians and researchers, in terms of developing a better understanding of how young people move between books and other media, and how they approach new forms of technology. The book will also appeal to professors and students of education and library and information studies.

Margaret Mackey is Professor at the School of Library and Information Studies, University of Alberta, Canada.

Literacies Across Media

Playing the text
2nd Edition

Margaret Mackey

LONDON AND NEW YORK

First published 2002 by Routledge
Second edition published 2007 by Routledge
2 Park Square, Milton Park, Abingdon, Oxon OX14 4RN

Simultaneously published in the USA and Canada
by Routledge
29 West 35th Street, New York, NY 10001

Routledge is an imprint of the Taylor & Francis Group, an informa business

© 2002, 2007 Margaret Mackey

Typeset in Times New Roman by
Keystroke, 28 High Street, Tettenhall, Wolverhampton
Printed and bound in Great Britain by
TJ International Ltd, Padstow, Cornwall

British Library Cataloguing in Publication Data
A catalogue record for this book is available from the British Library

Library of Congress Cataloging in Publication Data
Mackey, Margaret.
    Literacies across media : playing the text / Margaret Mackey. – 2nd ed.
      p. cm.
    Includes bibliographical references and index.
    1. Literacy–Social aspects. 2. Media literacy. 3. Technological literacy.
4. Children–Effect of technological innovations on. I. Title.
    LC149.M226 2006
    302.23–dc22   2006025815

ISBN10: 0–415–40746–X (hbk)
ISBN10: 0–415–40747–8 (pbk)
ISBN10: 0–203–96460–8 (ebk)

ISBN13: 978–0–415–40746–5 (hbk)
ISBN10: 978–0–415–40747–2 (pbk)
ISBN10: 978–0–203–96460–6 (ebk)

Contents

Acknowledgements

Many people helped me as I worked on this book, but readers will not get very far into the early chapters without realizing that my greatest debt is to the young people who participated in the project. Without exception they were extremely friendly, impressively intelligent, unfailingly helpful and always fascinating. The cooperating schools also lived up to that label in the fullest sense; administrators and teachers smoothed my way at every opportunity. My only regret is that I cannot name them all in order to thank them properly. I hope they will accept my profound gratitude on an anonymous basis.

Six graduate students worked on particular aspects of this project over a three-year period: Jennifer Branch, Kim Fraser, Mary-Lee Judah, Jyoti Mangat, Dan Mirau and Kristine van Leenan. Jenn and Dan, in particular, were central to the achievement of this project. They lugged quantities of equipment without complaint, played sample computer games with rather more alacrity, but, most of all, they contributed their own observations and reflections on all of the 1998–99 sessions. I will never think of this project without remembering what a good time we all had on our trips to the schools over that year.

Another crucial contributor to this project was Deidre Johnston, the world's most diligent transcriber. The conditions under which some of the tapes were made were far from ideal, and Deidre took extraordinary steps to ensure that as little as possible was lost to acoustic problems. Anyone who has ever recorded the dialogue accompanying a noisy computer game played in a room with a gurgling aquarium and then expected to read the results in a usable transcript will know the scale of my obligation to her.

My colleagues in the School of Library and Information Studies and the Faculty of Education at the University of Alberta also played a substantial role in helping me to make this book the best I can manage. Many people helped in various ways, and Jill McClay, Ingrid Johnston and Anna Altmann read many draft chapters and supplied excellent advice.

I also owe a more formal debt to the University of Alberta Education Faculty. In the autumn of 1999 they awarded me a Coutts-Clarke Fellowship, which freed me from teaching for a semester and enabled me to make a major start on my intimidating stack of transcripts.

This project would not have been possible without the generous support of the Social Sciences and Humanities Research Council of Canada. Research in the area of new technology is expensive as well as daunting, and SSHRC's support meant that I had to be troubled only with the daunting side of things. I am truly grateful.

Finally, as usual my family – Beth, Sarah and Terry – helped in both concrete and intangible ways too numerous to mention, and I thank them with all my heart.

Acknowledgements for the second edition

My obligation and my gratitude to the people and institutions mentioned in the first edition remain as significant as ever. As a consequence of writing the afterword to the final chapter of this second edition, I now also owe new debts to family, friends, colleagues and complete strangers in the city of Edmonton. A particular thank-you goes to two committed Oilers fans, Sarah and Beth Mackey. Jamie Burns and Dave Waldbillig also made helpful contributions to my thinking in this final section, as did Terry Mackey, Anna Altmann, Jill McClay and Ingrid Johnston. The responsibility for errors and misjudgement is, of course, mine alone.

On a more personal note, I would also like to thank Jenifer and Richard Allaway for their contribution, far beyond the call of duty, to our experience of the Oilers games.

Margaret Mackey
June 2006

Introduction to the second edition

This book reports on a longitudinal study of young people and their media use that took place between 1997 and 1999. It is a numerical accident that the project was completed at the end of the last century. No doubt the quirks of our psychological response to numbers makes these dates seem longer ago than they truly are. But there is no denying that the seven years that have elapsed since the completion of the last session have seen huge technological and cultural developments in a very short period of time.

It has not been possible to return to the participants of the study described in this book and gain updated insight into their media tastes and behaviours. As a result, in this new edition I have chosen not to re-open the main sections of the chapters, which remain as written in the 2002 edition (though Chapter 10 of the original version has been deleted to make room for new material). In this respect, the new edition presents the complexities of a longitudinal case study in unchanged form.

We are all aware, however, that there has been no shortage of more general evidence of rapid social, cultural and technological change. In this new edition I include samples of that evidence in separate afterwords appended to the end of each chapter. Although the details of our communicative lives are changing, I stand by the main conclusions of the original study; as an investigation of young people in times of cultural and technological flux, finding ways to interpret new media experiences, it still speaks to some of the main challenges of our times.

I was aware at the start of the project, as I collected diaries of daily media use from the participants, that I was gathering what might very soon seem like historical material. I truly had no idea just how much would change so quickly. A brief overview of some of the prominent changes over the past seven years is instructive. Napster has risen, fallen and mutated; DVDs have become ubiquitous; the electronic book has faded from the marketplace, though it may yet rise again; the Internet is a significant component of daily culture; the mobile phone offers more and more new features at remarkably brief intervals; and chatting, blogging, texting, and online posting of digital photographs and videos have all become normal and unremarkable forms of communication.

In the 2002 edition of this book, I raised the question of how generalizable my findings would seem after the lapse of only a few years. This new edition allows me to return to the topics I addressed in that edition and explore the robustness of my observations in the light of new developments.

I have not spoken to any of the participants in this study since we said goodbye in 1999. One of the drawbacks of anonymous participation in such projects is the artificial closure that follows the end of the study. In this new edition, instead of being able to establish how Janice, Jack and the others are faring today, I turn to alternative sources of evidence about young people and their relationship to information and communication technologies in the first decade of the twenty-first century, drawing on statistical studies for the most part, but turning to the vivifying potential of describing a single lively event in the final chapter.

The longitudinal nature of the original study gave me the opportunity to observe some forms of change in action and led me to consider an ecological model for exploring how today's young people direct their attention in a world of overwhelming story, information and noise. This new edition makes it possible for me to re-visit that ecology and look at how changes have affected what is now on offer to the kinds of young people represented in this book – children and adolescents who have grown up at home in a digital culture and attuned to the idea of constant change.

Chapter 1

Ecologies of literacy

Introduction

As we move from an industrial to a post-industrial information economy, one in which print literacy is not obsolete but certainly substantially transformed, then surely we need broader definitions of knowledge, literacy and pedagogy which will include study of the intertextuality of imageries, texts, icons and artefacts of new information economies, of media and of popular culture.

(Luke 1998: 27)

Today's children are growing up in the computer culture; all the rest of us are at best its naturalized citizens.

(Turkle 1995: 77)

A one-medium user is the new illiterate.

(Zingrone 2001: 237)

Snapshots in close-up

- Janice and Madeleine, both aged 14, are struggling with the confusing opacities of the computer game *Starship Titanic*. Although they have played other computer games, they have never encountered such a complex one as this, their experience being largely confined to the games enjoyed by their little brothers. Nothing makes sense to them, but they are enjoying themselves enormously, exaggerating their dramatic responses as catastrophe threatens to engulf their virtual starship.
- Gregory and Jack, also 14, are looking at an electronic book for the first time in their lives. Both boys are experienced users of different technologies, and they are perplexed by their negative response to the e-book. Clearly something visceral is bothering them and they struggle to express their disaffection, while affirming their enthusiasm for other forms of technology.
- Tom and Justin, aged 11, are exploring the background information that is part of the DVD version of the movie *Contact*. Having watched a scene where the space pod explodes, they are now viewing a description of 'how we made that scene', showing how different effects were layered into the final rendering.

Intrigued by the technical detail, they comment on how they now find it almost impossible *not* to watch out for particular elements in the composition.

Contemporary kids meet contemporary texts, and, while each of these particular experiences is a new one for the participants, the general experience of meeting novel kinds of text is not new. These young people have grown up in a world where they take textual developments and changes for granted. Their habits and preferences are established amidst a welter of new choices.

These six school students were part of a longitudinal study of young people and texts, which took place between 1997 and 1999. Sixteen students, aged between 10 and 14, explored texts in print, video, computer game, electronic book, DVD, CD-ROM encyclopedia and CD-ROM storybook. Sometimes singly, sometimes in pairs, they read, viewed, played and talked about these texts, encounters that were taped and sometimes played back to them for further discussion.

The focus of the study was on making a close-up record of ways in which young people process both new and familiar forms of text, but it was impossible to ignore the larger world of texts that surrounds all of us. Every time the students came into the room, they brought that outside world with them. They talked about current movie releases (*Men in Black* and *Titanic* at the start of the study, *The Phantom Menace* and *The Matrix* by the end) and their own tastes in reading and television programmes and Internet activities. They drew on previous experiences to make sense of the new formats on offer. They discussed school assignments and recreational preferences. They mentioned the impact of their siblings and friends on their textual activities in different media. For example, one 10-year-old girl owned *Where in the World is Carmen Sandiego?*, the CD-ROM game, and five different classmates mentioned playing that game on visits to her house. Little brothers and sisters often affected casual television viewing, and sometimes supplied reading material at moments of desperation. One boy spent every other weekend with his father in another city, and had two sources of domestic media materials and habits.

This book attempts to analyse the close-up record of the particular textual interpretive events that took place in this project, while simultaneously honouring the complexity of the larger background and exploring the social, pedagogical and theoretical implications of the ongoing revolution in media and technologies. It is a large agenda, but the significance of contemporary changes means it is an important one.

Changing definitions

The word 'reading' has always incorporated a number of complicated meanings, from the decoding of the alphabet, to the interpretation of complex instructions and descriptions, to the development of entranced absorption in a fictional universe. Not so long ago, however, the word 'reading' carried at least one permanent connotation: the turning of pages and the comprehension of print on paper.

Engagement with text, even if much of it is still alphabetic, is now a more complicated affair. In contemporary texts, words may be printed or sounded or both. Pictures, still or moving, may augment, contradict or replace words. In many cases, this communicative process continues to entail word recognition alongside the processing of information through other media. And we still very often call it reading.

A further complexity is added in texts where some form of reader control or interactivity is made possible, as in hypertext, web surfing or game playing. Here the blurring is between reading and writing, between receiving and directing the shape of the text. Readers have always interpreted, but in many of these contemporary texts a reader must make active decisions about which route to follow or which clue to pick up, and the text then changes accordingly. In many cases, simply noticing, remembering and connecting related aspects of a text are still necessary but now insufficient skills to bring to the task of text processing; a more dynamic intervention in shaping the text is also part of the process.

Take a complicated computer game, say *Starship Titanic* by Douglas Adams. To initiate this game you have to interpret visual cues in the graphics and use your mouse to take actions that seem to you to be appropriate according to your understanding of how computer games work. The initial story frame is conveyed to you through these graphics and through an audio description of the starship's problems as explained to you by one of the characters in the story. Before long, however, you are engaging in conversation with various characters through typing in your own comments and questions. Their replies appear in both audio and print form and the game's language parser means that these 'conversations' can be relatively complex within the tight parameters of the story's conventions. The boundaries between reception and production become very unclear.

The complex play of this game involves viewing, listening, reading, writing, making strategic decisions and acting on them, and then weighing the consequences. Those who learn how to engage successfully with this text have come to terms with a very complex set of interpretive processes. The nature of the story means they must also deal with stereotype, humour, irony, suspense and frustration. The game is a clear specimen of what Seymour Papert, in an inspired phrase, has labelled 'hard fun' (Johnston 1999: 12).

Reading embedded in daily life

As if the thickening plot of what goes on in contemporary text processing were not complex enough already, it is necessary to introduce another issue in order to talk about such processing as it occurs in ordinary life. Too often we talk about reading – at whatever level of complexity – as if it happened in some isolated way that transcended the pressures of the rest of daily life. Ellen Seiter reminds us that all forms of textual interpretation happen within the framework of the rest of our experiences:

> The primary contribution of ethnographic audience research since the 1970s has been its demonstration that media consumption is embedded in the routines, rituals, and institutions – both public and domestic – of everyday life. The meanings of the media, whether in the form of print, broadcast, or recorded video, or computer forms, are inseparable from and negotiated within these contexts.
>
> (Seiter 1999: 2)

Most people lead lives that are all too full of interruption, and any engagement with text must compete for time and attention with the rest of daily life. Of course, the social context of reading is not just a set of competitions and interruptions. Reading itself is socially developed, and the web of our daily lives informs our reading in positive and constitutive ways as well. We learn how to read in and through the company of other readers, not simply how to decode but how to place ourselves in relation to a particular text.

However, despite its social roots, much of our engagement with texts is not only private but also silent and invisible. It is not possible to look at a person who is reading and see what is going on inside his or her head. Some form of retrieval of this internal process needs to be organized if any outsider is to gain even limited access to what a reader is doing mentally during the reception of a text of any kind.

Such retrieval needs to take account of both the specific text and the specific reader. Sonia Livingstone, in her study of how people interpret television, provides a succinct description of why it is important to attend to both partners in the text processing activity:

> The creation of meaning through the interaction of texts and readers is a struggle, a site of negotiation between two semi-powerful sources. Each side has different powerful strategies, each has different points of weakness, and each has different interests. It is this process of negotiation which is central. And through analysis of this process, traditional conceptions of both texts and readers may require rethinking, for each has long been theorised in ignorance of the other.
>
> (Livingstone 1998: 26)

In other words, an exploration of the encounter between reader and text must respect the complexity and the energy manifested by both parties to the engagement.

Any study of how people deal with texts of different kinds must necessarily be very complicated just in order to deal with the factors outlined above. Attending to as many of the complexities as possible enables a rich and messy description of textual interpretation to emerge. It is just such a detailed and complex picture that I hope will result from my study of a small group of students and their text processing strategies. Yet much of the messiness and complexity will be accessible only to the peripheral vision, so to speak. The heart of this study lies in a close-up exploration of specific encounters between particular individuals and unique texts.

Changing ecologies of literacy

Seiter (1999) talks about the need to situate our understanding of media within a larger ethnographic awareness of daily social settings. Other scholars set the lens even wider and talk about a literacy or media ecology. Douglas Rushkoff, for example, talks about the datasphere in these terms:

> Today's activists understand the media as an extension of a living organism. Just as ecologists now understand the life on this planet to be part of a single biological organism, media activists see the datasphere as the circulatory system for today's information, ideas, and images.
>
> (Rushkoff 1996: 7)

David Barton and Mary Hamilton provide us with a succinct working definition of literacy. They also offer a useful outline of how literacy may be understood as a set of social practices in a rather more precise ecological perspective on literacy as rooted in its contexts. They describe literacy as follows:

> Literacy is primarily something people do; it is an activity, located in the space between thought and text. Literacy does not just reside in people's heads as a set of skills to be learned, and it does not just reside on paper, captured as texts to be analysed. Like all human activity, literacy is essentially social, and it is located in the interaction between people.
>
> (Barton and Hamilton 1998: 3)

Their six-point outline of how literacy functions as a set of social practices expands on this definition:

- Literacy is best understood as a set of social practices; these can be inferred from events which are mediated by written texts.
- There are different literacies associated with different domains of life.
- Literacy practices are patterned by social institutions and power relationships, and some literacies become more dominant, visible and influential than others.
- Literacy practices are purposeful and embedded in broader social goals and cultural practices.
- Literacy is historically situated.
- Literacy practices change, and new ones are frequently acquired through processes of informal learning and sense making.

(Barton and Hamilton 1998: 7)

Bonnie Nardi and Vicki O'Day also use an ecological metaphor to describe the interactions between human beings and diverse forms of media and technology:

> We define an information ecology to be a system of people, practices, values, and technologies in a particular local environment. In information ecologies, the spotlight is not on technology, but on human activities that are served by technology.
>
> (Nardi and O'Day 1999: 49)

The historical situation of literacy as it manifests itself today involves an ecology in which print on paper is not the only route to making sense of texts, and in which not every reader has equal access to new media and technologies. Even when we do define reading strictly as the processing of print, such print is no longer confined to paper but also appears on different kinds of screen. Furthermore, there is no question that what young people learn about approaching print is affected by what they know about texts in other media. For example, children who have watched many hours of television have certain expectations about the shaping of a story; children who gain a great deal of their information online or from CD-ROM encyclopedias learn to establish what is salient to their search by skimming and scanning. When it comes to making meaning, strategies can be imported across media boundaries.

Nowadays, of course, young people, in the West at least, can enter textual representations through a variety of portals: print, television, video, computer game, movie, audio text, interactive connection (multi-user dungeons, chat rooms, online games and so forth). It is now an unusual child who sticks completely to one medium alone. Our understanding of how literacy works for today's young people will be broader and more useful if we take account of how they accommodate and make sense of texts in different formats.

This study took place in Edmonton, in western Canada, so, to set the context of the students' media access, it is necessary to look at Canadian statistics. For the most part, these figures will be very similar to British statistics of domestic media access. There are a few small differences, at least partly based on the price of local telephone calls: wireless ownership is greater in Europe whereas home Internet access is higher in Canada. In the city of Edmonton where this study took place, 48.8 per cent of households had a regular Internet user in 1999, the last year of the study ('Did You Know?' 2000: B1). In general, however, differences between western Canada and western Europe are simply issues of differential timing; according to one report, the number of Internet users under the age of 17 in the United Kingdom grew by 44 per cent in the six months leading up to March 2001 (http://www.nua.com/surveys/?f=VS&art_id_905356746&rel=true). Certain specific contingencies of the setting of this study are Canadian but the overall picture is more generally Western.

Computer ownership, of course, is not the full story of how we use domestic communications technology. In North America, ownership of colour television sets is very close to 100 per cent and more than 85 per cent of all Canadian homes have at least one video cassette recorder (http://www.statcan.ca/Daily/English/ 971127/d971127.htm). Radio is even more ubiquitous, in cars as well as homes. CD-players, tape recorders, Walkmans and Discmans are commonplace. In addition, attendance at movie theatres is currently high, especially among young people.

It is a corner of this complex multimedia territory that I sought to explore with the help of a group of young people who have grown up with the new situation and take it more or less for granted. They provided me with specific responses to particular texts, grounded in the historical and cultural world of 1997–99. Yet the very individuality of the students' responses and comments offers us an opportunity to explore general questions in a way that generalities do not. Nardi and O'Day make the point well:

> When we are trying to understand something about the way an information ecology works, it is vital to gather real examples from daily practice. Each example may look like an exception to the 'rule,' but that is part of the point. It is far too easy to make generalizations that sustain common fictions about the way things work, smoothing out differences and idiosyncrasies. Real examples show diversity and interconnections that summaries often conceal. When people give general accounts of how things work to outsiders, they usually leave out what is locally unimportant or little valued. But sometimes these hidden details, seen from different perspectives, emerge as crucial to the workings of the ecology.
>
> (Nardi and O'Day 1999: 83)

Thus, the details serve as grounding, so that the workings of the textual ecology can be situated specifically in order to enhance the general utility of our understanding.

An ecology of attention

Contemporary Western young people learn about text processing within the broad and complex context of a social, cultural, educational and commercial textual ecosphere. The details of the technology and texts that form this environment change regularly. The particular responses of individuals to specific texts are equally complex when explored close up. How to find a useful way of exploring both the broad perspective and the individual detail without inducing vertigo is a problem with no simple answer, yet to ignore either end of the spectrum is to devalue the complexity of the issue.

One common ingredient that features importantly in almost any account of encounters with texts is the force that drives much of the workings of a textual ecology on any level: that very finite resource, human attention. Much of what we do when we process texts occurs automatically (see Logan and Compton 1998;

Mackey 1995; Robeck and Wallace 1990; LaBerge and Samuels 1985); we could not make overall sense of a text if we had to pay specific and conscious attention to every part of the process. Humans can really attend to only one thing at a time, although they have the power to switch attention very rapidly when it is useful to do so. Attention is shaped by experience and fuelled by affect; it manifests itself in different parts of the body, in the limbic system of the brain, and in the conscious processes of thought. Attracting, sustaining and directing attention is a major thrust of any text, whether designed for aesthetic, informational or commercial purposes, or any amalgam of the three.

An ecology of the workings of attention in text processing is a study with the potential to combine the long view and the close-up image of a complex mental operation. Such a study could explore details of individual reactions to particular texts within a context of social and technological changes. There are many questions to be addressed, even within the limits of a cumulation of singular experiences. What are the contemporary demands on attention? How do we direct and maintain our attention? What is the role of distraction? What is the importance of passivity? How do we learn to attend through different kinds of experience? What do we learn to notice? What do we learn to value? As we get older, how easy is it for us to mutate from what we learn to do as young people?

This study will not answer all of these questions, but it will provide a detailed look at a small number of rich examples of attention at work, in interaction with texts in a variety of media.

Attention and the body

An exploration of how attention is attracted and maintained also provides a useful route into a better understanding of how different forms of text work separately and together. Take two contrasting (and sometimes compatible) forms of communicating a text: through print on paper and through sound. Two comments highlight certain issues of how we pay attention in the reading of print, in contrast to what we do while listening. Tom Henighan notes: '[I]t's impossible to put a book in the background and turn it on' (1999: E15). In order to read, you really do have to attend. A print text really will not run in the background. Yet, as Adam Bresnick observes, it isn't quite that simple. Bresnick speaks of 'the relation of daydreaming and reading', and suggests that 'reading may well depend on a certain suspension and momentary abandonment of the text' (1999: 9).

In other words, attention is the engine that runs reading, but narrative or poetic reading, at least, also relies on association and a certain kind of licensed wandering of the mind. Simple, resolute and organized attention is not necessarily the full story of print reading.

Listening, on the other hand, is famous for its evocative powers of association, and a musical text can carry on in the background, barely attended to until a theme or a tune intrudes itself on awareness. Listening affects the body as well as the mind; it reverberates in the cavities of the body. In her discussion of radio, Susan

Douglas nicely expresses the conflation of the highly personal and the profoundly social:

> The fact that we hear not only with our ears but also with our entire bodies – our bones, our innards vibrate, too, to sounds, and certainly to music – means that we are actually feeling similar sensations in our bodies at exactly the same time when we listen as a group.
>
> In part because of this physical response, listening often imparts a sense of emotion stronger than that imparted by looking.
>
> (Douglas 1999: 29–30)

We have become accustomed to our relatively recent capacity to repeat the same piece of music over and over again, and Geoffrey O'Brien suggests that one aspect of this ability is our wish to recreate the way a piece of music has made us feel. Referring to rock and roll, he observes:

> The ultimate rock history would be a history of the listener's body as transformed by music, or of the imaginary body that the music makes possible, and that the listener can select from an expanding menu of options, in an era when music is often experienced as a literal appendage, attached via Walkman or Discman. What kind of body do you want? Pick your desired model of nervous response from the rack.
>
> (O'Brien 1999: 46)

Music, therefore, has a quality which can command our attention in a way that print on a page cannot do, yet in its ability to evoke wandering associations it shares a major element with many forms of aesthetic text.

Furthermore, in the immediacy of the impact of music, we meet questions about bodily relation to text that can usefully be transposed to issues of print reading. The same piece of music or oral reading of poetry raises different responses when heard in the immediacy of earphones, in the restricted space encompassed by a car radio and when surging grandly over a surround-sound system. Something we now take completely for granted – the volume control – has a major impact on how we hear. What do we learn if we transfer such issues to their print equivalents? How does a print text change if we read it in a well-designed paperback, in an electronic book, on a computer screen or in a cheap hardback with small print and tight margins? How do our bodies react to the physical arrangement of the book? What do our hands have to arrange in order to make the text legible, and is this process usefully comparable to the use of a volume control? Or does the volume control analogy work better with the electronic book's capacity to change print size on the screen? And what happens when print and audio are married? Does one extend, contradict or nuance the other, as words and pictures may do?

Such comparisons among media could be extended over many pages and would raise many interesting and important questions. What makes this issue particularly pertinent in a study of how attention is invited and directed in contemporary texts is that the boundaries between different forms of text are becoming much more permeable. Cassettes and CDs of the spoken word are perhaps the simplest form of convergence. The occasional book is now marketed with an attached CD of music that has some relevance to the printed text – music listened to by the characters, or music of the era in which the story is set. Text on the computer screen is often supported by background music and it is surely only a matter of time before developments in the electronic book make it routine for people to don their headphones for a spot of 'silent' reading. Exploring the role of attention in these new hybrid forms of text appreciation provides a thread, a 'clue' in the old-fashioned sense, for working through a rapidly changing labyrinth.

Similarly, Jonathan Beller explores the bodily implications of watching a movie. He speaks of 'culture as an interface between bodies and the world system' (Beller 1994: para. 14), raising questions of how our eyes learn to see in new ways according to the discipline of the camera and the cut:

> As an instrument capable of burrowing into the body and connecting it to new circuits, cinema and mass media in general are deeply imbricated in economic production and circulation in the world system. Indeed, cinema performs a retooling of the sensorium by initiating a new disciplinary regime for the eye.
>
> (Beller 1994: para. 52)

Beller's work offers interesting links between the role of our bodies in directing and being affected by how we direct our attention and the role of our social and economic engagement as we supply 'eyeballs' for industry to count for its advertisers. He confines his attention to cinema, but the argument becomes even more complex if we take account of the integration and competition of many different media.

The impact of advertising itself on how we pay attention has been explored by a variety of scholars (see, for example, Vanderbilt 1997; Savan 1994). The ecological metaphor offers us a useful way to explore how changes in one medium may have an impact on how we direct our attention in another; thus, advertising may alter our story schema to make room for short, snappy narratives. On the other hand, the idea of ecology is a metaphor that does not necessarily make enough room for the element of deliberate craft that is involved in the creation of both media and texts. A text is created on purpose to do particular things to somebody's attention; it is neither inevitable nor accidental. In this sense it involves a deliberate disruption to the forms of naturally evolving flow that we may romantically associate with the idea of ecology. Each text, once created, becomes part of the surroundings that shift and change with each new development. Commercial issues are important in this shaping and circulation of culture, and the role of the artists and other individuals who develop and create the texts that succeed or fail in engaging the attention of one or many people is also significant. And the issue of reception – who responds and how – is a vital and still unpredictable element in this changing environment.

Work and play

For the most part, this study explores that large corner of the textual universe devoted to voluntary recreational activities. But in different ways, other aspects of textual life keep appearing on the sidelines. The students occasionally commented on the commercial apparatus that surrounds many of their favourite texts. More often, they referred to the educational apparatus of their school lives, regularly mentioning text-based homework and study, and also making occasional reference to how school activities influence their recreational tastes. Such educational incursions into their leisure lives happen most consistently with their reading, but school decisions about what software to stock in the library or computer room also impinge, particularly on the lives of those whose computer exposure is largely at school.

Students also mentioned certain kinds of text that have a civic function alongside other, more playful qualities: the daily newspaper and the local radio station are two obvious examples. Again, some borderlines are fuzzy. Certain texts play strongly social roles, at least for a moment. In the spring of 1999, for example, no interview with the Grade 9 students (roughly equivalent to Year 9 students in the United Kingdom) concluded without some mention of the upcoming release of the new *Star Wars* movie, *The Phantom Menace*, and it temporarily participated in a kind of community-building. The quality of attention paid to the local ice hockey team and its associated media texts varied seasonally and in relation to the team's success. The textual ecology is local as well as global, fleeting as well as ongoing.

Questions about literacies across media

Given the realities of widespread media use in Western societies, it now makes sense to talk about reading in expanded terms that take account of an ecology that includes broad-based access to many different media. Very few Western young people indeed come to print texts without a vast background of exposure to texts in many other media. Understanding the consequences of this phenomenon raises a number of interesting questions:

- How do different media affect and direct users' attention?
- What are the consequences of multimedia exposure and experience for readers' tacit and explicit understandings of how texts work?
- What repertoires of strategies and behaviours help people to process story and information in different media?
- How does experience in different media and platforms affect people's strategic approaches to texts in different formats?

- What individual quirks or patterns of attention and response, if any, may manifest themselves across media boundaries?

The study

I set out to explore these questions in a longitudinal study of a small number of young people who were aged 10 and 13 when the work began. A total of eighteen students participated in all or part of the project, which lasted for about eighteen months; sixteen of them took part in multiple sessions. In the next chapter, I will outline the course of this project. For now, I want to focus on a few general points about the limits and the findings of this project.

Such a small-scale study elucidates the general textual ecology only in limited and particular ways. This particular study does not attempt to address the broader issues in detail. I introduced specific limitations right from the outset:

- The student volunteers in this study came from schools in areas that were relatively prosperous, though far from wealthy. My intention in selecting these schools in 1997 was to increase the likelihood that participants would have grown up with at least some access to computers at an early age. I succeeded in this intent, and the project therefore explores the responses of a particular minority of the population at large. My purpose was to explore the front line of textual processing among young people who are relatively nonchalant about interactive texts. The students in this study are not obsessively involved with their computers but they all, even those without a computer at home, do take computer usage for granted as part of their daily textual lives.
- The texts I offered to the students, with one exception, were texts designed mainly for recreational use. I was interested in exploring how they processed texts that in some way or another might resemble their recreational tastes. Such texts feature importantly in the larger ecology both in cultural and in commercial terms. Students themselves sometimes introduced references from that wider textual ecology.
- The study of the encounters with the selected texts featured a close-up, slow-motion focus on ways of reacting and responding to known and unknown texts in different media. I did not follow these students to observe how they function in a broader textual universe. The largest grouping of students within the study itself was a pair, so the social aspects of textual interpretation also remained in relatively close focus.

Such limitations made the study feasible for a single researcher, but they also provided the opportunity for a fine-grained observation of specific and individual responses to particular examples of narrative. Such a detailed account of an identifiable corner of the larger ecology contributes to a broader awareness of the complexity of the topic, but it is always important to remember its limits.

For a close-up understanding of forms of attention, the small-scale study has a great deal to offer. The individuals who took part in this project came to each session from a broader textual world in which they developed the knowledge, skills and attitudes that they manifested within the context of the study in their engagements with particular texts in specific circumstances. They demonstrated implicit understandings, gleaned from their connections with texts within that wider world; they also made explicit references to this larger environment in their diaries, their conversations and their responses to questions. Their school assignments, their personal choices among the television shows and movies that aired in 1998 and 1999, the books and magazines that they happened to be reading, their different experiences of online access and their developing computer sophistication – all these aspects of the broader world came into the room with them, when they came to talk, read, view and play.

Over the course of eighteen months, meeting singly and in pairs with me, and dealing with a wide range of recreational media, these young people contributed ideas and raised questions about our different ways of approaching texts with a view to making meaning. The details of these meetings are outlined in the next chapter.

The findings

A number of themes arose from the engagements of these young people with a variety of different texts. In subsequent chapters, I discuss these themes with relation to one kind of text or another, but this approach is an artificial strategy to make it manageable to talk about a project that was always on the edge of being unwieldy. I will address the issue of how these themes overlapped and reinforced each other in the final chapter, but at this stage I would like briefly to highlight the issues that became important along the way.

It was always clear that the students moved easily in a complex textual world, shifting gears both appropriately and nonchalantly as demands changed. Whatever their specific history of encounters with particular media forms, they were, in general, very experienced players of textual games. At the same time, some 'specialized'. A Grade 9 boy, for example, talked at length about his enthusiasm for the American television soap opera *The Young and the Restless*. Another Grade 9 boy was regarded by all his friends as a repository and resource for all known information on the subject of *Star Wars*. A Grade 9 girl was an expert on the subject of the Edmonton Oilers hockey team. Almost every Grade 9 student mentioned *Friends* and *The Simpsons*, television shows that I expected them to enjoy in common. Similarly, and less predictably, the Grade 5 students were familiar with a common list of novels, in this case created by the short list for the Young Readers' Choice Award, a programme organized by the Pacific Northwest Library Association and strongly promoted in their school. Both community and individual tastes featured in all the conversations, and students' repertoires of both texts and strategies manifestly drew on both school and popular culture, as well as individual preferences.

When it came to making choices about which texts were appealing to them, the students appeared to use two platform-neutral strategies to assess their responses to many different media. In case after case, it is possible to observe them making a trade-off between issues of *personal salience* and issues of *fluency of access*. In other words, they checked out a story in any medium to see if it held any individual interest for them, and balanced this element against the question of how difficult or how easy it would be to gain access to that world. Too many long words, too obscure a video opening, too complex a set of controls for a computer game, and they were ready to switch off – unless such difficulties might be compensated for by a particularly salient story. Similarly, many of them rejected texts that were too easy, unless they were extremely interesting to the individual making the choice.

Over the course of the project, the students looked at media with which they were already familiar (print, video, computer games and other texts) and also looked at newer formats (an electronic book, a range of DVDs). These latter encounters led them to consider issues of what Bolter and Grusin (1999) call *remediation*: the re-working of a text that moves from an old medium to a new one. The students themselves did not use this term, of course, but their comments on what worked and what did not work in new formats were exceedingly interesting. Remediation, in Bolter and Grusin's use of the term, involves an oscillation between looking through and looking at the text, and students did discuss some implications of this oscillation, though naturally without the framework of the technical vocabulary I am using here.

As texts change formats, they make many different kinds of demands on users. How these users focus and direct attention in these variant environments is a question of great interest. The readings of a picture book highlighted the important role of *hands-on engagement*: how the readers used their hands was surprisingly important. Tactile demands change from one format to another, and it was intriguing to compare the readings of a print picture book with the readings of a story-telling CD-ROM and a CD-ROM encyclopedia. The simple question of 'one hand or two' or even 'one hand or four' appeared to be much more important than I had ever anticipated.

Another element at work in more than one medium was the operation of *boundary crossing*. In the computer games, but also in relation to movies and television programmes, the students moved in and out of the diegetic world, that is the world of the story itself, without necessarily leaving the extradiegetic world of the game or the show in which this story was located. Strategic discussions over game-playing manoeuvres took place at this extradiegetic level, but so did other discussions about different texts, and students manifested the ability to move readily in and out of the core fiction in many ways.

The computer games also highlighted the need for players to draw on hybrid strategies. The older students played *Starship Titanic* and the younger players played *Myst*. The different demands created by these two games meant a differing emphasis on *narrative strategies* and *strategies for processing visual information*.

Again, it was interesting to make cross-media comparisons between the computer games and other graphic texts both online and in print form.

In short, the students encountered texts in many different media, yet many of the issues raised by their engagement with these texts were applicable across media boundaries. In addition, there was a question of what Lawrence Sipe calls the '*signature response*' (1998: 87). Some students did show a predilection for a particular form of response to texts, whatever the medium in which they were presented. A few expressed a preference with regard to the medium itself, though nobody was completely singular in this regard and questions of the salience and fluency quotients of a particular text appeared to be more important to them than a preference for one medium or another.

The participants clearly regarded this project as a licensed opportunity to play during school hours. In the final analysis of this study, the ideas encompassed in that very fluid and multifaceted word *play* became extremely useful in exploring some common questions of text interpretation in a variety of media.

This short digest of the findings does scant justice to a rich set of data. In the following chapters, I unpack these topics in much more detail.

Conclusions

The students in this project moved easily within their own textual universe. They also responded with alacrity and enthusiasm to most of the new texts I brought to their attention. They were confident in their reflections on new media formats, and swift to reach conclusions about the appeal of one text or another.

On the other hand, the students were reluctant to make either/or choices about one text *versus* another. If I pressed them for a preference, they would very often hedge, or specify that one kind of text would suit one social setting while another might work better in a different environment. They were clearly happy with multiplicity and often not willing to opt for a singular choice. In a similar vein, when I offered them a text adapted for more than one medium, they judged each version on its own merits and not simply as inferior or superior to the original; they were happy to live with variation. Multiple versions did not necessarily give them pause, although many of them said they would make some effort to encounter the original text first.

The project itself naturally affected the textual ecology within which the students lived and worked. I think there is no doubt that they found it interesting to explore the range of texts and media on offer, and it is probable that this exposure increased the sophistication of their responses. The Grade 6 students, for example, looked at a print picture book and then at a CD-ROM picture book, and it is likely that the contrast between the two actively affected the criteria they used for judging them. In any case, many students developed stringent criteria for adjudication: the text should tell a good story *and* it should exploit its medium to maximum purpose and effect. Either one without the other was simply not as interesting as it could be. These students live in a world where there is far too much textual choice on offer for them to put up for very long with a text they find uninteresting.

The young participants were lively, energetic and alert, with a great interest in exploring such textual questions as long as the examples they were offered caught their attention. It was a pleasure to watch them bringing their intelligence to bear on the materials I offered them. My analysis of the transcripts attempts to honour the complexity of these encounters, but I have no doubt I have overlooked as many issues as I have highlighted. What is clear from this work, however, is that these students, both singly and collectively, are adapting to a changing environment in supple and sophisticated ways.

Afterword: new literacy ecologies of the twenty-first century

Although the changes since 1999 have been substantial, the structure of this study makes it impossible to re-visit and update the data. Instead, I have opted for a separate afterword for each chapter, attempting to outline factors of change and development. Seven years is a short time but the rate of change has been significant, and there is much to discuss.

In Chapter 2, I address questions of domestic access to the Internet. In Chapter 3, I use Janice's instant messaging habits as a link to a discussion of texting. Chapter 4's presentation of Jack leads to a consideration of the rise and fall of Napster. Chapter 5 talks about layers of textual identity, but in my afterword I single out the mutating uses of radio for particular attention. In Chapter 6, I consider the issues of salience and fluency in connection with reading websites. Chapter 7 explores the contrasting markets for DVDs and electronic books during the first half of the decade. In Chapter 8, I consider the potential for adding soundtracks to the polysemic world of picture books. Chapter 9 re-visits the issue of narrative and game in *Starship Titanic* and other computer games. Chapter 10 raises questions about the future of print reading.

These afterwords were relatively straightforward to research and write. When I came to the final chapter of this book, however, I was baffled about what to update in a fairly abstract and theoretical discussion about play. Events in the city of Edmonton came to my rescue during the spring of 2006, and I decided that, rather than expand on the generalities of the final chapter, I would turn to a particular, local, contemporary and highly mediated example of play in action.

Chapter 2

The study
A description and a framework

The project

In the autumn of 1997, I began work with two groups of students who, at that time, were in Grade 5 and Grade 8 in the Canadian system (roughly equivalent to Years 5 and 8; the students were aged 10 and 13). Each of these students kept a diary of a week's out-of-school encounters with all kinds of media. Some students were selected for more detailed follow-up work. The numbers of participants fluctuated slightly throughout the project, which continued throughout all of 1998 and well into 1999. Most students committed themselves to several meetings. Over this eighteen-month period, these students looked at many different kinds of texts: novels, a picture book, a short story, movies on both video and DVD, computer games, texts in electronic book form, and an encyclopedia and a picture book on CD-ROM. Their responses to these texts were audiotaped and in some cases videotaped as well. Sometimes they worked in pairs, sometimes alone.

The transcripts of these encounters are very rich, and offer a variety of perspectives on the complexities of text processing behaviours. The diaries give a glimpse of how media use is embedded in the daily lives of these students. The recorded conversations between two readers working together on the same text often provide some sense of reading processes in action. With one text, the complex computer game, I replayed the video of their played game to each pair and they commented retrospectively on what they had been thinking as they went along. Aligning their concurrent and retrospective commentaries sheds further light on what is normally a very private process. Looking at what an individual achieves alone and what that same person achieves as one of a pair of readers is another illuminating approach. Finally, these encounters all provided the opportunity for rich and focused conversation on the role of texts in different media in the lives of the participants, and the content of these conversations also supplies valuable data.

Put together, all these sources of information do indeed build a complex picture of different readers in action with different forms of text, over a period of eighteen months. Yet, elaborate as this portrait may be, it is a long way from providing anything like a complete account of the complex textual ecology within which these readers move and develop on a daily basis. Instead, I would compare this study to the work of an isolation camera trained on a sporting event. Certain processes in the overall flow of the game are marked out for individual attention with the potential for close-up or slow motion or freeze-frame – all in the cause of explicating details in the larger pattern. It is a valuable and illuminating exercise, but I am under no illusion that it provides information about the entire game, the fan activity in the stands, the traffic patterns outside the stadium, and so forth.

I do not provide any kind of ethnography of these students' literate lives. Except through their own references, I did not explore their school literacies. What information I gained about their recreational literacies is all self-recorded, or obliquely derived from their behaviour with the texts I provided. My focus throughout this study was on their engagement with particular texts in different media, either pre-selected by me or chosen by the participants from a restricted set of options.

At the same time, however, the students' encounters with these different texts are rooted in their daily lives and their assumptions about literacy. They did talk about their school lives and assignments; they did refer to their own recreational tastes; and their descriptions of these connections are also recorded in the transcripts. As I manned the iso-camera, so to speak, I was very aware of the larger game going on around me. But that larger game is only peripherally the object of this study.

Barton and Hamilton's outline of literacy as a set of social practices includes this point at the end of the list: 'Literary practices change and new ones are frequently acquired through processes of informal learning and sense making' (1998: 7). This study explored the participants' reading practices as they explored a group of texts similar to some of their own text choices. In some cases, the readers met a text in a format they had never encountered before. How they chose to direct their attention as they responded provided oblique access to many of their tacit assumptions; their own comments and observations raised issues about which they were more explicitly aware.

I am well aware that I did not simply observe the textual ecology of these young people; I also actively affected it. I introduced media and formats and texts that were new to the readers; by the end of the study they were more sophisticated than at the start, in part because they had had the opportunity to explore so many different kinds of text. The advantage of this process was that it enabled me to see how they responded to completely new forms. Nobody in the group, for example, had ever seen an electronic book. Only a very few, in 1999, had had the opportunity to experiment with a DVD. On the other hand, all were familiar with the CD-ROM encyclopedia. Moving between media probably sharpened their sophistication about questions of format and platform. The more general activity of simply making space for the participants to talk, and to develop their awareness of their own attitudes and processes, may also have changed some of their ideas.

The chronology of the project

In the autumn of 1997, students from one grade each in two different schools were invited to participate in the study over the next two years. Their initial step was to keep a diary for a week of all their out-of-school media encounters. This initial stage caused one immediate and unforeseen problem: many more girls than boys first volunteered to keep the diary and then actually remembered to fill it out.

The second stage of the project involved setting up follow-up interviews with some participants. The constraints on this process were different with each group. In the Grade 5 class, seven girls and one boy completed the diary; of these, four girls and one boy were selected for further work, in consultation with the class teacher. In the Grade 8 class, seven students completed the diary and returned the consent forms, and all of them took part in a subsequent stage. Again the gender imbalance was very strong: the group consisted of six girls and one boy.

Those students who participated in the second stage, in the winter and spring of 1998, took part in a session in which they looked at the openings of fifteen different texts: five first pages of novels, five opening credits of films on video, and five initial stages of different computer games. In each case, they were asked two questions: would you carry on with this text if you had the opportunity, and what kind of story do you think it will turn out to be? Discussion of these specific texts also fed into more general discussion of their tastes and preferences in different media. All the sessions were audiotaped.

This process took us to the end of the school year. In the autumn of the new school year, I made some changes. With the help of the schools, I recruited more boys, now in Grade 6 and Grade 9. Without the barrier of completing a diary, they were now willing to take part. The sole male participant from Grade 5 had left the school, and his place was taken first by one and later by two boys from the same class. In Grade 9, we were successful in recruiting four more boys. Over the course of that year, 1998–99, I made every effort with these boys to reproduce substantial sections of the informal interview I had conducted with the others the year before. I did succeed in gaining something of a picture of their domestic media lives, though without the corroborative detail of the diaries.

The second change of Year 2 was that I began to record the sessions on videotape as well as audiotape. The camera was at all times trained on the text under consideration rather than on the students; even so, one Grade 9 girl chose to drop out rather than be videoed. This left me with five girls and five boys in Grade 9, four girls and two boys in Grade 6.

During that year, the younger students participated in two sessions. They played a computer game in pairs, except for one boy who played alone because his friend had forgotten to return the consent form in time; in their case, the game was *Myst*. We videotaped their game for about forty-five minutes, then played the tape back to them and asked them to comment retrospectively on their decisions: why they had made them and what they had expected to happen. Thus, we have a videotaped record of the game as played, a transcript of the pair's comments and suggestions to each other as they played, and an audiotaped and transcribed retrospective commentary on the decision-making process of the game.

The Grade 9s were involved in an identical session, except that in their case the game was *Starship Titanic* by Douglas Adams.

The second session, in the winter of 1999, was similar for all participants except that the Grade 6s had one extra text to consider. The students, again working in pairs, were asked to look at a variety of texts in different media: an electronic book from which they could choose one of a small number of texts, a DVD movie, which they selected themselves from a limited range of offerings, a picture book (*Shortcut* by David Macaulay was used in all cases) and a CD-ROM encyclopedia (*The Way Things Work*, also by David Macaulay). The Grade 6 participants also looked at a CD-ROM picture book, *Lulu's Enchanted Book*. (The Grade 9 sessions were well under way by the time I obtained this text, so the older students did not get the chance to respond to it.)

Finally, the Grade 9 students had a concluding session in May 1999 in which they read a single short story, 'Tunnel' by Sarah Ellis, from her collection *Back of Beyond* (1996). Participants were given a copy of the story, asked to make a tick on any word or phrase that caught their attention on the way through as they read it silently, and then asked to provide a retrospective think-aloud commentary on what had struck them as they read. These sessions were audiotaped, and the marked-up copies of the story collected from the students. Participants worked individually for these sessions, which concluded with an informal exit interview.

With the exception of the sessions on 'Tunnel', which lasted one hour each, all the other sessions took a full school afternoon, two hours in total. The Grade 6 sessions were interrupted by a break; the Grade 9 sessions ran straight through. In each case, we worked in a room made available by the school and students were removed from an afternoon's classes, singly or in pairs, to take part. Students were generally very positive and enthusiastic about their participation, and expressed regret when the project came to an end.

The texts

The selection of texts involved a number of balances. I wanted students to look at a variety of different media. I wanted to include at least some texts that could be processed in their entirety and achieved this with *Shortcut* and 'Tunnel'. I also wanted to record at least one extended encounter with a text of some complexity and accomplished this aim with *Myst* and *Starship Titanic* – though it has to be said that nearly all students wanted to play for much longer than they were able to do within the confines of our agreement with the schools.

The first set of texts was the largest, comprising fifteen opening scenes of stories in three different media: print, film and narrative-based CD-ROM. I used a different set of texts at each grade level, with some overlap of titles. I aimed to offer a range of complexity, in which I succeeded, and also to collect a set of titles that students might not be familiar with; I was far less successful on this count.

The set of texts for the second meeting was much smaller, consisting of two games on computer: *Myst* for the Grade 6s and *Starship Titanic* for the Grade 9s. I wanted to find games that would stretch even the most experienced computer users. I was a bit concerned that students would already know *Myst*, which is one reason why I did not use it with the Grade 9 students. In the event, all the Grade 6 students said they had never played it before, although some had heard of it. None of the Grade 9 students knew of *Starship Titanic* at all.

The third meeting involved a variety of different texts in different platforms. My electronic book held a small number of texts; *Alice in Wonderland*, *The Secret Garden*, *The Age of Innocence* and *Unleashing the Killer App* were four that students chose to look at. This text selection was the most highly constrained of the entire project; in early 1999 there were few available e-book titles likely to interest teenagers or pre-teens. Of the books explored by the students, only *Alice in Wonderland* was illustrated, with the familiar black and white Tenniel drawings.

With the DVD, most students were allowed to make a choice from a small selection that included *Ace Ventura – Pet Detective*, *The Secret Garden* (the 1994 version), *Little Women* (the 1993 version) and *Contact*. The most popular selections were *Ace Ventura* and *Contact*. In some cases, I directed students to check *Contact* after they had looked at other choices, simply because I wanted to ask them about that DVD's excellent range of extra features.

I chose the picture book *Shortcut*, by David Macaulay, for several reasons. I liked the overlap caused by having a picture book and a CD-ROM provided by the same author. I wanted a book that would challenge even the Grade 9 readers and that would most likely provide valuable information from both first and second readings. *Shortcut* is also interesting because of its organization, which shares some features in common with hypertext; small elements of the story link to other sections much later on in the book. Although it is organized into what claim to be sequential chapters, it is a very non-linear telling of a story that is, in the final analysis, a linear sequence. The fact that the book is funny was an important bonus.

I acquired *Lulu's Enchanted Book*, a picture-book CD-ROM, while I was half-way through recording the Grade 9 sessions, and decided to reserve it for the Grade 6s only. It was interesting as a bridge between the comparatively straightforward text of *Shortcut* and the hypertext of *The Way Things Work*. It also provided unintentional fodder for discussion. I find it a fairly dull story told in an interesting way, and some Grade 6 students also made some observations to this effect. Like *Shortcut*, *Lulu* is organized into chapters with text and picture more or less confined to a page frame. However, unlike what we often perceive as the 'traditions' of CD-ROM story-telling, this book offered much more interaction between words and pictures than is common. As is often the case, the pictures can be animated by clicking the mouse on the image; in this story, however, the pictures can also be animated by clicking on various points in the text. The story is ultimately a metafiction, but no players had enough time to reach that point of discovery.

Finally, the CD-ROM encyclopedia *The Way Things Work*, also by David Macaulay, offered a number of features not explored elsewhere in this study. It was the only non-fiction text of the collection, and even that description is provisional, as its factual information about machines is animated and illustrated with the fictional doings of a woolly mammoth. It is hypertextually organized, with a number of different routes into various kinds of information, and a good working set of indexes. I expected more students to be familiar with it than turned out to be the case.

The final, story-reading session was done only with the Grade 9 students, mainly because the school year was nearly at an end. I selected the story 'Tunnel' by Sarah Ellis for several reasons. It is an ambiguous story that involves several changes of tone and of direction throughout. For example, many readers assume that the first person narrator is female until explicitly told the contrary. It is a part of a young adult collection of stories, all of which contain some supernatural element. This particular story, the first in the book, is also funny in places and speaks directly to experiences that Canadian junior high students might reasonably be expected to recognize, such as the limitations of work experience and the tedium involved in babysitting. The ending is open to more than one interpretation, which was a very helpful element from my point of view, as I wanted to observe how determined different readers might be to come up with a definitive explanation. I gauged that this story would be accessible to all the readers in my study, yet would provide room for them to be challenged as readers. My observations of the students' engagement with the story confirmed that I achieved this particular aim, though I would not say that every reading was equally successful.

The activities

I was interested in sampling as broadly as possible within the territories that I will earmark as 'before', 'during' and 'after' the interpretive encounter with the text. In other words, I wanted to catch students' responses at the very initial stage of engaging with a text, which was accomplished by the use of the fifteen different openings. I also wanted to explore how they responded during the actual activity of processing, and achieved this directly with the discussion during the playing of the computer games *Myst* and *Starship Titanic*, and the reading of *Shortcut* and *Lulu's Enchanted Book*. In a different way, I picked up various aspects of processing activity in the retrospective accounts of the reading of 'Tunnel'. In addition, I was interested in exploring what happens after a reading is complete; discussions following the completion of 'Tunnel' and *Shortcut* provided the main routes to exploring this stage of the reading process. It is probably worth noting that both these examples are print texts, not because I particularly wanted to set it out in that way but because the nature of much video and computer text is that it is far too extensive to complete in a two-hour session.

Finally, there was a different category of activity that can probably be classified with the 'during' activities but which involves a kind of play and exploration rather than straightforward text processing. For example, students experimented with the electronic book for relatively extended periods of time without actually reading very much. They moved backwards and forwards in the DVD movies they selected (partly because I refused to let them simply settle down and watch the movie, which many of them would have been happy to do!), and tried out different sound tracks and special features. They explored different elements of the CD-ROM encyclopedia *The Way Things Work*, with varying levels of attention to the actual information included. Some made serious attempts to be systematic in their exploration of the organization of the text; others simply played. I am not attempting to pass judgement on these activities; to a certain extent they were fostered by the nature of the sessions and the students were simply doing what I asked them to do. On the other hand, it is worth noting that, judging by their responses, students enjoyed and could justify a certain form of engagement with text that is possibly best described as 'tinkering' rather than anything involving serious processing. It was also clear from their comments that this was not an entirely novel activity for most of them.

The issue of text tinkering is a fascinating one. To what degree is it encouraged by the organization of certain media? To what extent is it more likely to occur when young people are engaging with a text in the company of a peer? What is the ultimate value of such behaviour as a pastime and as a way of deriving at least an overview of the kinds of information on offer? These questions resonate, particularly for concerned adult onlookers, in an abundantly mediated world. How much of what these students were doing as they played around in these texts was desultory and largely aimless? How much should rather be seen as the essential building of skills and the development of an overview of the vast and complex potential on offer in these different texts? How much of this kind of tinkering is a useful preliminary to more focused work, and what is lost if we encourage students to bypass this initial playful stage and move straight to activity more readily defined as purposeful by adult agendas? On the other hand, what is the danger that at least some students will never move on to the level of purposeful inquiry and will instead find it easy and attractive to keep themselves constantly occupied at this initial and perhaps perfunctory level?

Clearly these are questions about attention and about personal decisions concerning salience and purpose. On the other hand, there is an equally important question of fluency of access, and it may be that the initial tinkering is a long-term investment, however footling it may appear at first glance.

The participants

The students who participated in this study came from two elementary-junior high schools in the same broadly middle-class neighbourhood of a western Canadian city.

The personalities of the young people will emerge through their own words, but a brief outline of who took part at which stages of the project may be useful.

Not all the students were white but it will become obvious throughout this report that all of them were fluently at home in Western popular culture and the issue of ethnic background was not pursued. Similarly, in view of the small numbers, I have not attempted to reach any substantial conclusions regarding gender, though I take note of a few issues as they arise.

It is worth noting that a research project has its own ecology, and that something less than a perfect model is bound to evolve. Altogether, eighteen young people took part in at least one session in this project. Of this group, ten students engaged in every possible meeting. Five more missed only one session.

Grades 5–6

Claire, Megan, Angela and Lisa participated in both years of the study and took part in every session. Colin was a participant in Grade 5 but at the end of the year he left the school and this project. Tom and Jordan were recruited to replace him but a delay in Jordan's return of his consent form meant that Tom took part in both of the Grade 6 encounters and Jordan in only the last one.

Grades 8–9

Anita, Catherine, Kelly, Janice, Madeleine and Jack participated in both years of the study and took part in every session. Nasrin completed the diary and met with me for the first session to explore the openings to the fifteen texts. Subsequent meetings were videotaped, which led her to withdraw from the project. In Grade 9, Jeff, Leonard, Gregory and Kyle joined the project and took part in all three of that year's sessions.

The data

In addition to the diary documentation which is all in the students' own words, there are several sources of information about the various sessions: the texts the students explored, the audio and video recordings and their transcripts, and the notes taken by a graduate student at each encounter. The video camera, which ran for two sessions, recorded the text at all times, so that with the computer games, for example, the delineation of each played game on the screen, as it developed through the decisions of the playing pair, is recorded completely. What is lost through this decision is a visual record of the demeanour of the players, with one exception that proved surprisingly informative. This exception is that the videotapes do sometimes record the hands of the participants, and their manual activities in processing different kinds of text are very illuminating. I had deliberately set out to record how students handled the electronic book; I did not anticipate that the manipulation of the picture book would be, if anything, even more fascinating.

The transcripts, of course, provide access to only the public observations of the readers. John Fiske has commented astutely on the implications of this basic fact:

Discourse is the continuous process of making sense and of circulating it socially . . . [D]iscourse is both a noun and a verb, it is ever on the move. At times it becomes visible or audible, in a text, or a speech, or a conversation. These public moments are all that the discourse analyst has to work on, but their availability does not necessarily equate with their importance.

(Fiske 1994: 3, 6)

It is overwhelmingly likely that the conversations recorded in this study represent only the tip of the iceberg in terms of the participants' complete responses to any given text. It is also likely that my own personal intuitions about text interpretation will be a factor in how I attend to the transcripts. Antonio Damasio suggests that researchers exploring the workings of the mind must not attempt to reduce their account of what is happening to that which can be 'scientifically' observed:

It is fine for us scientists to bemoan the fact that consciousness is an entirely personal and private affair and that it is not amenable to the third-person observations that are commonplace in physics and in other branches of the life sciences. We must face the fact, however, that this is the situation and turn the hurdle into a virtue. Above all, we must not fall into the trap of attempting to study consciousness exclusively from an external vantage point based on the fear that the internal vantage point is hopelessly flawed. The study of human consciousness requires both internal and external views.

(Damasio 1999: 82)

These comments apply to reading processes as well as to a more blanket case of consciousness, and raise an important issue. There are different approaches to research into reading and other forms of text processing. Some routes deal only with what can be publicly measured in some way; others attempt to take account of personally 'felt' questions and responses that are often never articulated. It is possible to be reductive either way, since the 'felt' issues can often only be raised in the context of the researcher's own personal reading experience. Nevertheless, Damasio's point is well taken, and I have undoubtedly drawn on my own internal understandings of text processing in the development of my analysis. I would argue that this approach seems like the less reductive route in the long run, although I have tried to be alert to its necessary drawbacks. I have also tried to be explicit about how and where I have connected to my own experiences, but, given the shadowy and ubiquitous nature of implicit awareness, I doubt that I have been completely successful in this aim.

To hope that the consequences of an extended study like this one may be that we wind up 'less vague' about what is happening in contemporary literacy is certainly a modest ambition. Perhaps I am limiting my expectations too much, or perhaps, given the invisible and amorphous elements of text processing, I am simply being realistically temperate. Talking to these students and observing their responses to a variety of texts was illuminating, and the analysis of the records of these engagements yielded further information. The transcripts and the videos allow for close-up, slow-motion observations of the public manifestations of a private experience. These public manifestations are both audible and visible. In some cases, the videotapes provide information that is completely absent from the transcripts of the audiotapes, and these transcripts had to be extensively annotated to provide a useful account of the activity that had been recorded. It is likely that a second camera trained on the readers themselves would have provided even more information, communicated by their demeanour and their physical links with each other and with the text. Sitting across the table from the participants as they read, played and talked, I certainly got a different view of their engagement with the text than the one the camera recorded from behind their shoulders. Only the tone of their voices on the audiotapes (again, untranscribable to a large degree) conveys anything of the quality of engagement I saw in the enthusiastic faces and alert bodies opposite me.

All data about reading processes are partial and never likely to be otherwise, even when MRI technology allows us to record inside the brain of a reader. I set out to observe and record as systematically and as broadly as possible, but I am under no illusions that I possess anything remotely approaching a complete record of what happened in these encounters.

The data analysis

The collected data set was massive: sixteen two-hour videotapes, twenty-eight two-hour audiotapes and a further ten one-hour audiotapes, five very large binders of transcript, plus fifteen diaries. I took these records, one activity at a time, and immersed myself in them, reading and re-reading, establishing potential categories and testing them against the material. Only in the case of the computer game, where the students had used different texts, did I work separately with the transcripts for younger and older readers; otherwise I treated each activity as a single unit.

Early in the project, I recognized that speed of reporting was an issue in this kind of work; the shelf life of some of these text forms is short and our need for a clearer understanding of the complexities of contemporary text processing is immediate. Thus, I decided that it would be more useful to offer generally grounded observations than to produce a laborious coding of every line of the transcripts. Nevertheless, I have not made any generalizations without the backing of multiple examples from many different readers, though space constraints limit the number of samples on offer here. My conclusions are grounded solidly in the transcripts – and also in my reading of theorists who deal with the processing of texts in a wide variety of media.

I did not work exactly the same way with each different segment. In the case of the fifteen openings, my observations on salience and fluency came straight out of the transcripts. With the work on the electronic book and the DVD, however, I specifically searched for a theoretical account of how texts are re-worked in new media to support my investigations of the transcripts, and found it in Bolter and

Grusin's *Remediation* (1999). Exploring the responses to *Starship Titanic* with an open mind, I was quickly reminded of earlier work with Rabinowitz (1987). When I tentatively applied his 'rules of reading' to the transcripts of the computer game playing, I found the goodness of fit to be illuminating. With the work on *Myst*, on the other hand, I early established that I needed to learn much more about visual processing if I wanted to do any useful grouping of responses. My analysis of the manual activities involved in the reading of *Shortcut* was multiply determined as I describe in that chapter. The most striking element of the responses to 'Tunnel' was the individuality of the actual experience for each of the ten readers, an aspect of reading which I have explored before (see Mackey 1995 in particular).

The theoretical and practical precedents

At the heart of this project lies a commitment to exploring the temporal processes of interpreting texts, to investigating what happens *during* the activity of reading, viewing or playing of a text, paying due attention to both person and text involved. While there is an enormous literature bearing on this complex topic, and I read a great deal of it, a small handful of particular texts turned out to be of special importance to my thinking over the course of this project. Not by coincidence, many of them share the attribute of a present participle in the title; it is the ongoing nature of the activity that is the focus of their attention.

Like many researchers in this territory, I first gained a glimpse of its complexity and promise through reading Wolfgang Iser's *The Act of Reading: A Theory of Aesthetic Response* (1978) and Louise Rosenblatt's *Literature as Exploration* (1970). Both of these theorists provide a clear delineation of the important issue of 'unfinishedness' in any form of text processing. Reading and other forms of text processing are indeterminate and contingent *while they are actually going on*, a fact radically concealed by our post-reading efforts to develop and present to ourselves and others a coherent idea of the whole.

Peter Rabinowitz's *Before Reading: Narrative Conventions and the Politics of Interpretation* (1987) provides a fine-grained account of the conventions we may apply as we read print narrative. His approach provided a surprisingly clear and helpful lens through which to explore encounters with other media as well. A study that takes a more active look at readers learning how to make use of these conventions is Margaret Meek's *How Texts Teach What Readers Learn* (1988). In this book Meek investigates the activities of small children learning how to understand the page as well as the print.

A main focus of this project is to understand how our understanding of narrative conventions may cross media boundaries, even to involve the interpretation of unfamiliar platforms. As Florian Brody puts it, 'A new medium is new only until it is established and no longer new; but since any usage of a medium is based upon communicative conventions, a new medium is somewhat of a contradiction' (2000: 139). The application of already understood conventions to new forms of material requires skills already acquired by many contemporary readers, viewers and players. Such skills are developed, in many cases, in exactly the same way as Meek's young readers learned about the conventional movement of the eye over the page: in social contexts and in the service of particular texts.

In my own doctoral work, 'Imagining with Words: The Temporal Processes of Reading Fiction' (Mackey 1995), I explored the activities of readers reading and then re-reading a single, complex print fiction. Moving into the realm of narrative in many different media, I kept a constant eye out for work that would fuel my understanding of how we may explore the durational elements of text processing. Torban Grodal's *Moving Pictures: A New Theory of Film Genres, Feelings, and Cognition* provided ways of investigating 'symbolic manipulation as the nucleus of the development of play, art, and fiction' (1999: 26). Grodal clarifies one of the prime elements of fiction in all media: 'In standard fictions, as in real life, the future has not yet taken place' (1999: 47). In his book, Grodal explores minutiae of our detailed construction of a mental world in which the future is contingent, a world paradoxically created out of a finished set of symbols. Like Rabinowitz, he does not use examples of actual viewers, but his construction of a theory to account for moment-by-moment responses is nevertheless vivid and useful. His work pairs usefully with Jerome Bruner's elegant discussion of the subjunctive mode in *Actual Minds, Possible Worlds* (1986), and both writers explore detailed applications of conventions in highly helpful ways.

Similarly, Richard J. Gerrig's *Experiencing Narrative Worlds: On the Psychological Activities of Reading* (1993) produces a detailed account of the felt life of a narrative as constructed in the mind of a reader. And Steven Poole, in *Trigger Happy: The Inner Life of Videogames* (2000), explores the same kinds of mental activity, but with reference to a different platform. Poole is more explicit than the others in drawing on his own experiences with different texts as a source for much of his developing understanding of how our minds move through a story world.

Sonia Livingstone's book *Making Sense of Television: The Psychology of Audience Interpretation* (1998) supplies a similar focus on the durational elements of text processing, drawing on television viewing for her source material. She, however, pays considerably more attention than some others to the necessity of attending to both individual readers and specific texts.

Shorter works have explored some complexity of engaging with CD-ROMs and computer games. Lisa Sainsbury (2000) explores conventions, and Lydia Plowman (1996a, 1996b) looks at structures of multimedia texts that enable decision-making, and investigates the responses of young people to particular examples of interactive multimedia texts.

Work by Saskia Tellegen and Jolanda Frankhuisen (1999) on young people's engagement with computer games and with reading explores the impact of the environment on textual activities. The studies of Teresa Dobson (Dobson 2001; Dobson *et al.* 1999) with novice readers of hypertext highlight the effects of strangeness and newness, and the impact of unfamiliarity on aspects of attention. Although she does not use these labels, her work draws attention to aspects of salience and fluency.

Many of these examples either posit a notional reader or draw on the reactions of individual readers working and responding on their own. The challenge of working through new or repurposed conventions, however, is often more successful when it is a social activity. Being part of a conversation about the challenges of a text is a powerful heuristic, a fact that will be amply demonstrated in subsequent chapters.

Furthermore, in this project, I was exploring not any one of these different media but their cross-fertilization. The New London Group's work on multiliteracies (1996) was very helpful in foregrounding the kinds of negotiations among literacies that make up contemporary culture. Shirley Brice Heath's work on visual literacy (2000) was also useful in its cross-disciplinary sweep. Both these pedagogically oriented studies explore readers, but I was also influenced in how I looked at texts by Janet Murray's prophetic work *Hamlet on the Holodeck: The Future of Narrative in Cyberspace* (1997). This book was published in the year my study began and, throughout the course of the work on this project, I could see Murray's speculations taking firmer form in the world around me.

All kinds of text interpretation are profoundly private as well as intrinsically social. For a first pass at this paradox, I consulted Gadamer's (1989) account of play and compared it with Bakhtin's (1988) more plural analysis. A more broadly theoretical account of changing text processing activities remains to be done; in the end, this study is rooted in the actual activities of readers.

Conclusions

Sixteen students are at the core of this study, offering their insights into a broad range of media and texts. They worked both alone and in partnership with another. They also spoke extensively of their textual encounters outside of those provided by the project. The transcripts of these encounters provide a view of young people with some very sophisticated processing skills and strategies.

At the same time, it is fair to inquire to what degree these students were skilled and strategic because they were *asked to be*. It would undoubtedly be a great mistake to assume that they approach every recreational text with their repertoire of judgement criteria on full alert. Some of what they read, watch and play they undoubtedly select for its lack of challenge rather than for any more positive reason. The textual ecology within which they live and operate offers them ample opportunity for textual engagement of the most desultory kind, and many of them referred to such encounters as a regular part of their lives.

Nevertheless, what comes across clearly in these discussions is a rich and complex textual life for all of these young people. They were clearly eager to meet new media and intrigued by new texts in old media as well.

Afterword: new literacy ecologies of the twenty-first century

How would this study be different if I conducted it in the latter part of the first decade of the twenty-first century? At least some of the participants in the original study were early adopters and all were enthusiastic about some elements of new technology. How would these tendencies manifest themselves seven years later?

To some extent, I am asking a hypothetical question, but there are some areas where the answer is clear cut. The single biggest difference I would make if I re-ran the study today would be to focus much more closely on participants' use of the Internet.

Although 1997 is not so very long ago, it is instructive to remember some of the conditions of research in schools in those days. At least three factors weighed against adding actual Internet use to the project. Firstly, I was warned that the school board would be much more likely to grant consent for my project if I left the alien territory of the Internet out of my proposal. Secondly, I could not assume that every school had a reliable Internet connection that I would be able to tap into; many of the schools that were connected had access only through administrative offices, for instance. (It is easy to forget the patchy and uncertain nature of school computer access just a decade ago. In 1996 I worked on a project that involved introducing a CD-ROM of *The Secret Garden* to some young people; that component of the project was made possible at the very last minute, after the rest of the project was completed, when, randomly but in the nick of time, a local firm happened to donate some used computers with CD-ROM readers to the school.) Thirdly, I was concerned that parents would be far less likely to sign consent forms if I suggested that I might take their children online; the Internet was still so new that parents were even more apprehensive about its potential than they are today.

Today, if I sought to replicate this project, I would certainly expect to add the perusal of Internet sites to my list of activities. I would assume that any urban school could offer me decent access, that Canadian children would be accustomed to using the Internet in school and at home, and that this frame of reference would affect the willingness of both school board and parents to trust me to go online safely and sensibly.

Some (not all) of the participants in this study did go online regularly at home. What they described to me was often a highly sheltered and supervised activity. By 1999, some of the Grade 9 students did experiment more independently (Jack with his chat room monitoring and Janice with her instant messaging offer glimpses of the future). But there is little sense in any of the activities recorded in the diaries or mentioned in the conversations of the Internet as a ubiquitous force in the lives of these young people.

The Media Awareness Network in Canada has been gathering statistics about young people and their computer use. In 2001 they produced a major survey of Canadian young people and at the end of 2005 they published a follow-up survey.

The 2005 figures involve responses from 5,272 school students ranging in age from Grade 4 to Grade 11. This study offers some startling figures.

For example, in 2001, 79 per cent of the survey respondents had Internet access at home, a number that had risen to 94 per cent by 2005 (Media Awareness Network 2005: 14). These numbers are high but it is clear that families with children are more rather than less likely to own computers and provide domestic Internet access, a finding duplicated in the United Kingdom (Livingstone and Bober 2005: 2) and the United States (Lenhart *et al.* 2005: 1). Eighty-six per cent of the young Canadians surveyed in 2005 have an e-mail account, and 30 per cent of secondary students have a personal website (Media Awareness Network 2005: 14). Thirty-seven per cent have a computer with Internet access available for their own personal use (Media Awareness Network 2005: 15).

For the purposes of comparison with the participants in my study at the project's end in 1999, I looked at the favoured activities of Grade 6 and Grade 9 students in 2005. 'On an average school day', 60 per cent of Grade 6 students and 77 per cent of Grade 9 students talk to friends on instant messaging. Fifty-seven per cent of Grade 6 and 78 per cent of Grade 9 students download or listen to music. Sixty-one per cent of Grade 6 and 75 per cent of Grade 9 students use e-mail. Seventy-five per cent of Grade 6 and 76 per cent of Grade 9 students do homework. Eighty-five per cent of Grade 6 but only 69 per cent of Grade 9 students play games on the Net (Media Awareness Network 2005: 20). Boys are consistently more likely than girls to game; girls top boys in the use of instant messaging. The popularity of gaming in particular declines from Grade 4 to Grade 11, radically for girls and slowly for boys (Media Awareness Network 2005: 19).

Given these figures, it seems likely that all the participants would have domestic access to the Internet if the project were to be replicated today. It is not hard to picture that Madeleine, who in 1999 had to maintain her e-mail correspondence with a couple of visits a week to the school computer, would now blossom into a state of constant connection with her friends via chatting. Yet as more and more young people now take ongoing access for granted, the implications for those who are left out become more severe. Madeleine in 1999 could 'pass' as connected by means of brief visits to a public computer. The inability to chat on a regular basis cannot be so camouflaged; it is a condition of chat that you have online access that is regular and extensive, if not necessarily constant (Seiter 2004). The politics and economics of access to chat are different in different countries; in Canada, where texting on a mobile phone is less commonplace than in Europe, the role of computer access becomes more significant.

Chapter 3

Janice

Ecologies in close-up

This project was organized according to activities, and for the most part I will keep to that organization as I describe the outcomes of the work. Before proceeding with general description and analysis, however, I would like to introduce two young people in rather more detail than is possible with all sixteen of the core participants in this study. Janice and Jack were both in the first term of Grade 8 when the project began. They took part in every stage of the study and worked with me until the last month of Grade 9. A detailed look at their interactions with texts of various kinds – both as they performed and as they reported such interactions – provides a sense of the rich interpretive texture of their lives, in a way that cannot be conveyed by descriptions of particular activities.

Janice

Janice participated in this project from just before her 13th birthday until she was 14½. She kept her media diary for a week, and we met on four different occasions extended over fifteen months. On two occasions we met one to one; the other two meetings also included Madeleine, Janice's classmate and good friend.

Janice has one brother three years younger than herself. From her description, he is more interested in the computer than she is, and she frequently made reference to games he might like.

At the time she kept her media diary, early in December 1997, Janice was heavily involved in extra-curricular activities. Her diary refers to oboe and piano lessons, dancing class and concert band. She is a keen ice hockey fan and actually got to attend a National Hockey League game on the Friday of the week she recorded. In addition to all of this activity, she sampled a range of media.

Janice's media week

On Monday, Janice looked through the local newspaper and read some articles, notably one about a teen stabbing. She listened to her own radio and also the radio in her dad's car on the way to her oboe lesson. She talked to her old babysitter on the telephone.

On Tuesday, Janice watched television (*The Simpsons* and *Fresh Prince of Bel-Air*), went online to create an e-mail address, listened to the radio, and read the comics, the horoscopes and the political cartoon in the local paper.

Wednesday involved listening to the radio first thing in the morning and last thing at night. She also read the comics, the horoscopes and a 'new year' section in the newspaper and went online to check her e-mail.

The Thursday listings involve the radio again, the same two television programmes as on Tuesday, and another stint on the Internet, during which she checked her e-mail and played a game called *Rodents' Revenge*. She also talked on the telephone.

Friday was a teachers' professional development day so Janice was off school. She read the comics in the paper and listened to classical music on the radio in her mother's car on the way to do a variety of errands. That night she went to the hockey game and listened to a popular radio station in the car on the way to and from the stadium. After she got home she watched television from 10.30 till midnight ('way past my bedtime', she notes in parentheses) and saw one show from the Friday night amalgam *TGIF* and then *20/20* and *The Simpsons* again.

On Saturday, Janice records a simultaneous entry: 'Talked on the phone – went on computer' between 11 and 11.20 a.m. She used the computer to check e-mail. She read the colour comics in the paper and read *Seventeen* magazine. In the evening, she records a cryptic but intriguing note for 6 to 7 p.m.: 'Made a movie – homemad [*sic*] with my friend called "Toyland".'

Sunday, Janice mentions reading newspaper articles, comics and the political cartoon from 'many newspapers'.

Janice and books

In all of this diary, there is not a single mention of a book, even though 'reading a book' was prominent among the prompts offered to the diary-keepers. Ignoring for the moment the very real possibility that this oversight represents a certain perfunctoriness in the diary-keeping, it is possible to see Janice as a classic example of a young teenager too busy to read.

From our meetings, however, it is clear that such an interpretation would be a simplification. Janice does find it hard to get time clear to read, but she claims that she nearly always has a book on the go, she refers knowledgeably to particular titles and authors, and she is definite about the advantages of reading. In our first session near the end of Grade 8, Janice looked at the introductions to five novels, five movies and five CD-ROM games. After we had finished talking about specific texts, I asked her the question I asked most of the participants:

MARGARET: Suppose I said that you were going to a desert island and you could have a plug-in tree or something and all the equipment you need, would you take a book with you or a video or a CD-ROM, do you think?

JANICE: Probably a book.

MARGARET: Why?

JANICE: Reading just lasts so much longer and you can always go back, and video games too, but books are so much more – you can just imagine it, you know.

MARGARET: Let's take the extreme other period of time. Suppose it's a rainy Saturday morning and you have half an hour to kill, would you be likely to turn to a book or video or a CD-ROM?

JANICE: Probably, I'd probably read.

MARGARET: You'd still probably read; why is that?

JANICE: Just because I don't get to read very much. Like, I can watch TV or movies, like, I watch a movie with my mum often, and video game, my brother has a few so I play with him and – but reading is the sort of thing that you do by yourself, a quiet time.

MARGARET: Right. Suppose you were going to do something with a friend, what would be your choice then?

JANICE: A movie.

MARGARET: A movie?

JANICE: Yeah.

MARGARET: No question about that?

JANICE: No question, oh yeah, we'd watch a movie.

MARGARET: Would you ever – you play video games with your brother presumably sometimes, would you ever think of doing it with your friends?

JANICE: Well, I used to. Not these kind of video games but just little card games on the computer.

MARGARET: Right. Suppose you took *Virtual Springfield* [a computer game based on *The Simpsons*] home, is that the kind of thing you would do with a friend?

JANICE: Yeah, that would be fun. I'd do it alone too.

E-books and picture books

Halfway through Janice's Grade 9 year, I met with her and Madeleine. It was my second meeting with both girls together, and we explored a variety of formats. This time the two girls looked at an electronic book, a DVD movie of *The Secret Garden* shown on the computer screen, a picture book (*Shortcut* by David Macaulay) and a CD-ROM encyclopedia, *The Way Things Work*, also by David Macaulay. I asked them to choose which one they might like to take home and Janice chose the picture book.

A short while later Janice returned to the question of books. She and Madeleine had already been fairly dismissive of the electronic book. '[With] radio', she said,

> you get to think of images in your head and listen to it. And then TV you get to watch and listen to it so it's like no imagination, and then with a book it just like, totally like, you go over the library and pick it up, and then with these

[electronic] books it kind of ruins the image . . . I'd rather have a book because it seems cosier almost.

Janice and Madeleine saw many advantages to paper as compared with an e-book:

JANICE: And not everyone has the book so you can pass them on to your friends. It's kind of hard to pass on electronic books.
MADELEINE: Yeah, because once you have it you have to, like, once you find a book then you're stuck with it.
JANICE: Yeah. Like, I like trading for, like, if it's like a new book and you get it and stuff and you can trade in books or with your friends and stuff. It makes you able to do that, and get books from the library.

The girls rejected the technological feel of the e-book but it seems clear from this exchange that they also found it difficult to picture how the e-book would function *socially* as effectively as a paper book does. The reading of paper books comes across in this discussion as rooted in a social exchange system that the girls perceive as an integral part of the reading experience.

The Way Things Work: CD-ROMs versus books

Over and over again, it became clear that Janice on her own and Janice and Madeleine in concert were making very specific judgements about appropriate platforms for particular texts in particular situations. Almost immediately after their rejection of the electronic book and their endorsement of the cosy pleasures of a print book, they moved on to talk about *The Way Things Work* and perceived different virtues and flaws.

MARGARET: There is a book of *The Way Things Work*; would you rather have this in the CD-ROM format or in the book format?
JANICE: In the CD format probably. It seems more fun having like, it is kind of more fun like, having a guy move. Like I think, like the books are really fun, but it's also fun having this kind of thing, that's not just kind of a good book on a screen. This is more fun.
MADELEINE: Yeah, it's like, the diagrams move. In the books it's just 'blah'.
JANICE: As it shows you actually how the little things work.

A media ecology

In the environment of young secondary students, ease of access to materials in different formats is clearly related to expense. One of the pleasures of books is that you can trade them with your friends and maximize your investment in that way. Janice also referred to sales at the library and elsewhere where she could pick up books for fifty cents. The implication is clear that you are happier about trading something that did not cost you a great deal of money in the first place.

Many adolescents must aim for a delicate balance in achieving independent access to texts. Computer texts are difficult because they are so expensive, and the amount of unfettered control over purchases is correspondingly limited by parents and by what will please more than one person in the family. I have worked with adolescent readers for many years, and have always asked about number, age and gender of siblings. It is striking how much more relevant such questions appear to be in a discussion of some kinds of texts as compared to others. If you have a 13-year-old girl and a 10-year-old boy in your family, that demographic fact may affect what kinds of computer texts you invest in. Purchased and even rented videos are sometimes treated similarly, with a choice made on the basis of compromise between interested parties – and access to the television set may be an issue of greater or lesser importance depending on the number of sets in the household.

Books (possibly with the exception of books chosen to be read aloud to all the children) are a much more individual issue. It is unusual to hear a teenager talk about book choice as being constrained by the presence or absence of siblings – though access to a sibling's collection may sometimes enhance choice. Yet other real limitations on possible book selection exist. The range of available library books depends on the size and location of the library. Book purchases are often curtailed by one factor or another. To buy a new book and have a correspondingly broad choice you need the full price of a paperback. Whether you have access (independently or with transport required) to a chain or an independent bookstore also matters significantly. If you buy secondhand, you can get more books for your money but you are then restricted to the choice from whatever happens to be on sale.

Similarly, the price of movie admission gives you a broad choice of current screenings (limited in some cases by the need for parental transport); the price of a video rental (possibly with similar transportation constrictions) gives you an open choice, subject to the kinds of family considerations outlined above. If you are restricted to what is available on television (either in real time or taped for later viewing), the price is better and access is easier to organize, but the selection is again reduced.

Janice and Madeleine's conversations about the best platform for particular texts need to be interpreted in the light of their roots in a complex financial and ecological environment. If a CD-ROM is much more expensive than other kinds of text, then it must offer enough advantages for you to be able to make a case for it to the person who holds the purse strings. Access to different media needs to be negotiated for on different terms, so that transport is a major issue with movies and perhaps the potential for an educational return factors into the discussions over an expensive text such as *The Way Things Work*. It is worth remembering that, in such an environment, a book may appear to be relatively hassle-free; once you have managed to lay your hands on it one way or another, temporarily or permanently, the need for other kinds of negotiations is reduced. Both Janice and Madeleine spoke positively about their independent access to at least secondhand books. Magazines did not feature in our conversations but it is likely that at least some of their appeal lies in a price that can be managed within the limits of adolescents' incomes. And part of the great appeal of television and radio to young adolescents certainly lies in the price and ease of access.

It would be a fascinating exercise to map an adolescent's geographical 'footprint' in the local and extended neighbourhood, in terms of acquiring texts in different media. How far afield is a 13-year-old allowed to travel, on foot, by bus or on a bike? What kinds of textual access require the scaffolding of adult and car? Which texts arrive as gifts, acquired through an adult's broader range of access? What is the role of libraries and video rental shops versus outright purchase? Access, in the abstract, is plentiful, but a teenager's actual limits are often both tight and idiosyncratic.

Re-visiting texts

Early in Grade 9, Janice and Madeleine played *Starship Titanic* together and were excited by its complexity. Discussing its potential for replaying led them into an interesting disagreement on the virtues and values of re-reading:

MADELEINE: I find games kind of boring after a while. Except for *Starship Titanic*.

JANICE: Yeah, that was a good one. If there's games where you do keep finding new things like even *Virtual Springfield* – you're always finding new stuff.

MADELEINE: It's like, some games are so repetitive, you just go three levels and you can't get, just like, one thing – so I get annoyed and I'm just, like, 'I'm not playing this any more. I keep getting killed by these little fishes.'

JANICE: Yeah, there's some that are really good but some are –

MARGARET: Well, you can say the same thing of books, couldn't you?

JANICE: Yeah. I usually, if I read a book more than once, I usually notice different things after the second time.

MADELEINE: I'd never read it again.

JANICE: No? I've a couple that I've read over and over. I just love them so much.

MADELEINE: Oh, when you have to do a book report, and then I find it very annoying –

JANICE: To go back.

MARGARET: Yeah, readers are very different that way. What are the books that you read again and again?

JANICE: Um, I have some from when I was little. They used to take me, like, weeks to read and now they just take for me, like, an hour.

MADELEINE: When I was little, characters, like, looking at pictures I could read them over and over; and now, the novels, I get sick if I have to read it again.

JANICE: Yeah. I had one of them, I don't remember, *The Ghost, The Doll in the Garden*, I think it was, and it was by Mary Downing [Hahn] . . . Yeah, I like that one though, because I got it – I had a gift certificate and that was what I was into at the time and I was wanting to read it and I couldn't find it anywhere, so I bought it.

It is easy to look at the huge range of books published for adolescents today and dismiss questions of access as academic. But Janice's memory of a particular book – she wanted it so much she spent her gift certificate on it because she couldn't get it any other way, and she then re-read it more than once because it was to hand – testifies to a world where specific issues of access are simultaneously random and powerful. If Janice had not had the gift certificate at the psychological moment, she might never have read this particular book that now features prominently in her reading history. Selection processes are important elements in the ongoing creation of readers, but they often work in a context of coincidence.

Publicity is also important; most readers in this study mentioned the Young Readers' Choice (YRC) Award at some point, and this competition clearly features large in the personal selection policies of students in the two schools where the study was located. For example, nearly every reader recognized *The Watsons Go to Birmingham – 1963* as a YRC title, a solid testimonial to the power of good library practice (and one I had not anticipated when I chose the title for use in the study).

One solution to the problems of limited access to titles is to re-read books and re-watch videos you already own. Janice was open to this solution to an extent:

> There are some movies that I wouldn't mind watching again or, like, mystery movies, you don't understand them the first time you see them and you just notice new things every time you see them. That's what, with movies, and with books too . . . But I wouldn't see [*Titanic*] more than twice . . . I like to think about them rather than see them again and again and again.

Janice has similar views on re-reading:

MARGARET: With a book like this that you like very much [*Anne of Green Gables*], would you read it more than once?

JANICE: Yes.

MARGARET: Do you read a lot of books more than once?

JANICE: Not really. I've read a few of my favourites more than once, and if I have them then I do. If they are from the library, then I usually don't, or if I go buy them then of course I'll read them more than once.

MARGARET: So when you say more than once, would you read them a lot of times or just two or three times?

JANICE: Probably two or three times or, if I didn't have a book to read, I wouldn't mind reading it again.

Issues of reading such as what to select, how to find time for reading, and so forth are often much more contingent than they appear in the abstract. At one level,

Janice, a relatively privileged young person in Western society, has historically unparalleled access to a wide range of texts. Yet on different occasions she described her text processing life as rather more circumscribed than such a general image would imply; the specific limitations on the life of a young teenager play a substantial role in how she engages with texts of different kinds.

The school Janice attends has an Uninterrupted Sustained Silent Reading (USSR) period of fifteen minutes every afternoon. At one point Janice referred to this daily session and said that she was reading a novel by Mary Higgins Clark (one of her favourite writers) but that it was too good to read in just fifteen-minute instalments so she had to read it at home as well. Presumably, fifteen minutes is sometimes plenty, but she is clearly familiar with the phenomenon of being taken over by a book.

To paraphrase a well-known bank advertisement, people become readers one book at a time. Depending on questions of access and selection, Janice's reading is more or less avid and more or less challenging at different points of the year. The role of the specific text weighs heavily. Unlike Madeleine who never re-reads, unlike other readers who will re-read anything, Janice's attitude towards re-reading is strongly text-dependent. Seen in this light, her fairly random access to what happens to be available in the fifty-cent library sale takes on a new importance to her personal literary history.

Communicating with computers

On more than one occasion, Janice referred to the pleasures of reading. 'Within our school, even though we don't have all computers, they're just, everything else, they're just in our science lab and everything, it's just nice to read a book you know. Just a plain old book.'

But Janice and Madeleine were also happy to talk about the virtues and values of different technologies:

MARGARET: What's the best technological thing that you know of? What's the thing that you think works best and does most?
JANICE: Curling iron! [laughter]
MARGARET: Okay.
JANICE: No, I like my computer.
MADELEINE: Probably medical stuff, like stuff that keeps people alive.
JANICE: Oh yeah. The technology advances in the medical field.
MADELEINE: The technology where they can, like, cut people without a knife. Save people like that.
JANICE: Yeah, that's the best.
MARGARET: In your lives, your daily lives?
JANICE: The computer, I like my computer.
MARGARET: And what's the best thing the computer does?
MADELEINE: Typing stuff for you.

JANICE: Yeah, for homework, it makes it a lot easier. I am even faster at typing than I am at writing, well not at writing –

MADELEINE: It makes it neater.

JANICE: – but it makes it neater, like, presentation is a lot better.

MADELEINE: Oh, the best thing is e-mail.

JANICE: Yeah, oh yeah. Internet of course. [laughter]

MADELEINE: No wait, wait, wait! The phone!! [laughter]

. . .

JANICE: I have a friend in Florida that I can instant-message so, it will be like eleven o'clock their time and eight o'clock our time and we can be chatting in the Internet, so . . . It's not like, big long e-mails, it's just, like, really fast, 'Hey, how're you doing, great, oh I have to go, bye.' So it's very short, just catching up.

By the end of the two years, references to instant messaging were becoming common in the conversations with the Grade 9 students. This project actually occurred over the period of time in which chat rooms and instant messaging became more popular. In this dialogue, the girls toss around ideas about what technology they like best: e-mail, the Internet or (Madeleine's suggestion) the telephone. At the time of these interviews, Madeleine was using the school computer to check her e-mail, but, of course, it is much more difficult for such an intermittent user to draw on all the advantages of a chat room. It is not surprising that she reverted to the benefits of the telephone. Yet for those teenagers with constant access (which probably means home access) to computers, the end of the 1990s was a time when a lot of daily conversation transferred from telephone to chat lines (or the chat room augmented the already steady use of the telephone). Canada's low rates for local telephone calls undoubtedly feature in this ecological development.

The girls also talked about other valuable uses of computers:

MARGARET: Here's another question. If the computer is the best thing in your daily sort of life, is it better for producing your own stuff or for doing the kinds of things we're doing here, reading things and looking at things?

MADELEINE: Both.

JANICE: Yeah. I tend to kind of, just, type my homework and draw pictures and stuff. We don't have, like, we have some games, they're mostly my brother's. He has, like, hockey, he's on all the time playing that.

MADELEINE: Yeah, my brother's more into games.

JANICE: Yeah. I'm more into just homework doing on it because it's just so helpful for homework.

MADELEINE: Yeah. I don't really do games. I just do e-mail and homework.

JANICE: Yeah. E-mail and homework.

MARGARET: So, somebody said that boys use computers more for games and girls use computers more for communication.

BOTH: Yeah.

MARGARET: Is that true of you?

JANICE: Yeah.

MADELEINE: Definitely.

JANICE: Well, in our case, yeah.

MADELEINE: In mine. I find games kind of boring after a while. Except for *Starship Titanic*.

It is worth pointing out that e-mail and other Internet activities offer many advantages of independent control at a reasonable price – at least for the teenagers who are not paying for the equipment or the online connection. In a world where computer games were cheap and readily accessible, it is possible that these girls, on their own or with the guidance of their friends, might have discovered more games with the appeal of *Starship Titanic*. As it was, they were astonished to realize how engrossing such a game might be. If their main exposure is to computer games that appeal to 10-year-old boys, their amazement is not so surprising. It is clear that many of the stereotypes of gender divisions in computer use apply to these two girls and their little brothers, yet at the same time it is also clear that the girls are relaxed and confident about their own uses of computers.

Heading for high school

Late in Grade 9, Janice's exit interview for this project confirmed many of her earlier predilections. As we spoke, she was reading *To Kill a Mockingbird*, partly to get a head start on high school, where the novel is a common choice in Grade 10. Sometimes, as an alternative, she picked up *The Little Prince*. She spoke of a selection of recent reading: *Cat Tail Moon*, *Rats Saw God*, *The Golden Compass* (first published in the UK as *Northern Lights*) and 'The Lottery'. She read for fifteen minutes every day in reading break, and added somewhere between half an hour and a full hour at home most nights.

Asked to name her best books ever, Janice referred to S.E. Hinton's *The Outsiders*; to the Mary Downing Hahn book she discussed in Grade 8, *A Doll in the Garden*; to a book by Mary Higgins Clark, *All Around the Town*; and to a newcomer to her pantheon, *Chicken Soup for the Teenage Soul*. This last she values because it is so easy to pick up and put down. She would like to read *Jonathan Livingston Seagull*. It is noticeable that her list of favourites is considerably less demanding than the recent reading she described.

Her television favourites fell in the same broadly popular territory: *Dawson's Creek*, *Two Guys and a Girl and a Pizza Place*, *Dharma and Greg*. She also watched *Friends*, *Charmed*, *Felicity* and *Candid Camera*. Hockey continued to be important through the playoff season: 'we're a hockey family'. She was more likely to re-watch a television show than re-read a book. But an important proviso to all of these allegiances is that, as we spoke in May, she was watching less television and was more likely to be out roller-blading. For all of the young people in this northern city, their text ecology was definitely seasonal, as they took to the outdoors with great enthusiasm as soon as the weather finally broke.

The asset model

Kathleen Tyner (1998) uses an interesting and helpful phrase about approaches to media education, speaking of the 'asset model'. 'An asset model for media teaching assumes that mass media and popular culture can work as a benefit to literacy instead of as a social deficit' (1998: 7). Taking her experiences with different kinds of texts into account, what kind of asset model can we develop from Janice's self-descriptions?

As we will see over the course of this book, Janice, like the other students in this project, approaches a variety of texts with a range of skills and understandings. She knows a great deal about how stories work, and is able to make intelligent predictions and judgements about them. She is completely at home in decoding print and moving images, and also shows that she is able to build on less developed skills in playing with an unfamiliar computer-based fiction. She moves confidently between diegetic levels of stories in different media and assesses different versions of the same fictional universe with confidence.

Her account of her recreational media choices is a reminder that even young teenagers are substantially independent text users in contemporary Western society. This fact is so taken for granted that it is almost invisible. Issues of access and of time act as very real constraints, yet it is clear in all the conversations that Janice is in charge of her own text and media choices in her domestic life. She makes relatively little reference to required reading and does not mention arguments with parents over her text choices. In fact, she speaks as a full participant in a world of extensive choices, despite the limits on her access to remote or expensive texts. Working within the politics of classroom decision-making and resistance, teachers may sometimes underestimate the degree to which young people are full agents in their own private textual lives. Janice's confidence in her ability to tackle even unfamiliar formats in part arises from this sense of agency, an important asset for adult life.

There is much public discussion focusing on the dangers of young people having too much uncontrolled access to violent computer games, inane television pro-grammes, overly sexual movies and websites, and so forth. Such debate, while it raises important questions, makes it easy to forget the importance and complexity of *learning to select* from the huge range of alternatives that citizens of the West take for granted from a very early age. The contemporary ecology of enormous choice calls for different skills from those needed to function in a society where a few texts are used intensely. All of Janice's decisions may or may not be wise ones, but she is possessed of many selection skills and speaks of them with confidence.

Another asset that Janice manifested at every session is also undervalued to the point of invisibility. When asked to talk about her text choices, Janice was fluent and confident. Just being able to take part in the ongoing social conversation about texts is an asset in itself. During the course of this project, I was struck by a hidden virtue of the school's compulsory daily reading time: it meant that every one of the junior high students was able to join in a conversation about books with an interested stranger. The value of any one particular conversation may not be very great, but the ability to join in should not be underestimated. Children whose parents ban television know how much the playground conversation matters and often become skilled at bluffing a certain expertise on matters televisual. The Grade 8 and 9 students in this study are not all committed readers but they all have enough exposure to books for the ongoing conversation about print not to be closed to them.

Janice and Madeleine testify to the importance of being able to take part in a conversation about certain kinds of texts by the enthusiasm with which they make reference to *Starship Titanic*, a game that appears to represent their first successful exposure to an appealing and complex computer game. They had other comments about games they had played at home, but they clearly enjoyed not having to filter their discussions about such games through their little brothers' choices.

I think it is easy to underestimate the ongoing half-life of a text, the extension of the pleasures of the initial engagement into subsequent discussion with others. In the kind of society where choice is so extensive, people need to be able to join in at different levels. You may not have seen the exact episode of *Friends* being talked about, but you know the series and can follow the details. You haven't read one book by an author but you have read others, or you have read books by different authors in the same series, or you have seen a film adaptation. You haven't seen the movie but you have seen the back story of its filming on the television programme *Entertainment Tonight*. Being able to join in the conversation in one way or another is a valuable asset in contemporary social life. One element of the compulsory reading time in this junior high school is that it keeps books in the mix of the ongoing conversation among these students. Issues of access to computers also matter at this level of joining in the conversation as well as in questions of skill and competence. In the case of Janice and Madeleine, on the evidence of their conversations with me, they could talk happily about e-mail but much less extensively on the subject of games. This limitation is self-perpetuating to the degree that they are closed out of other conversations about games, thus closing down one route to expanding their repertoire and expertise.

Undoubtedly Janice possesses other assets that fuel her relationships with many kinds of texts. The final element I will describe here is an intangible ingredient in her text-related life: enjoyment. Janice sparkled with enthusiasm throughout our encounters. If appearances are not misleading, she thoroughly enjoyed the chance to play with the texts and to talk about her textual pleasures.

Conclusions

Janice is well on the way to becoming a fully literate citizen of the twenty-first century. She not only knows how to take advantage of the different qualities of different formats and media, but she knows why she wants to do so and is clear about the virtues of specific formats. She is not intimidated by unfamiliar technology but not immediately ready to jump on any passing bandwagon either. When pressed to choose one option over another, she often opted for print, but her domestic and scholastic lives clearly include an expanding relationship with the computer as well.

Janice's life is a full and busy one. Her musical and sporting enthusiasms are very positive ingredients in the ecology of her personal experience. School plays a major part in her life, and her textual experiences are interwoven with school requirements in many interesting ways.

Talking with Janice was always enjoyable and instructive. As with the other participants, I was sorry to say goodbye to her at the end of the project. Observing her responses to many different kinds of text was always illuminating; her evident pleasure in the challenge of the project was a bonus.

Afterword: new literacy ecologies of the twenty-first century

Janice was already adept at instant messaging in 1999, but there is no mention in all her interviews of any form of texting on cellphone or mobile telephone. The issue of text messaging is a reminder that literacy ecologies may be geographically as well as technologically specific. North America lagged far behind Europe and Japan in its adoption of cellphones, even for regular conversation, never mind texting; and Canada was slower even than the United States to climb on board this particular technological bandwagon.

In October 2005, Statistics Canada reported that, by the end of March 2005, 'there were 47 wireless subscribers for every 100 people in this country, a level reached in the United States in mid-2002' (Partridge 2005: B3). By the end of 2004, the United States figures stood at 61.7 wireless subscribers for every 100 people, but 2005 figures suggest far greater wireless penetration in Europe:

> 103 per cent of the population in Britain, more than 109 per cent in Italy and 119.4 per cent in Luxembourg. These seemingly impossible percentages stem from a growing phenomenon of users subscribing to more than one wireless service, one for the office and one for personal use, for example.
>
> (Partridge 2005: B3)

With fewer than half of the population even owning a cellphone by early 2005, it is not surprising that Canadians are not big text messagers. But why are the discrepancies so startling? Why is the media ecology of Canada so out of sync with other parts of the world in this particular area? Why does a rich country like Canada rank at twenty-seven in a study of wireless penetration among thirty member countries of the Organization for Economic Cooperation and Development (Partridge 2005: B3)?

Cost is one element of the answer to this question. Prices are still comparatively high in Canada, compared to the price for a land line (which is relatively cheap, compared to many other countries). Competition among carriers is not as intense in Canada as in some other countries, and Canadians are not yet able to take advantage of number portability: if they change carriers to get a better deal, they have to change phone numbers. The inconvenience of this arrangement is not likely to entice users to experiment.

But cost is not a one-off simple yes-or-no factor in cellphone usage. Even if the overall price of a cellphone package is high, the design of that package may foster certain forms of use. A pricing package that allows for free evening and weekend use may tip the balance towards lengthy conversations at particular times of day – and if talk is cheap for at least part of the day that may reduce the pressure to switch to text messaging as an alternative.

Whatever the reasons, there is no doubt that texting has been very slow to take root in Canada, but it appears that the shift is finally beginning to take effect. A 2004 survey indicated that use of texting among Canadians 'has doubled since 2003, with 23 per cent saying they send or receive an SMS message on a monthly basis' (Bloom 2004: B9). Such figures must seem risible to Europeans and Asians – fewer than a quarter of the population engaging in text messaging even once a month. But this study also showed signs of encroaching change: 'Nearly *half* of young Canadians (aged 15–24) say they use text messaging on a *weekly* basis' (Bloom 2004: B9, emphasis added). A different study established that 300 per cent more text messages were sent in Canada in 2004 than in 2002 (more than 710 million messages in 2004 versus 174 million in 2002). By February 2005, 3.4 million text messages a day were being recorded, a rate that would extrapolate to an annual tally of 1,241 million, another huge increase but almost certainly an underestimate since it is built on the idea that the February rate would remain constant for the rest of the year (Wilson 2005: B1). Even if older Canadians are slow to take up texting, it seems likely that the kind of young person represented in this study will soon be catching up to global peers.

Chapter 4

Jack

Jack

Jack had just turned 13 when he undertook his media diary in his first term of Grade 8. He worked with me until near the end of Grade 9, when he was 14½.

Jack lives with his mother and his sister, who is three years younger. Every other weekend he and his sister travel three hours each way to stay with their father, stepmother and two small half-siblings. I never asked about his personal life and he volunteered no opinions about this arrangement, but it occasionally surfaced in relation to texts: he has two sets of text-related behaviours, two sources of books and videos. For example, he said, 'We usually rent a video or two when we go to my dad's or one, maybe once a month with Mom.'

Jack's media diary

Jack's diary differed from the others in that he supplied the record for a single day only, but provided considerable detail about that day, a November weekday in 1997. From 7.40 to 7.45 in the morning, he used the computer and printer to print out an extra working copy of his science fair project. From 7.50 to 8.00, he read the newspaper, as follows: 'read comics, and some scanning of the current events, and the Canadian dollar'. From 8.10 to 8.25 he listened to a popular radio station in the car on the way to school, 'as usual'.

Returning from school, he listened to a tape, 'usually an alternative . . . kind of tape'. Between 4.00 and 5.00 Jack went online, browsing for Hebrew computer fonts and Hebrew translations and transliterations for his bar mitzvah. From 5.30 to 6.00, he listened to a CD and the radio at a friend's house, while working on the science fair project. Then he and the friend spent twenty minutes playing what he described as 'some bad graphics, slow speed golf games on my friend's 1985 computer'. This particular activity, he explained in a footnote, was not usual and only occurred because of the science project.

On his return home, Jack worked on his own computer between 7.30 and 8.00, typing up some 'stuff' and doing some homework. Between 8.30 and 9.00 he watched 'Teletoons' on television with his sister. From 9.00 to 9.45 he read his book, *The Three Musketeers*, after which he fell asleep with the radio playing.

Reading this single page of dense listings, it is easy to see Jack's media encounters embedded in the fabric of his normal daily life. Apart from the bad computer golf game, which appears to have been somewhat forced on him, he clearly selects medium and text very specifically for his particular needs, and ranges back and forth between media in a purposeful kind of way. Yet at the same time, the contingencies of what happens to be available are still part of his daily routine. The friend's bad game and the juvenile television show watched with his little sister contrast with what he chooses for his own purposes: Hebrew fonts and *The Three Musketeers*.

Jack and computers

Jack was one of the more experienced computer users of the group participating in this study. His experience and expertise manifested themselves in many ways, but one particularly striking consequence of his knowledge was that, much more than many of the others, he felt a sense of control over his options with regard to computer materials. Where Janice and Madeleine talked about occasionally playing their little brothers' games, Jack surfed the Internet looking for demo games, and occasionally purchased a computer magazine with a demo CD-ROM full of samplers.

When I showed Jack the computer game of *Men in Black*, he was pleased to see it:

JACK: Ah, ooh!! I love that game!
MARGARET: You know this game?
JACK: I know that game.
MARGARET: Have you played it?
JACK: I have the demo, actually . . .
MARGARET: How did you get the demo?
JACK: I got it off a CD.
MARGARET: What kind of CD?
JACK: It's a demo CD. *PC Gamer* . . .
MARGARET: Are you a regular reader of things like *PC Gamer*?
JACK: Every once in a while. Yeah, I don't really go out and get them often, but I think I would have downloaded this anyways, actually.
MARGARET: You can download the demo . . . Do you do that very much?
JACK: When I see something that I like, like, you know, but sometimes it's just not worth it to spend more time on it.

Of the assortment of computer games shown to the participants at various times in the study, the *Men in Black* game is the only one that works via keyboard controls rather than through the mouse. Jack was familiar with the set-up of the game and played far more confidently than any other participant. He actually prefers keyboard controls: 'I like the keyboard because I think you have more control. You know where you're going; you can't skip.' Alone among the students who tinkered with *Men in Black* he said, 'I think it's easy to navigate and it makes sense.'

The role of partners

In a Grade 9 session, Jack played the computer game *Starship Titanic* in the company of Anita, who had probably less computer expertise than anyone else in the entire group, a fortuitous pairing that was set up by the school to accommodate students' afternoon schedules. To his considerable credit, Jack was punctilious about trying not to insult Anita's lack of skill and understanding. It is, of course, impossible to say how he would have behaved in the unlikely event that they had played less publicly. As it was, Jack was careful to explain some elements of the game to Anita as they moved through the screens, and he was quick to praise ('You did the right thing!' 'Good job, Anita!' 'You were right – I wouldn't have thought of it.')

For all his care in bringing his partner along with him, Jack found some activity so automatic that it did not occur to him to explain it to anybody. He saved the game incessantly and resorted to help keys more methodically than any other player. An interesting contrast in style between the two players was manifested in a snatch of retrospective dialogue. Jack said, 'That's when I started pushing F1 and stuff to try and get the, what we're supposed to do', and Anita replied, 'I thought we could do something in the [on-screen] TV that was going to help.' Jack was looking for rules; Anita was looking for content.

In the *Starship Titanic* session, the players spent about forty-five minutes engaged with the game as the video camera recorded the screen of the computer. At the end of that time, we played the video back and asked the participants to comment on what decisions they had made and why, what they expected at certain points, and so forth. My two graduate assistants and I watched Jack and Anita work their way through a game that we observers had played ourselves and often seen played by others. It was only as we replayed the video, however, that any of us registered that Jack had been saving the game every ninety seconds or so. His action was so automatic as to be invisible, even to people paying close attention to the screen but not looking for this particular strategy.

At one point in the game, the players encounter a time bomb. There are many warnings not to touch it, but most people manage to set it off and a countdown ensues. Anita inadvertently set the bomb ticking, but Jack instantly reloaded the game from the point a few seconds earlier where he had saved it. His action was so swift that none of the observers picked up exactly what had happened and it was only on the retrospective investigation of the video of the game as played that anyone queried it:

MARGARET: What did you make at this point? Did you think the game was going to come to an end?

ANITA: I just thought the thing was going to blow up.

JACK: Yes, I did.
MARGARET: And that would end the game or . . .?
JACK: Well, after, I think we were supposed to solve the puzzle.
MARGARET: Yeah.
JACK: If it looks like a puzzle.
MARGARET: So what did you do?
JACK: I loaded it. That's why I saved it in the first place.

In his retrospective observations on a second engagement with this bomb, Jack's commentary shows us how his game-playing strategies affect his imaginative engagement:

ANITA: Why did you go in there in the first place?
JACK: I was looking around.
ANITA: Oh, okay.
MARGARET: Why did you ignore all the signs saying 'Keep Out, Dangerous, High Voltage, Don't Say You Weren't Warned'?
JACK: I saved.
MARGARET: You saved, okay, that's – once you've saved, you're invincible, hey? It doesn't matter how much you mess it up?
JACK: That's right!
MARGARET: You back it up. Okay.
JACK: Well, I wanted to see what was in there.
ANITA: Curiosity, okay. Just wondering.
MARGARET: That 'save' thing does make a difference to how reckless you can be, I guess, doesn't it?
JACK: I guess so.

Jack's discussion about the consequences of his constant saving has its tentative aspects, but his actions during the game playing itself were quick, decisive and apparently automatic. He appeared to save as a reflex action and readily conceded that this strategy had developed from considerable experience in game playing. The impact on his imaginative processing of the game is intriguing. Asked a question from within the context of the imaginative world of the game, 'Why did you ignore all the signs saying "Keep Out, Dangerous, High Voltage, Don't Say You Weren't Warned"?', Jack replied with a strategic answer from the world of the game player rather than the game: 'I saved.' What does this shift tell us about the nature of the implied player of a computer game? Does the game address an interpreter who, it is assumed, will find some way of dealing with the threat of a ticking bomb? Or has Jack's playing strategy actually diminished his engagement with the game because he knows he can escape from the consequences of almost any action by reverting to the last save-point? (It lends a whole new resonance to the phrase, 'With one bound Jack was free'!) Instead of working through the endless maze-like complications of the game, he is able to streamline a steady progress through the story. It could be possible to describe this as a kind of 'cheating'; yet the tactic is well known to seasoned game players and the game may well be set up to be played in just this way. Certainly Jack did not find a way to make the game simple, and it is doubtful if he ever would have managed that, even with a more experienced partner and all the time in the world.

Those of us who observed Jack's game ranged in experience from Anita with almost no exposure to computers at all through to the student cameraman, an experienced game player in his mid-20s. None of us had attained Jack's level of automaticity in running a series of game maintenance strategies alongside the content processing of the material.

The pairing of Jack and Anita was accidental but had definite consequences: some that facilitated the aims of this study and some that hampered it. Jack did his best not to leave Anita behind but her inexperience undoubtedly restricted his explorations. On the other hand, her diffidence about making decisions led him to be more articulate about his reasoning than he might have been with a partner with whom he could have taken more for granted.

It was never a condition of this study that we would see the participants engaged in any natural engagement with texts. From beginning to end, the study was designed to offer opportunities to observe text processing in close-up and in slow motion, and the artificiality of such a set-up is simply part of the nature of the study. Given the ordinary conditions of his daily life, it is very difficult to imagine Jack volunteering to play this complex game with such an inexperienced partner. There is no way to tell how courteous and careful of his partner's feelings he would be if such a situation did arise more privately. What we saw was a teenage boy doing his best to make room for his partner to participate even though their skill levels diverged very broadly. But by default, what we also saw was a reading that could only be processed by two readers simultaneously and that was therefore shaped by both. The interactions between Jack and the text did not exist outside of the context of the interactions between Anita and the text, and the interactions between Anita and Jack. The imaginative space was created jointly by all three, and affected as well by their occasional references to those of us watching who were more familiar with the game than they were. This constraint was not necessarily to Jack's liking. He said on more than one occasion that he preferred the *Men in Black* game. Partly, it was clear, this preference was because he felt more in control of that game; he had learned how to attend to it privately and without having to bring a partner along with him. He was the only person in the study to describe the *Men in Black* CD-ROM as less frustrating than *Starship Titanic*.

Jack's choices

Many years of working with adolescent readers have taught me never to make assumptions about what will appeal to a reader, and Jack's responses to a range of texts confirmed this observation. The first page of *Anne of Green Gables* always strikes me as long-winded and leisurely with no attempt to draw the reader into any developing action. The plot does not really get going until well down the second page, after we have learned a great deal about the Avonlea brook and Mrs Rachel Lynde, a minor character. Jack, however, was positive from the first glance onwards. He first read a photocopy of page one and was then given the whole book to look at:

JACK: I would definitely keep going because it sounds like a book that would tell a good story. It would tell a descriptive story that made a lot of sense.
MARGARET: You like the way it's written?
JACK: I do like the way it's written.
MARGARET: Well, okay, have a look at the whole book and see if you still think so.
JACK: I do, because I've read it . . . I liked this book . . . I liked the way it was written. Yeah, I mean, I found some old books that I wouldn't read [*unclear*] recently, and it was all like, 'Bob said . . .' and it was written, not, they were good stories but it wasn't written well enough to keep me interested, so I like this book a lot.

The motif of preferring books that were well written was one that Jack returned to when he looked at the first page of *The Golden Compass*:

JACK: Huh! *The Golden Compass*! I love this book. I read it this year and I read it because my friends read it and they said it was good. I picked it up and I looked at it and said it doesn't look that interesting to me, but they said it was a good book so I opened it and I read it and I got sucked in. I just *loved* it! It was written so well, it was a totally incredible story.
         . . .
MARGARET: If your friends hadn't told you anything about that book, would that first page be enough?
JACK: Yes, but I don't know if I'd even have opened it.
MARGARET: Right, right. But assuming that somehow you came across that first page –?
JACK: Yeah, I definitely would.
MARGARET: What in that first page then would make you want to find out more?
JACK: It's well written! It's really descriptive right away and you know where you are and you know you're in some place that isn't where we are right now and you want to learn about it.
MARGARET: What tells you that? In that first page?
JACK: Well, her daemon and that she's in her Master's room. That it's someplace that I don't know about and I'd like to learn about.

The powerful role of a reading community in the development of readers is well known, but Jack's comments about the friends who talked him into reading *The Golden Compass* reinforce the importance of having someone to talk to about your reading, to stretch your tastes and keep you going.

A description of Jack's reading tastes is not exhausted by an account of this relatively refined approach to particular titles. Like many Grade 8 readers, his reading covers a broad continuum. He said he reads a lot and I asked him if he reads every single day:

> Yeah, definitely! I have *Hardy Boy* books that my dad had and his brothers and sisters that were lying in my room, and I hadn't read them before because they were kind of scary and, you know, I was little. But I read, like, one a day now and I think they're really good. I love mystery stories.

Like Janice, Jack has his sources for acquiring new books:

> My sister *loves* to read. She wasn't a great reader before, I remember, but now she can't stop and she keeps taking books from my room. I have to take books from her room because I've read all the books in my room. Yeah. And I, yeah, there's this place called the 'Book Nook'. It buys, sells and trades books, and we go there. But you know, they're also like little kid books like *My Teacher is an Alien* kind of thing. I got $300 at Chapters [Canada's book superstore chain] for my bar mitzvah, and, so we go there a lot and get books.

Like Janice, Jack is describing a world where many of his sources for books are random rather than organized. His reading is embedded in a matrix of domestic and commercial access. To what extent the flavour of his actual reading is affected by the source of a book is a matter for speculation, but it would not be difficult to imagine that his reading of one *Hardy Boys* book per day might be nuanced by his sense of participating in a tradition established by his father and his aunts and uncles. Sometimes access to a particular book is relatively neutral but often it is marked by personal and/or institutional relationships. Books from friends, books from parents, books from Chapters, books from the 'Book Nook', old copies of the *National Geographic* from his grandfather – all will come bearing a certain charge from the source. This study did not investigate the impact of this effect – all the texts explored by the readers in this project were supplied by me as a visiting researcher, and available for sampling only rather than extensive reading. However, the conversations about reading often returned to questions of access and selection as part of the ecology of the literate lives of these students.

The textual world of *Men in Black*

One of the many ingredients that makes contemporary literacy such an interesting brew is the fact that the ecology within which young people learn to negotiate their literate habits and strategies is one profoundly marked by commercial proliferation of texts, adaptations and multimedia versions of the same story. Jack, who was a fan of the 1997 hit movie *Men in Black*, has clearly developed a tool kit for making decisions about how he will navigate this multiplicity of texts. His conversation about the different versions of the story was an interesting one.

At our first meeting, which was in the spring of 1998, I showed him the opening scenes of both the video and the computer game of *Men in Black*, and in the course of our conversation we ranged over a number of other manifestations of the story. Jack was a fan of the movie, which he had watched three times (once in the movie theatre and twice on video): 'I *loved* it . . . I liked the way that it has a storyline that kept you interested all the time.' He was cool about the spin-off animated television version, on the other hand:

> I watched it, half of it, once . . . It didn't seem too interesting. It didn't seem like something that would keep me interested when I know that there's other things on. Because . . . it didn't keep me interested on a minute-to-minute basis. That there wasn't stuff happening enough.

Yet given a choice between watching the movie for a fourth time or watching the animation, he would opt for the animation; for the time being, at least, he had saturated the potential of the movie and would choose novelty over perceived quality.

Jack would read articles and watch television shows about the making of *Men in Black*: '*Definitely*! I really like that kind of stuff.' He was more hesitant about whether he would read the novel:

> Maybe. It usually, they're not as good. I mean the, if the movie's based on the novel, it's always the novel that I would choose. If it's based on the movie, I would know that that, um, it would be something that somebody tried to make some money off but I think I'd read it. It might be interesting.

Asked about the role-playing game book, however, Jack began to reach a point of diminishing returns. 'Maybe not. I don't think so. There's a lot of hype about *Men in Black* and it's got kind of annoying actually.'

Later in our conversation, when I offered Jack the chance to experiment with the computer game version of *MiB*, his enthusiasm returned. He had already played the demo version of this game and was seriously considering purchasing it. Having practised the game previously, he attacked the keyboard controls with confidence. 'I think it's easy to navigate and it makes sense', he said. 'There's a story that begins to develop, and ah, yeah, it's more fun!' When I asked him if he would ever resort to the walk-through cheat text offered on the Internet, he was scornful, though he admitted that he might turn to it if truly pressed. 'When I'm stumped, you know, I'd get a clue or two, but I really don't [like it].'

Jack moved back and forth among the different versions of the story with panache. It is clear that story in multiple format is a familiar concept to him, and he has set his personal hierarchies for processing such texts. If the movie is based on a novel, he may prefer to read the novel first, for example, while a novel based on a movie is something to be wary of. He is interested in behind-the-scenes information but cautious about hype. He is also clear when he has had enough; after three viewings of the movie he would rather pass the time by watching an inferior but novel cartoon version of the story. He is happy to invest his money in the computer game but only after checking out a sample. Clearly this is a boy whose strategic tool kit for processing a multiply-told story is well stocked.

Jack moved among different versions of the story with ease. He discriminated between those texts he truly enjoyed and the ones that he described as the product of hype or money-spinning. These critical distinctions were drawn within the context of the *MiB* multiverse; at no point in our conversation did he draw on any critical perspective on the movie original except to say that it was possible to watch it enough times to prefer novelty to a repeat experience.

The aesthetics of the e-book

On the occasion that Jack looked at the electronic book, the DVD movie, the picture book and the CD-ROM encyclopedia, he was paired with Gregory. Their conversation about the e-book was one of the most interesting of the whole project. Neither boy liked the e-book, although they could not entirely articulate what it was they didn't like, and they were both very surprised to reach this conclusion.

Although neither of them had ever seen one before, Jack and Gregory explored the e-book with ease, looking up words in the dictionary, changing the font size, writing and attaching notes, and changing the page orientation, with very little assistance or advice from me. But they were very clear about the book's lack of appeal:

MARGARET: Can you ever see yourselves using something like this?
GREGORY: Um, I don't think I could.
JACK: I don't think so. I mean, like, it's neat. You have so much stuff, but –
GREGORY: Without even having to read anything! [laughter]
JACK: That's true.
MARGARET: Yeah, well, no, you're playing here really, aren't you?
JACK: I think that I prefer to sit down with a book. Like, a book.
GREGORY: Yeah.
MARGARET: Why?
JACK: I really like technology and all that, but I think that this – I don't know.
GREGORY: Yeah, it's hard to explain.
JACK: The other thing is this is, like, it's a little, it's just complicating it. I mean, you read a book, you're getting the story. I think this takes away from the story, you know, you're playing with it, you've got to move your finger and that kind of thing.
GREGORY: You're going to find yourself getting distracted. The only thing I do like, though, is, like, the dictionary.
. . .

MARGARET: Now, you're looking at it at the moment as a novelty and, you know, obviously you are in a situation where you are not going to sit down and read. Can you imagine that if you were used enough to reading with it that you would stop being distracted? Can you envisage that if –

JACK: I guess you probably could, but I still think it, like, scroll there and go.

GREGORY: Yeah, because if you're, like, reading it and you accidentally hit the screen with, like, your thumb or something, and then it flips through an entirely new page.

JACK: And, like, for me that would be difficult to, like, get used to, but um, I guess if I had to I could.

GREGORY: Yeah.

JACK: I don't see why I would have to.

I put it to these boys that one of the advantages of the electronic book is that you could carry just one instead of a stack of ten. Even this consideration was not enough to move Jack, who said:

> But if I was taking ten books or something, I think I would pack the ten books, you know, like, I don't know if I would have even bought this in the first place . . . I mean, if I had it, I'd take it.

I suggested that it might be a convenient way to organize a large set of textbooks. Jack said he would use the e-book if that were an option, but then added:

> If I was in my dorm or my room, I wouldn't pick this up . . . I mean, even with my notes and everything. Well, maybe I'd read them later, but I would pick up the textbook, that's easier for me and that's like, yeah, I really don't know how to say it.

Jack continued to be doubtful. In a series of remarks, he expressed a resistance that surprised even himself:

> It's convenient. I don't think it's a great way of reading and learning, though . . . I mean, it is great. I wouldn't use it . . . I prefer the book. I don't know why . . . I mean, I actually don't know why. This is amazing, it has so many neat functions and you can, like, put notes and bookmarks, but I like a book.

Asked what improvements to the e-book might make it more appealing, the boys came up with a sensible list in very short order: less glare, better fonts, a higher pixel count, colour, better menus, a double-page opening, bigger pages, and a way of reducing the impact of fingerprints. They continued to be surprised at their own resistance to the e-book.

Up to a very late point in this conversation, the boys had been looking at the e-book inside its leather jacket. They both expressed a dislike of this jacket, which is indeed cumbersome, and were surprised to learn it could be removed. The bare e-book, which rather resembles a high-grade Etch-a-Sketch, pleased them quite a bit more, but their final vote was still categorically in favour of the paper book.

It is interesting to try to disentangle the factors at play in this exchange. The boys were clearly intrigued by the e-book, even as they disliked it. Their observations on how to improve it are clearly functional in focus but there seem to be aesthetic issues at work as well. For instance, they objected to particular letters in the italic font that was loaded on to my e-book; the p and the f were designed in a broken shape that they greatly disliked. They complained about the relatively small number of words that could be screened at a time, again a functional issue but a question that possibly also reflects the way the e-book 'page' is full to the edge, with no margins and no sense of white space or deliberate design.

Unlike Janice and Madeleine, Jack and Gregory did not go into the social implications of the electronic book. It is possible to read into Jack's reference to himself at some future time in his dorm the implication that he can readily imagine a social setting for using the e-book. Given that both boys appear to be confident and at home in the world of technology, this seems a reasonable supposition. Even so, there was something about the e-book that caused them to resist it strongly.

Yet both boys thought it likely that the e-book would catch on in the long run. Gregory's observations on that score are extremely interesting:

> And a lot of people, they're still, like, amazed how, like, a lot of the technologies, like if you're around technology a lot you get used to it, and when something comes out it's not as big of a deal each time, but for the people who aren't around it all the time, they just go, 'Wow, I'm going to go out and get that!'

These two boys like technology in general; both are very explicit on that score. Yet they are not so impressed by any and all technologies that their judgement is overwhelmed by lust for the new. The considered, even puzzled, tenor of this conversation testifies that familiarity can breed not necessarily contempt but instead some sense of proportion. A new piece of technology is not necessarily 'as big of a deal' *per se*; function and content matter more than bells and whistles.

Jack on the way to high school

At the end of Grade 9, Jack and I had our final conversation, which ranged across a variety of his literate habits and behaviours. Once again, it is possible to see traces of his daily life adhering to many of his textual choices. He was currently on a blitz of reading James Bond books, as the consequence of a friend's recommendation. He reads for about fourteen or fifteen hours a week – 'a lot' – and, although he is not utterly committed to the idea of reading everything by a single author, he finds that other people tend to pick up on his choices and reinforce them:

People say, 'Oh, you like that book. I have some more Jeffrey Archer books' ... I read a Jeffrey Archer book and Mom said, 'I have some more. Would you like to read them?' And I was in [the city where Dad lives] and my dad said, 'Oh, we have some Jeffrey Archer books in the bedroom', so I ended up with the whole bunch, but it's not because I feel that I have to read every Jeffrey Archer book.

Jack was categorical about his enthusiasm for reading. 'I love reading. I guess I pick up books and I don't stop.' He was very interesting about what makes a book worthwhile:

MARGARET: What's the best book that you've ever read?

JACK: I don't know. I used to think it was *Shiloh* because I loved that book and it made me feel, it evoked an emotional response. Except that I've read a lot more books since then. That's five years ago. And, ah, I really don't know.

MARGARET: Can you think of a more adult book that you've read that evokes such a powerful emotional response?

JACK: Mmm – [pause] wait a second. I read *Cain and Abel* and, you know, I didn't think I really cared about these people, you know, it was a story, but then he died in the end and I was on the verge of crying. And it really, like, it made a difference. It got to me.

MARGARET: Right. That's a very interesting question to raise. How important is it to you to care about the people that you're reading about?

JACK: Well, I think it means that I would like to keep reading the book and, like, to read more of the same kind of books.

MARGARET: Right. So it does make a difference?

JACK: Yes. But, if it's a good writing style and it's a good book, it's a good story.

MARGARET: A good yarn is enough?

JACK: Yes.

MARGARET: Right. So it's a bonus then if you care about the characters as well?

JACK: Yeah.

MARGARET: How much do you care about James Bond?

JACK: Well, I think he's cool. I like the gadgets and stuff. [Laughter] And they're neat stories.

MARGARET: Right, but you're reading them for the stories rather than for the deep –

JACK: It doesn't make me cry or doesn't make me – yeah.

Jack re-reads very little, and hates re-watching television programmes. His favourite television programmes are *Friends* and a programme that was new at the time of our interview, *The Family Guy*. The latter programme appealed to him because it was funny; with *Friends*, his reasons were a bit subtler. 'I like the people. And it's good stories and you get to know these people.'

Jack's account of his different forms of television viewing is rooted in the ecology of his daily life. With *Friends*, for example, 'if I'm there I'll watch it, and I try to be there, but it doesn't really matter to me unless it's the season finale'. His sister watches re-runs of *Friends* all the time, but Jack doesn't like to do that. If he is unable to be at home on Thursday, his second recourse is to his own friends. 'For important things, you know, if somebody tells me, "Oh, this happened", then I might borrow it from somebody because everyone tapes it.'

Similarly, his video watching is socially conditioned. The video movie at his dad's house every other weekend is simply part of the package of going there. Likewise his relationships with his friends can have an impact on his viewing:

> A lot of movies I won't watch twice. I saw *Something about Mary*, like, eight times because it was, 'Oh, we rented *Something about Mary*. Do you want to see it? . . . I've seen it . . . That's okay, let's watch it again. It's funny', but that got kind of annoying. Except there are funny parts!

The last movie Jack had seen before our interview was *From Russia with Love*, because his friend had videos of all the James Bond movies. The last movie he had seen in a movie theatre was *The Matrix* (he said he was waiting for the lines to die down before he went to see *The Phantom Menace*). Like many of his classmates, he was impressed by *The Matrix*:

JACK: It was *very* interesting. Like, it was a theory, like, of what might be happening now or what might happen in the future. I thought that was very interesting. A lot of people said it was *bad* –
MARGARET: Bad as in violent and bad for you, or badly done?
JACK: No, bad story and badly done. But I liked the point of it. It was very interesting.
MARGARET: Did you think it was an interesting point badly done or did you think it was overall a pretty good movie?
JACK: I think it was a pretty good movie. I mean, it could have been done better, I guess, but it was, ah –
MARGARET: What would you say to the people who object to the violence in it?
JACK: Well, I don't think – no, the violence is not really the movie, though.
MARGARET: No?
JACK: I mean, it's there and it adds to the movie. And it's part of it that this guy has to be gotten rid of for this, for things to happen, but it's about the fact that we're all, you know, people being harvested by aliens or by machines.
MARGARET: So there's a theme beyond the violence?
JACK: Yes.

Jack appears to have been intrigued by the demands made by *The Matrix* on the intelligence of its viewers. Yet when it came to naming his favourite movie, he struggled to come up with a title and eventually described a movie that seems to have appealed to the same instincts as *Shiloh*: 'There was one movie that really, um, *Patch Adams*. I don't like crying in movies. I don't like being emotional, but it was *very* well done. It was funny and it was *very* good.'

Jack spends maybe four or five hours a week watching television, but his computer time is much more extensive: three or four hours a day, twenty-five or thirty hours a week. His list of computer activities is broad but includes very little time on games:

> Write to friends. Chat with friends. I'm really interested in – I don't play a lot of games. I'm really interested in, like, computers and programming, and that sort of stuff. I do some basic programming. Um, just talking to people and surfing the Net . . . Sometimes things interest me. There was www://aprilfools. com, which has a lot of neat stuff and I was there for weeks just playing with all the stuff.

I asked Jack to describe his favourite activity on the Net and his answer surprised me:

JACK: Bother people. [laughter]

MARGARET: Can you be a bit more explicit about that?

JACK: Well, ha ha, there are some people on the Internet that don't have great intentions.

MARGARET: Uh-huh.

JACK: And me and my friends like to [pause] ah, not be very nice to them. Not just swearing and stuff, just picking on them and annoying them.

MARGARET: And how do you track down these people to badger them?

JACK: A lot of them, they're on the chat rooms, and we've loaded the programs to learn to find them. There was one person that bothered me, and I gave him his address, so he left. Um, there's a million ways to get stuff on the Internet.

MARGARET: Right.

JACK: And so –

MARGARET: Would you describe yourself as a very knowledgeable Internet user?

JACK: Yes, I would.

MARGARET: Yeah, it sounds like it. How much, let me think how to put this, so I'm trying to put it neutrally, because I'm not trying to reach judgement on things. How much of what you do on the Internet would you say is positive and how much is reacting to other people like what you've just described? How much is you doing things because you want to do them and how much is in response to the behaviour of other people?

JACK: Probably half.

MARGARET: Okay.

JACK: I [pause] – well, more, yeah.

MARGARET: More which one?

JACK: I mean probably 90 per cent me wanting to go look up stuff, but when there are people that do –
MARGARET: Right. Do you see yourself as a kind of, um, Net vigilante or something? [laughter]
JACK: Well, I don't, I'm not –
MARGARET: People bothering you, or do they –
JACK: Just – bothering me. I'm not going in the Net hunting, or –
MARGARET: Right, right, okay. [laughter]

In our first interview when Jack was in Grade 8, he had just discovered chat rooms; in the fourteen months in between, he had clearly explored the systems to considerable effect. It is difficult to interpret his activities with any precision, as he was himself reasonably vague in his description. With the clarity of hindsight, I think the word 'vigilante' frightened him off a bit, which is too bad, because my intention was simply to establish how he perceived his own activities; perhaps if I had used a more neutral word he would have been more forthcoming. The conversation veered away at this point, and we did not return to this question. Whether he and his buddies are simply indulging in a technological version of being adolescent and annoying, or whether they are attempting something more serious is not entirely clear from this exchange.

What is very clear, however, is that Jack's computer skills gave him a considerable sense of his own autonomy in addressing the Net. If he didn't like somebody's behaviour on a site, he had a set of steps to take to remedy the situation, apparently to his own satisfaction.

It is also very clear that both the computer itself and his own growing mastery of it are sources of great satisfaction to Jack. I asked him what he likes best about computers:

JACK: [pause] Their incredible logic. I think it's amazing that, I mean, you can tell it to do something and it does what you say and then it reacts to situations, but only as programmed.
MARGARET: Right. So it doesn't have much imagination.
JACK: It doesn't, but it also, it will follow the program. And it will, it won't stray for anything.

An asset model

Jack is a confident and versatile user of texts in many different media. He brings many strengths to his engagements with various media. The story of Tom and Captain Najork (Hoban 1974) provides a useful clue to Jack's strengths. Many adults trying to come to terms with the computer apply Captain Najork's approach, relying on complex instructions and protocols. Jack's approach, like that of many adolescents, particularly boys, is much closer to Tom's: fool around enough and then when you need to use an application you will find you already possess the requisite skills and confidence. As assets go, this one is hard to overvalue. Clearly Jack and Tom both possess the chief ingredients for successful and productive fooling around: plenty of spare time, plenty of patience, and a lively curiosity about where a particular piece of fooling around might lead. Jack was usually firm in his views, but with the electronic book he surprised himself. Full of enthusiasm at the prospect of fooling around with an e-book for the very first time, he soon discovered that its utility and appeal fell far short of its reputation. He found it difficult to analyse exactly what it was that bothered him about the e-book, but he was certainly able to articulate his discomfiture.

Indeed, Jack was always articulate, no matter what challenge was placed in front of him. His account of how important it is for a book or a movie to tug at his emotions undermines many stereotypes about 14-year-old boys, yet he made these observations very readily. (It is probably worth mentioning, however, that these disclosures were made in the final interview, when he was on his own rather than paired with one of his classmates.) Similarly, when he read the short story 'Tunnel', he drew thematic connections with an emotionally challenging issue in his own life; we will return to his reading of the story in a later chapter.

Like Janice, Jack is fledging as an independent reader, making systematic choices about where he wants his reading to go next, occasionally stretching himself with a more challenging title. He demonstrates one of the hallmarks of a committed reader in his opportunism: if somebody supplies access to a number of Jeffrey Archer or James Bond books, he immediately takes advantage of the offer. His enthusiasm about reading is undeniable, and appears to co-exist very comfortably alongside his excitement about his computer.

Conclusions

Jack is a lively, intelligent, curious and critical user of texts in many forms and formats. He is the kind of student who would be a joy to any open-minded high school English teacher, but it is not clear if any of the local English classrooms have enough hardware and software to challenge and develop Jack's multiple literacies to the extent he deserves and would benefit from. He is approaching high school at a time when the potential gap between students with his range of experience and many of their teachers is broader than it may ever be again. Undoubtedly much of his exposure to print texts in high school will stretch him, regardless of what other opportunities are available to him, but it would be a shame if his schooling did not find some forum to engage and strengthen his other literacies as well.

A short description of this quandary is that there may be a clash between Jack's home and school experiences. Jack's domestic and personal textual ecology is extensive and sophisticated. What will happen if school offers him a much more limited ecology? Questions of access are very complex. On the face of it, Jack is exceedingly lucky, and schools need to be attending to those students who have far less domestic access to computers. Yet it is clear that Jack would benefit from being challenged on many fronts and in many media. The more tacit knowledge and understanding he acquires through his domestic access to different media, the more he needs to find ways to make his knowledge explicit and to grow as a computer user as well as a reader.

Be that as it may, this study leaves Jack at the end of his junior high years, intelligent, inquiring, and privileged in his domestic access to many forms of text. How he develops over the next five or ten years is a question full of interest and significance, both in terms of Jack's personal future and in terms of how schools and society find ways to draw out the critical understanding and creative techniques of young, bright computer amateurs.

Afterword: new literacy ecologies of the twenty-first century

I first met Jack in the late autumn of 1997, well under ten years ago as I write this afterword. I last spoke to him in late spring of 1999. Inevitably, in the years following this study, I found myself thinking of the participants from time to time, wondering how they were growing up in general and wondering how they were responding to new technologies in more particular ways. The story of Napster's rise and fall frequently put me in mind of Jack, even though I have no way of ascertaining his actual reaction to the events that made free online music more and then less available to users.

On first principles, however, Jack was a natural for Napster. He certainly had both the curiosity and the computer know-how to be an early adopter. Perhaps even more importantly, he had a well-honed capacity for opportunistic pick-up of readily available texts. Such examples as the James Bond books and the downloaded demos of computer games illustrate a user who either finds a way to get what he wants or finds a way to like what he can get – a mindset perfectly adapted to exploring the advantages of musical file-sharing.

The official lifespan of Napster was a short one, just two years from 1999 to 2001 (Coleman 2003: 177). McCourt and Burkart remind us how staggering was its rise, how precipitous its fall:

> Between February and August 2000, the number of Napster users rose from 1.1 million to 6.7 million, making it the fastest-growing software application ever recorded . . . In late July, at the [Recording Industry Association of America]'s request, Federal judge Marilyn Patel ordered an injunction against Napster, finding that the service was used primarily to download copyrighted music and rejecting Napster's arguments. In February 2001, a three-judge panel unanimously upheld the injunction, and Napster soon began filtering its system to block copyrighted material. Napster declared bankruptcy and ceased operations in 2002. Despite the RIAA's claims that Napster-driven piracy was eating into profits, recorded music sales in US reached an all-time high of 785.1 million units in 2000, up 4 percent from 1999. The RIAA claimed

that sales of CD singles dropped 39 percent in 2000 and inferred that Napster was to blame, yet fewer CD singles were released as the industry cut production. Some market research suggests that users did not utilize Napster primarily to 'steal' music through non-payment. Instead, they used Napster to 'sample' music before purchasing it. Users also were drawn to the huge array of music it presented, the obscure as well as the popular – a vast catalog (including out-of-print material) that was otherwise inaccessible.

(McCourt and Burkart 2003: 339–40)

The period when the addition of selected music to your life was almost completely free did not last long; today, even if users still engage in covert ripping and burning to supply the texts, the channels for such online music have changed and become more expensive. MP3 players of various kinds and legal tariffs for downloading songs are not cheap (at least not relative to Napster music, which was 'free' to anyone who owned an adequate computer), and they do require some kind of acquisition budget on somebody's part. If Jack were 14 today, he might well be considering spending his bar mitzvah money on a player rather than at the bookstore.

But during the heyday of Napster, Jack was perfectly situated to take full advantage of its opportunities; he had access to a computer and access to the kind of understanding necessary to take all the required steps. There was no need to find extra money for any component of his listening pleasure. It is hard to overestimate the importance of this fact for young teenagers in particular. Their grandparents may wax eloquent about the importance of hard work and thrift in their own youth; in the case of Napster, many youngsters like Jack were bootstrapping their own computer competence in ways that were also, though differently, thrifty. In return, they enjoyed the benefits of a potential that, in a different context, adults might well label as renaissance in its variegated splendour and profusion. Many of today's young people have had the opportunity to develop a rich and experimental musical background with their sampling. For a short period and for those in the select group with good computer access, Napster served some of the functions of an unlimited public library – though of course it was never really 'public' in the same way.

In addition, Napster users became more fearless in the way they attacked the Internet. The lure of free music was the kind of 'killer app' (Downes 1998) that engaged a generation of computer users in extending their skills and sharpening their attitudes. With a focus on the goal of locating their musical choices, young users acquired a set of new abilities that were perhaps all the more valuable for being almost completely tacit. Napster's shelf life was short, at least in its illegal manifestation, but its impact on those who were growing up with computers at the turn of the century was significant.

Chapter 5

Layered textual identities

The diaries

Layers of text and textual identity

All the young people in this study move among many levels of textual environment. Texts are woven into their relationships at home, at school, with their friends, with the wider society they live in (as represented in many diaries by local radio stations and the local newspaper) and in their aesthetic and/or consumer relationship to the broader world of commercial texts mostly marketed to them for entertainment and for a promise of increased knowledge. These students watch television with their siblings, play computer games and go to movies with their friends, bargain for transport or the price of a video with parents, make decisions about where to research their homework (in books, in CD-ROM encyclopedias, online). They layer their media exposure, adding radio and CDs in particular to many other activities. They use media knowledge as cultural capital in their dealings with each other and with adults (though not all adults value what they know).

In part, how these students perceive themselves and think of themselves as perceived by others is tied up closely with their knowledge of and taste for particular texts. In many cases, these texts are sold to them, and so is supplementary knowledge about the text that may serve to increase their cultural standing among their peers or simply lead to pleasure in increased insight for its own sake. It is important to remember that books are part of this commercial ecology as well. Too often books are bracketed out of discussions about the popular cultural marketplace as if they belonged to a more rarefied, less commercial zone, but a book is also a saleable commodity of a particular kind.

How these teens and pre-teens choose to present themselves in relation to particular texts is a subject of considerable interest. Gregory was an unabashed *Star Wars* zealot, happy to be known as a repository of arcane information and happy to live with the label of fanatic that his friends used to describe him to me. Janice expressed her allegiance to the local NHL hockey team in the form of ten individually painted logos on her fingernails as the team moved into post-season play; she attended games and checked the team website. Jack had no hesitation in deciding and describing which texts of *Men in Black* would offer him a worthwhile experience and which could be dismissed as mere hype and marketing. Leonard was an ardent aficionado of the soap opera *The Young and the Restless*. Such expressions of allegiance are more than public statements of how these young people wish to be identified by others, however; they also mark a certain kind and quality of imaginative experience that the individuals value and that is being interwoven with their other experiences of daily and intellectual life.

Tia DeNora would go even further in terms of assessing how people use texts to develop what she calls a 'technology of self' (2000: 46). In her study of the role of music in everyday life, she says, 'music is appropriated by individuals as a resource for the ongoing constitution of themselves and their social psychological, physiological and emotional states' (2000: 47). Her discussion concerns how people actively use music to control mood, focus and/or sense of self, but other texts may often be used in similar ways. It is not difficult to conceive of a reader managing mood by active selection of stories, or of a television viewer constituting a particular self through choice of programmes. DeNora's study makes more room than many for an account of individual agency that actively uses texts as part of developing a sense of self, both in macro terms of public self-placement and also in micro terms of emotional self-management.

Daily fiction

In 1974, Raymond Williams was inaugurated as Professor of Drama at Cambridge University. In his inaugural address, he spoke about the reach of television into our everyday lives, and said:

> It is in our own century, in cinema, in radio and in television, that the audience for drama has gone through a qualitative change . . . [F]or the first time a majority of the population has regular and constant access to drama, beyond occasion or season. But what is really new – so new I think that it is difficult to see its significance – is that it is not just a matter of audiences for particular plays. It is that drama, in quite new ways, is built into the rhythms of everyday life. On television alone it is normal for viewers – the substantial majority of the population – to see anything up to three hours of drama, of course drama of several different kinds, a day. And not just one day; almost every day. This is part of what I mean by a dramatized society. In earlier periods drama was important at a festival, in a season, or as a conscious journey to a theatre . . . What we now have is drama as habitual experience: more in a week, in many cases, than most people would previously have seen in a lifetime.
>
> (Williams 1983: 12)

It is now a long time since Williams produced his very stimulating assessment of how both our daily rhythms and our developing understanding of the world are affected by constant access to dramatic fiction. In that period, the pace of change has, if anything, speeded up. But in the quarter of a century since Williams spoke about our constant access to drama, other, perhaps smaller, cultural shifts have also taken place: for example, as well as coming into daily contact with many stories, we now are also bombarded with stories about the making of stories. Books, television programmes, newspapers, magazines and many, many websites are devoted to discussing movies and television programmes in terms of the background, the production decisions, the special effects, the actors, the budgets and the box office, and many other aspects of the behind-the-scenes world. Books are still more austere in these terms, but author tours and interviews proliferate far more widely than they used to do, and publishing decisions rate more attention than before. A flourishing market in sequels, prequels and parodies also draws more oblique attention to the constructed nature of print stories. It is almost as if much popular culture now comes in the form of a central core (where the story is actually told) and an outer zone where we remain in the world of the show or the game but are not completely within the world of the story. As we will see throughout this study, these students moved in and out of these zones with great ease.

Another major change over the past quarter-century is the development of interactive texts. The consequences of this development are not all clear, but one important change is that many texts now explicitly provide a different experience for each individual user. No two readers have ever engaged with a fixed print text in exactly the same way either, but at least they generally encountered the events of the story in the same order and with the same quotient of available information. A computer game, on the other hand, may have a clear-cut set of objectives, but each player will reach the goal by a different route and the social framework of textual engagement is correspondingly altered.

A 1997 snapshot

This project occupies a particular time frame. As I wrote up the study during 2000, I began to think of these diaries from late 1997 as historical documents. In certain important ways, these diaries represent a single moment in time, when young people used their computers for research and for a few games – and, in some cases, for e-mail exchanges – but not for ongoing real-time conversation with their friends, or for access to chat rooms, or for the exchange of music.

For the most part, these students spent more time watching television than any other media activity according to the 1997 diaries; but in the twenty-first century that perspective may seem rather quaint. It makes sense to contrast these young people with their Canadian counterparts only three years later, but the trends are similar in all Western countries. By 2000, according to a study conducted by Northstar Research Partners for Youth Culture Inc., 85 per cent of Canadian teenagers were online, three-quarters of them from home (Ferguson 2000: 38–9). Counting e-mail time, their average time online was 9.3 hours per week (McHardie 2000: A1). Ninety-three per cent of them used the computer for homework research, 68 per cent of them joined chat sessions or discussion groups and 59 per cent of them used instant messaging (Ferguson 2000: 29). And a full third of the teens said they now spend less time watching television (McHardie 2000: A1). Sue Ferguson called it 'one of the survey's most surprising findings: teens who use it are about as likely to click on the Net as they are to flick on the TV' (2000: 40).

The diaries kept by some students in the project tell where they were at the beginning of the study, and the chances are great that their behaviour by its end was probably closer to the pattern of the teens surveyed above. In 1997, not everyone in this project had a computer at home; nevertheless, all the diary-keepers noted time on computers as part of their weekly record. Their activities on the computer varied. All of them did homework and most of them played computer games. Only the Grade 8s recorded Internet time, however. There is not enough information to suggest whether the Grade 5 homes did not have online access in November 1997, or whether the parents of the younger children had stricter rules about going online. Certainly some younger students later mentioned looking at Beanie Baby sites or checking out a National Hockey League team, but in their diaries of a single week there is no mention of Internet access.

The other interesting difference between the Grade 5 and the Grade 8 students is that only one Grade 5 participant made any mention of listening to the radio or a CD or tape. The older students all spent substantial periods of time listening to one or the other, often as they read or did homework or travelled in the car. Culturally, the move from childhood to adolescence in North America is often marked by an increase in time spent listening to popular music, and most of the radio stations cited by these young teenagers are popular local organizations. Again, however, the impact of different forms of electronic audio texts may alter this picture over the next decade, and the younger siblings of these students may well listen less to conventional radio and more to Internet audio.

Five girls

The most complete and interesting diaries were maintained by five Grade 8 girls. All of them recorded periods of viewing, listening, reading and interacting with computers over the course of the week. Yet, their profiles diverged substantially, as can be seen in the following descriptions.

Catherine

Catherine was by far the most confirmed viewer of the group, recording 1,150 minutes of television viewing and a further 180 minutes of movie watching. Yet, at the same time, she also recorded the highest total of book reading time, 470 minutes, and mentioned several book titles through the week. Her reading time was further augmented by 30 minutes of newspaper reading and a full hour and a half reading catalogues and fliers that came to the house with the newspaper. The date of the diary perhaps sheds some light on this attention to catalogues; she kept this diary in November and the imminence of Christmas may well have been a factor. She spent 130 minutes on the Internet and, in 1997, was the only Grade 8 student to refer to online chats as one of her activities; she also surfed the Internet.

Madeleine

Madeleine was one of two girls who actually spent more time listening than viewing (430 minutes of viewing versus 470 minutes of listening). Although in later conversations she often referred to reading as hard work, she still recorded two hours of reading a book and a further 105 minutes on magazines, in this week under scrutiny. Furthermore, neither book she mentions (*Running Out of Time*, *Galax-Arena*) is completely simple or straightforward; both are young adult novels and, while not enormously challenging, still far from anodyne. Madeleine was one of the students without a home computer but she still managed 30 minutes of computer time, doing e-mail, during this week. The oddest entry in Madeleine's diary is the total of 25 minutes devoted to bits of movie viewing, during which time she watched parts of *Marvin's Room* and *Contact*. It is difficult to believe that this experience could have amounted to much more than simply passing some time. The potential to become fully engaged in a movie during a spell of less than 25 minutes is surely slight – yet, if you have seen the movie before, it may be that a sampling has its own satisfactions.

Nasrin

Nasrin was the other heavy listener, recording 300 minutes of listening to a popular radio station and 75 minutes of listening to CDs and cassettes (she mentioned cultural music and Jewel). In contrast she watched only two hours of television (much less than any other girl) and a further 130 minutes of movies. She too read newspaper inserts and fliers, for a total of 35 minutes – rather more than the 15 minutes she devoted to reading the newspaper itself. She spent 45 minutes on a computer project. The radio and the book stand out in her profile, and she combined them on more than one occasion.

Janice

Janice, although she talked about books in many of her conversations, was the only girl to record no book reading. She did spend 95 minutes with newspapers over the week and it seems clear from talking to her that at least some of her 150 minutes of Internet time were devoted to reading about the Edmonton Oilers. Her main Internet activity was e-mail. Three hundred and ten minutes of television viewing represent her major time commitment, but it was clear from all our conversations that Janice was a girl with rather less time to spare for media engagements than some other participants in this study.

Kelly

Kelly was another big viewer, with 420 minutes of television watching and another 240 minutes with movies. Her reading was distributed between books (135 minutes), newspapers (175 minutes) and magazines (30 minutes). Kelly spent just over an hour playing computer games such as *Solitaire*, *Doom* and *Minesweeper*. She listened to the radio for 230 minutes.

Commonalities and divergences

Expressed in this way, these activities sound fairly similar, although each girl clearly works out a different balance among them. At the level of specific titles, however, there is much less agreement. I expected the book titles to differ completely, which they did, but thought that the television and movie titles would be much more uniform. In fact, the distributive power of video is such that no movie title is mentioned twice. Television is a bit more homogeneous: three girls mentioned *The Simpsons* and *Fresh Prince of Bel-Air*, though to my surprise only one recorded watching *Friends*. (Later interviews elicited many mentions of *Friends*, and it is, of course, possible that there is a simple explanation for its absence from most of the diaries: that week's episode may have been a repeat.)

From the evidence of these diaries, the common element in the culture of these young teenage girls is radio. All five of them mention Power 92, a particularly popular local station, and the only point of unanimity in the whole record – though some listened to it exclusively and some listened to other stations as well. Jack kept a day's diary instead of a full week, so I have not attempted to compare his entries to the girls', but it is worth noting that he also mentioned this station.

In this confusing and fast-developing technological world, radio has acquired a fairly old-fashioned aura; but its role in the lives of early adolescents may still be as powerful as it was a generation ago. I can think of a number of reasons why this might be so. One is a general sense of community. Susan Douglas reminds us:

> orality generates a powerful participatory mystique. Because the act of listening simultaneously to spoken words forms hearers into a group (while reading turns people in on themselves), orality fosters a strong collective sensibility. People listening to a common voice, or to the same music, act and react at the same time.
>
> (Douglas 1999: 29)

At the same time, radio offers access to a specific sense of community. Power 92, the station listened to by all these Grade 8 students, is local radio, speaking to the concerns of a particular city as well as providing access to a more anonymous, continent-wide popular culture. It may seem difficult for serious adults to sustain the idea of citizenship being developed by this flippant and sometimes raucous radio station. However, to 13-year-olds who are beginning to develop some sense that they belong to a wider world, it may well be that Power 92 represents a very real step into one kind of civic life. And it is a community that values their participation; the station regularly runs contests and invites listener participation. Furthermore, the announcements about local concerts and so forth address, if not their direct interests as 13-year-olds, then perhaps a virtual version of how they see themselves developing.

Thirdly, radio and other audio texts have the virtue of being good partners to other activities. You can listen while reading, while surfing, while doing e-mail or homework. All the other media explored in this study resist being such pure background and, in the cases where television comes close, it is surely its audio qualities that make it possible.

Finally, of course, the price is right and ease of access is guaranteed. Many teenagers have a radio in their bedrooms so no negotiation with parents or siblings is necessary. They do not have to find the price of a CD or a tape, and they are assured of a certain amount of variety in their listening.

However, again there is a strong possibility that these diaries recorded the end of a particular historical era. It is very likely that, a mere two and a half years after these diaries were written, most of the diary-keepers spend at least some time now listening to downloaded online music instead. In some ways, this development may increase their sense of agency and control with regard to their listening, but it is also possible that a very real element of community is being lost.

A 2000 study suggests that, unlike the situation with television, radio use did not fall as Internet use expanded (Harding 2000: 11). Of course, it is not necessary to turn off your radio to go online, and the compatibility of computer use and some kind of background audio is well known. Radio offers a link to the local community that other forms of audio cannot match, and it will be interesting to observe the robustness of that link over the next few years.

Relative to the dazzle of new technologies, radio's niche in the media ecology is in many ways modest. How it survives will at least partly depend on how it, in the words of a famous beer commercial, 'reaches the parts other [technologies] do not reach'.

Internet use

Largely because online access in schools was a complicated operation in 1998 and 1999, the students and I did not do any exploration of the Internet during our meetings. I did explicitly ask them about their Internet use on more than one occasion. Most of the participants in this study are casual Internet users, and it is easy to see them simply adding the Internet to their toolboxes of communications options.

Nardi and O'Day talk about four basic applications of Internet communications: connecting people with information, services, goods and other people (1999: 188). The young people in this study made clear reference to all four categories. A number of them used the Internet to research school projects. They consulted the

Internet for material concerning the Beanie Babies and computer games. They also used e-mail and chat rooms to communicate with other people, mostly already known to them but in some cases strangers or the friend of a friend. Anita went online shopping but never actually bought anything. Madeleine saw e-mail as a supplement to her preferred method of communicating with her friends by telephone.

Collectively, this small group of young people availed itself of a broad range of Internet possibilities. Separately, they were actually quite selective about what they do. Anita went online shopping and wrote e-mails, but found chat rooms scary; Jack, on the other hand, was intrigued by what he was learning about one chat room in early 1998, and by mid-1999 was a seasoned user. Colin and Catherine used the Internet to hunt down new games. Jack and Gregory looked up information about particular games, and Gregory checked out the *Star Wars* site almost daily; Kyle did research for his homework. Janice took advantage of certain AOL magazine features such as the horoscope and pursued her own local interests such as the hockey team and the local radio station. Angela also took an interest in a different hockey team, but for family reasons: her cousin is a team member. Madeleine made the most sweeping statements of interest and approval and talked about the pleasures of just browsing. She was committed enough to the idea of using the Internet to go online once or twice a week, even though her only access was at school.

If I were to apply a single adjective to this eclectic list of activities, it would be 'domesticated'. The Internet plays a role in the lives of these young people, but it is a modest role and one shaped to their own interests. In many cases, they say or imply that their Internet use is largely determined by questions that engaged them before they gained access to the Internet.

Another adjective that might usefully apply to this set of activities is 'social'. The students talk of going on the Net with a sibling, of corresponding with friends, of joining a chat room because a friend suggested it, of using the Net to support school projects (that are also socially framed, albeit differently). This particular set of young people, at least by their own accounting, appears to regard the Internet as an interesting but subordinate element in their lives. They were nonchalant in their references to their Internet experiences; I got no sense that they were straining for activities to describe to me. They find it interesting but they are not over-impressed or startled by it. Once again, we are talking about a single strand in a complex tapestry.

Finally, an interesting question was raised almost casually by Gregory, as he talked about his interactions with the Internet:

MARGARET: Can you see yourself, for example, as you get older spending more time on the Internet?

GREGORY: Since we've got the Internet I've been finding myself spending less time on it. Less and less.

MARGARET: Is that right? Why is that?

GREGORY: Well, there's only so much you can do that'll interest you really. I mean, there will be a list of topics you like, you'll find the best site on each of them and then you'll go every now and again. It's not updated as often. It's usually not updated as fast as you keep going back on.

MARGARET: Right. Right, and you don't ever just sort of surf at random?

GREGORY: No.

MARGARET: When you set out to find a site on something that you're interested in, are you reasonably successful fairly fast? I mean, do you find it straightforward to track down what it is that interests you?

GREGORY: It depends if what I'm looking for is general or specific. If I'm looking for just something general, say, I don't know, just take the moon just for example. You like, type in the moon and you get tons of sights, you get pictures, you get NASA, you get this, you get that. If you want a certain fact, all that you'll find yourself clicking on this site, no not there, getting out, clicking on this one, keep going down. It takes a bit longer.

Gregory is clearly very familiar with the sites that address his interests and, in the last remark quoted above, demonstrates that he understands the need for different kinds of searching strategies. But his developing ennui with the sites he selects as best for his purposes shows an interesting gap between the kinds of expectations that Internet use can foster, and the ability of even as vast a documentary universe as the World Wide Web to meet those expectations over the long run.

Signature responses

Of the older boys, only Jack kept the diary in Grade 8. All five boys participated in the exit interview in Grade 9, however, and it is fascinating to compare and contrast some of their differing approaches to texts.

One question that interested me was whether attitudes and behaviours cross media boundaries, whether at least some students would manifest what Lawrence Sipe (1998) calls a 'signature response'. These boys, all friends and acquaintances of long standing, with many background elements in common, offered some fascinating examples of how individuals can respond very differently to the same potential input.

Gregory is a boy who went in for enthusiasms, and this propensity showed up in many ways. This is how he described his reading:

I find that I go in kind of, with a lot of things, I go in bursts. Like, for one month *every* night I'll be in my room reading and then I won't even touch it for the next few. I think right now I'm in one of those stages. I've just had a big reading one a couple of months ago.

Similarly, his viewing of a particular movie comes in waves: 'You can watch it, like, three or four times a month then again you'll leave it alone for a while then a few months later you'll come back you'll watch it three or four more times and leave it.' His game playing seems to operate on similar lines:

MARGARET: If you get a computer game that you really like, are you like the same as with your reading? Do you have a stint of playing it a lot?

GREGORY: I'm pretty consistent with how much I play, but how much I *do* play is never very much in the first place. I'm not one of those people who can sit down for six hours a day, but when I do play it will be, like, one level today, one level the next day then pretty much every day play another level. I'll never play more than one level a day.

MARGARET: Right. So how much time when you've got a game on the go would you say you spend in a week?

GREGORY: In a week? If I just got it, about ten hours. If I had it for a couple, a few months, maybe five. I don't even play it in a month right now.

It may be that one reason Gregory was waning in his interest in the Internet lies in his preferred approach to texts. The kind of steady sampling over an extended period of time which makes best use of the sites he favours actually runs counter to his personal preference for a more binge-oriented kind of engagement.

Kyle's particular 'signature' is a predilection across media for texts that stimulate his intellect by intelligent use of details:

MARGARET: What's your favourite movie?

KYLE: My favourite movie? I would have to say *The Matrix*.

MARGARET: Uh-huh. What is it about *The Matrix* that you like so much?

KYLE: I really liked the kind of, the whole idea behind it that we all lived in an arti . . . virtual world and it's all in our mind and we've never actually seen reality. I thought that was really interesting.

MARGARET: So you like your movie to have a little bit of an intellectual challenge to it?

KYLE: Yeah.

      . . .

MARGARET: What's your favourite computer game?

KYLE: Probably a game called *Half Life*.

MARGARET: What's the appeal of *Half Life*?

KYLE: It's really realistic. It's ah, and actually it's a first person action game. But the thing is, the appeal that I think is really good about *Half Life* is most action games don't have much of a plot or much thought behind it. You just grab a gun and kill everything you see and that's kind of pointless. But in *Half Life* it's, there's actually a story behind it and, um, the game designers put in a lot of details like, you can read like, things posted on the wall and you can, it's just very, very realistic. There's all these little details that you've never noticed, but then you get to really appreciate because then you think, 'oh, that's so neat how they did that'.

Asked if these tastes represented a general preference, Kyle became quite eloquent:

KYLE: I just really appreciate when, like, the details is the difference between a good movie and a bad movie or an interesting book and a not-so-interesting book. If I think that the director of the movie or the author of the book puts in the, makes sure that everything kind of rings together, everything makes sense and also kind of, it just brightens up the book by adding details and I really like that.

MARGARET: Right. Do you like it if the plot is quite intricate? If there are a lot of little twists and turns inside alleys and that sort of thing or is it just the sort of background, the notices on the wall or both?

KYLE: Both really, but sometimes, too many twists in the plot I begin to find kind of annoying, because for example, in certain movies, if, if at the very, very end of the movie, um, one of the main characters is killed or [*indecipherable*]. Like for example, in *Star Wars*, one of the things I didn't like is whenever, um, one of the characters, the queen I believe, the queen, I don't know, I forget her name.

NOTE TAKER: Amidala.

KYLE: Yeah. Whenever she seems to be captured by somebody, it always turns out that it was actually a decoy and the real queen is somewhere else and I believe they did that two or three times in a row. And to me that just shows that, ah, the scriptwriter, or George Lucas I suppose in this, didn't really think out carefully the entire story while he was writing it. And I really, really like movies that where everything is kind of already thought out so that this leads to that and it all kind of –

MARGARET: Is under control?

KYLE: Yeah.

Neither Gregory's binge and famine approach to different kinds of text nor Kyle's preference for intelligently worked out details in plot and character is particularly striking or unusual in itself. What is of interest here is that these tastes appear in their accounts of several different media. Not every user of texts may have such a clear-cut crossover, but in these examples it is very evident.

Social elements of personal tastes

One of the virtues of a small sample group is that the specific particularities of individual tastes show up, rather than being averaged out of recognition. The quirks of this little group of students showed up especially in the interviews from the final session with the Grade 9 students; their conversations open windows on to their own idiosyncratic tastes.

Leonard, for example, admitted, a bit bashfully, that he is a fan of the American daytime soap opera *The Young and the Restless*. As it happened, the graduate student who was taking notes for that session also watches it. The instant change in the tone of the conversation when Leonard realized he was talking to a fellow fan was both amusing and instructive:

MARGARET: What about television? Do you watch much television?
LEONARD: No, I only watch, and I hate to admit this, *The Young and the Restless*.
MARGARET: Okay. How do you manage that?
LEONARD: We record it so we watch it like, from eight like, nine to ten or something, but I hate to say it, but it's very good. It is.
MARGARET: Do you watch every single instalment or just pick it up from time to time?
LEONARD: No, no. You can pretty well get everything in the storyline if you watch every two or every three. Whenever I'm not doing anything and it's on, I'll watch it.
MARGARET: And this is taped religiously every day in your house?
LEONARD: Yes, except my mom forgot to tape yesterday so I was *most* disappointed. [laughter]
NOTE TAKER: Nothing happened.
LEONARD: You watch it too?
NOTE TAKER: Yes.
LEONARD: What do you think of Chet?
NOTE TAKER: I don't like Chet! [laughter]
LEONARD: What about Victor? Are you hoping Michael and Jack or Brad and Jack will take over?
NOTE TAKER: Well, Brad wants to get Nikki back, that [*indecipherable*] storylines. Brad's mad because –
LEONARD: I was thinking about that except Nikki doesn't seem too keen on Brad.
NOTE TAKER: No.
LEONARD: [to Margaret] Do you follow this discussion?
MARGARET: No, no, this is leaving me completely blank. I'm fascinated.
LEONARD: When I had my operation I got to watch soap operas twenty-four hours a day, but that was horrible. None are as good as *The Young and the Restless*.
MARGARET: Is daily too much of a good thing? I mean if you could, would you watch it every single day?
LEONARD: No, no, that's okay. It's okay to relax and I guess watch it. Watch one show a day.
MARGARET: Do you watch any other television shows?
LEONARD: No, not really. Not on a regular basis.

The discovery that he was talking to another member of the club instantly altered the register of Leonard's conversation; all of a sudden he was deep into specific plot and character questions, his diffidence about his TV taste immediately translated into the intensity of the enthusiast. This little dialogue offers an accidental testimonial to the degree to which ordinary and daily text processing may run deep social roots.

Kyle's account of watching *The Simpsons* contains some of the same social ingredients, fitted in at brief moments in ordinary daily life:

KYLE: I think that it's just the type of humour that it doesn't matter who you are you still find it funny because it's kind of slapstick humour.

MARGARET: Sometimes they make quite complicated jokes in *The Simpsons*.

KYLE: Yeah, sometimes.

MARGARET: Do you care if you always get those jokes?

KYLE: Not really, because then I come to school the next day and I talk to my friends and then we kind of –

MARGARET: So you decipher it between you?

KYLE: Yeah.

MARGARET: How much time in an average day do you spend talking about *The Simpsons* if you've watched it the night before?

KYLE: Um, maybe a minute between classes.

MARGARET: Right. So it isn't a huge preoccupation?

KYLE: No.

Thus are media texts woven into the daily fabric of social life in schools, and thus do these young people gain a strong sense of each other's strengths and preferences as text interpreters. The diary format made no room for it, but the final interviews and many of the preceding conversations are full of references to other students' tastes and abilities. The students were operating out of their own community, but they were also drawing on the fact that they knew the two graduate students and I were also developing our own connections with those of their friends who were participating in the study. Although we never met as a complete group, the references from one student or pair of students to our encounters with other students helped to weave a community spirit around the enterprise of this project as well.

Conclusions

The diaries show all the students sampling a broad range of media and sampling very deliberately to serve their own particular interests. Undoubtedly there have been a number of changes since 1997, and the behaviours of today's Grade 5 and Grade 8 students are probably different from those recorded here. Nevertheless, this window on to young people's domestic and recreational media use does serve as a reminder of how flexibly and purposefully young people move between different kinds of text. The supplementary information provided by the exit interviews with the Grade 9 students casts further light on how these young people draw on each other's strengths and repertoires as well as their own.

These students also use popular texts to develop and present themselves in pragmatic ways. Tia DeNora expresses it this way: 'individuals not only experience culture, but also . . . mobilize culture for being, doing and feeling' (2000: 74).

Example after example in the transcripts shows these young people making exactly such use of their favourite texts.

Afterword: new literacy ecologies of the twenty-first century

Local ecologies change with little but local notice, and it is perhaps not surprising that the local Edmonton radio station, Power 92, which attracted the attention of all the Grade 8 diarists in 1997, has since undergone a change of format. According to Wikipedia, Power 92 shifted from top 40 to 'hot AC' (adult contemporary music) in June 2003, and many Power 92 fans moved to a new station (http://en.wikipedia. org/wiki/CKRA-FM, accessed 26 March 2006). A particular locus of teen loyalty thus mutated and the local ecology shifted.

It is clear, however, that this small regional change is the least of the story. Since 1997, teenage attachment to radio has significantly fallen. A study of Canadian radio habits conducted by Statistics Canada in the autumn of 2004 shows a substantial drop-off in teenage radio hours:

> Radio still has very little appeal for teenagers. In the fall of 2004, they tuned in for only 8.5 hours a week, the least amount of time devoted to the medium by any age group.
>
> In addition, the gap between adult listening time and teen listening time continued to widen. In 1995, adults listened to 10 hours a week more than teens. In the fall of 2004, this had widened to 12 hours.
>
> Over the last five years, adults reduced their listening time by close to one hour per week, while among teenagers the decline amounted to nearly three hours per week.
>
> (Statistics Canada 2005)

Nobody suggests that teenagers have stopped listening to music, but MP3 players of various kinds, podcasts and satellite radio are all making inroads into territory once shared across a region. Power 92 was never exactly ground-breaking in its choice of music, and it is very possible that some or many listeners are now taking in a much more sophisticated mix. Nevertheless, some local bonding is eroding.

'The one thing that radio still does better than your iPod – or your satellite – is talk', says newspaper columnist Russell Smith, discussing the erosion of radio in Canada:

> Political analysis, sports and humour are still what people are consistently tuning in to on the radio. People in the commercial radio industry are predicting that broadcast radio (radio that is free to everybody with a radio receiver) will shift almost entirely to talk, and people will find their music from more specialized sources.
>
> (Smith 2005: R4)

The young people in this study, tuning in to the radio for music, may well have picked up a little bit of talk along the way, and begun to gain a bit of a sense of the complex weave of local events that make up a city culture. But they are now gaining access to their music in very different ways. A report released by the Organization for Economic Cooperation and Development (OECD) in early 2006 claims that Canadians, per capita, download more unauthorized free music than anybody else (in part because Canadian courts are more ambivalent about the illegality of such a procedure) (McCoy 2006: C4). The numbers are still relatively small (1.2 per cent of Canadians versus 0.9 per cent in the US and 0.6 per cent in France and Germany), reflecting the legal challenges to downloading free music discussed in the previous chapter, but the iPod and its ilk undoubtedly represent a large pool of legal downloads as well. Personalized music choice is ubiquitous.

Sports news, another potentially big draw for radio, is also leaching out into a huge range of formats, including live updates directed straight to your cellphone. Even the car, listed in almost every diary as a prime location for radio listening, is now adaptable to iPod listening with a simple converter – though it is likely, in a city like Edmonton, that live radio coverage of the Edmonton Oilers games still prevails in many car journeys.

I would not want to be sentimental about the fading and eventual loss of Power 92 as a cultural factor in the life of the city of Edmonton. Even in its heyday, the station adhered to a predictable and banal regime of pop music with raucous and undemanding commentary in between the songs. But the local news and the little factoids concerning upcoming events of city organizations did provide a very accessible scaffold for a developing sense of community among teen listeners. Such sense of a wider world will now very often, for many of them, involve a developing allegiance to a virtual, broad-spread community of like-minded podcasters and listeners. It is a change worth noticing.

And it is a change worth placing in an international context. The Canadian figures seem quite clear cut in terms of an overall reduction in radio listening. But at the same time, a British news article suggests that radio listening in the United Kingdom is still increasing, and that the critical focal points for change in that country involve digital audio broadcasting and competition between the BBC and commercial channels (Gibson and Day 2006). In this area as in so many, media ecologies are affected by local and national agreements and arrangements; technological possibilities on their own do not determine the nature of change.

Chapter 6

Salience and fluency
The beginnings of stories

The fifteen text openings

In their first session with me, students looked at five first pages of novels, five opening credits of videos and five initial sequences of narrative computer games. They were asked to say whether they would continue with this text if it were left entirely up to them, and to explain what kind of story they thought it would be, and why. Their responses were audiotaped and transcribed; the responses raise many interesting questions.

With the books, students first looked at a photocopy of the first page and expressed an opinion about whether they might read further; they were then given the complete book and asked if it made a difference to their response. With the videos, they simply watched the opening scenes. They were given control of the mouse and the keyboard to experiment with each of the games, but did not have access to any off-screen instructions. Some students mentioned help screens but there was very little attempt to actually make use of one, possibly partly because, by this point in the session, the students were used to dealing with just the very introductory stages of each text.

In the many cases where students already were familiar with a text, they were asked first if they thought they would keep on going if they were meeting this text for the first time, and then if they could reconstruct what in fact they did think when they first met the text. Usually I asked a follow-up question about whether they had actually enjoyed the text.

The texts

The complete list of titles is given in the table.

The fifteen openings of texts in print, video and CD-ROM form were selected with a number of criteria in mind. I wanted various kinds of overlap. I wanted, for example, to include some titles in more than one format, and succeeded most completely with *Anne of Green Gables*, which I found on all three platforms. *My Teacher is an Alien* (print and CD-ROM) and *Men in Black* (movie and CD-ROM) also fulfilled this specification. I wanted to include texts with cross-media

Grade 5:	Books	Videos	CD-ROMs
	Anne of Green Gables	Anne of Green Gables	Anne of Green Gables
	The Secret Garden	The Secret Garden	Oregon Trail
	My Teacher is an Alien	Toy Story	My Teacher is an Alien
	The Watsons Go to	Air Bud	The Jolly Post Office
	Birmingham – 1963	Little Women (animation)	Alien Tales
	The Golden Compass		

Grade 8:	Books	Videos	CD-ROMs
	Anne of Green Gables	Anne of Green Gables	Anne of Green Gables
	My Teacher is an Alien	Toy Story	My Teacher is an Alien
	The Watsons Go to	Casablanca	Virtual Springfield
	Birmingham – 1963	Men in Black	Men in Black
	Cat's Eye	Benny and Joon	Discworld II
	The Golden Compass		

connections including but not confined to texts that are adapted from a print original; for example, I picked the CD-ROM of *Virtual Springfield* partly because of its base in a television cartoon, *The Simpsons*.

I also wanted texts that could be used at more than one age level and texts that could not. I purposefully included one Disney title (*Toy Story*) and was rewarded with specific comments on Disney's appeal. I included a black and white movie at each level (the 1949 *Secret Garden* for younger participants, *Casablanca* for older ones) and asked specifically about the old-fashioned qualities of each movie as well as the black and white filming.

The most difficult challenge was to include enough openings of texts that were unknown to the participants. Both schools have strong library and reading pro- grammes, and I found the students had already read more of my sample print texts than I had anticipated. It was even more difficult to locate videos that the students would not recognize; my biggest success was *Benny and Joon*, a movie which had been reasonably popular about five years prior to this study but which was unknown to most of the participants (although some recognized Johnny Depp). It needs only to be stated to be recognizable as a truism: students, even very young ones, will be familiar with a much higher percentage of all available and appropriate texts in video than in print or in computer form. The immediate implication of this observation is that what might be called their cultural literacy quotient is higher with contemporary films than with books or computer texts in that the ratio of known to unfamiliar texts is much higher with movies.

Salience and fluency

Overall, these participants were relatively indifferent to platform. They showed no signs of having an automatic preference for one medium over another; instead, they judged each text on its merits. Nobody either selected or rejected all the texts in a single medium without qualification.

In very many cases, students applied a yardstick to the text in question that can best be described as a balance between issues of salience and issues of fluency or ease of access. They queried whether the text was saying something that they wanted to hear, for whatever reason. They also queried whether they could gain access to that text without undue aggravation or difficulty. These questions arose in all media and were sometimes answered differently for the same title when it appeared in more than one format.

Example 1: the Grade 5 students

Questions of salience as weighed against fluency came up in many different forms. Here, for example, is Colin on the book version of *My Teacher is an Alien*. He would not read further than page one in this book:

> I don't really like books about boys and they pick on little people and then there's little people trying to find ways, like, to get away from the bullies or whatever . . . It's about, kind of like, like school kids that kind of, like, he likes to read and, like, he's getting picked on by the bully guy.

Colin's aversion to reading about bullies was his primary response to the book. He was much more attracted to the CD-ROM version of the story, which, not surprisingly, places a much stronger emphasis on the game-playing side of things. Colin played the game for as long as I would let him, and said he would play much more, given the opportunity. It was the different salience that he commented on, rather than the shift of medium. He would expect that 'you would keep on going to different classrooms and find different things and then find the classroom with the Principal guy in it'.

Colin also took fluency into account with some of his decision-making. He rejected the black and white video of the old movie version of *The Secret Garden*: 'I don't really like movies in black and white because it's kind of hard to decipher one thing from another.'

Megan looked at the book of *Anne of Green Gables* and also made a decision based on ease of access: 'I don't think I would read that one. They use big words and it's sort of confusing.' Asked what sort of story she would expect it to be, Megan said, 'Like, one where she ventures a lot and stuff. I've read one like it.' The combination of big words and lukewarm plot is clearly unappealing.

Yet Megan did not reject dense text outright. Given the first page of *The Golden Compass*, she said she would read it because 'it describes a lot, like the things.

I like that because you can, like, picture it'. And Megan did not reject the 'ventures and stuff' of *Anne of Green Gables* when presented with the story in video form, where the emotional impact of the unwanted orphan is more instantly established. She would watch more, she said, because 'I would want to see, like, what happened to Anne'.

Megan's responses show an active balancing between how difficult and how interesting she found the stories. Chapter One of *The Golden Compass* is entitled 'The Decanter of Tokay', and the fourth word of the chapter is 'daemon', a more challenging introduction than any of the words or ideas in the opening page of *Anne of Green Gables*. Yet the leisurely discourse of the Montgomery book does not offer her any reason to persevere with the story, even though, as she demonstrated over and over again during this project, she is a reader who actively enjoys description. The direct narrative compulsion of the opening page of *The Golden Compass* clearly caught her attention in a more dynamic way that outweighed any obstacles that unfamiliar words might present.

Megan and Colin present an interesting contrast when shown the early stages of the video of a Japanese animation of *Little Women*. Megan rejected the idea of watching any further; she had read an abridged version of the novel and not cared for it; furthermore, 'I don't really like the way, like, they're drawn and stuff. They're sort of different. I don't like it that way.' She also rejected the plot line: 'Like, the father is gone and everything like that. And that's like, what they talk about a lot and so it's mostly, like, there's stuff happening but they also just talk about that lots.'

Colin, on the other hand, was reminded of a family-oriented Japanese animation he described as his favourite movie. He would watch more of *Little Women*, he said, because 'I like the animation and it's kind of gotten an interesting start'.

Angela was explicit about issues of adaptation. She preferred the movie of *Anne of Green Gables* to the book by a slim margin, having experienced both:

> Well, it's kind of hard to say. You had to sit quite long through the movie. It was pretty long but it, you could, it almost expressed what was happening better 'cause you could actually see. Like when she dyed her hair green and whatever. That was, I think, better. I like imagining it well enough but the movie was pretty good.

Yet Angela normally prefers the book version:

> I don't usually always like the movies. Sometimes they change things a whole bunch. So they're not – well, to some people they might be better, but to me, I like them the way they kind of were in the book. Like, sometimes they, some movies that they've made, they just twisted the stories around and if I had read the story first I probably would have liked it because it was more realistic and original.

As a reader of *Little Women*, Angela rejected the Japanese animated version for two reasons: 'it's not really like the book and it's . . . the characters look like *Sailor Moon* characters. Like, I would watch it but it wouldn't be a main priority.' Asked whether she thought the animation did justice to the characters of the book, she said:

> They're not exactly, well they have the same hobbies and everything, but they just don't seem the way they are in the book so – maybe not the same, well I noticed that Meg didn't have the same hair or whatever, or they didn't – usually they act all together and not separate. And well, I know that Jo likes to write stories and she's a bit of a free will, but, I mean, in cartoons I don't think it looks as good.

These Grade 5 students explicitly drew on intertextual references to help them establish issues of salience and accessibility. There are many versions of 'I read/saw/played one like this and it was satisfying/frustrating', both in terms of content and in terms of processing. Similarly, questions of provenance and recommendation arose often. In conversation students often made reference to how and in what circumstances they had encountered a book and what impact this had on their selections. A friend's seal of approval, a formal award or some recognition that someone else had enjoyed this story might predispose these participants to look more favourably on an opening scene. Such a recommendation appears to act as a (provisional) certification of salience.

Example 2: the Grade 8 students

Nasrin, an eighth-grader, was explicit about questions of salience and fluency in her discussion of *Anne of Green Gables*. On first looking at a photocopy of page one of *Anne of Green Gables*, Nasrin said, 'This seems a little too advanced, of what I would normally read, but if it was recommended by a friend or had won an award, then I'd probably read it.' Questions of fluency would undermine her interest in the book, on the strength of the first page only, but might be over-ridden by some form of recommendation. As she picked up the book and looked at it, however, we can see issues of salience take over. After a single glance at the back of the book, she said:

> Now I'd probably read it! The back simplifies it, from the first text, from the page on the first text so I – actually I like books like this because I, I'd also pick it because I'm not an orphan and I'd probably want to know how it feels to be an orphan, so just for the experience of it, 'cause a lot of books, they can do that.

The leisurely and loquacious introduction to *Anne of Green Gables* antagonized many of these young readers, but not all, and one exception was a reminder that gender stereotypes are not necessarily the whole story when it comes to describing readers. Jack was an eighth-grader who would keep reading *Anne of Green Gables*: 'I would definitely keep going because it sounds like a book that would tell a good story. It would tell a descriptive story that made a lot of sense. I like the way it's written.'

One of the interesting elements of the students' responses is that issues of salience and fluency apply to all the media we explored. Here, for example, is Anita on whether she would watch more of the movie *Casablanca*:

> Probably not because even from the start I didn't even understand it, so, it seems more like a history movie to me. Although I don't really think that's what it's supposed to be, but I think I probably just wouldn't pay attention. I'd just lose track. It would be a waste of my time.

Fluency and salience are both affected by repertoire in this instance. Anita makes a genre link to a history movie of the kind that would be offered in a social studies class. This is not an unreasonable connection given the introductory map and the newsreel-style voiceover at the outset of *Casablanca*, but it causes her to categorize the film as educational rather than interesting. At the same time, she recognizes that she does not have an immediately accessible repertoire of background information that would render this movie quickly transparent to her, so she rules it out on grounds of fluency as well.

The computer game of *Men in Black* provided some interesting examples of differing responses. The question of fluent access arose very sharply for many users. Unlike all the other games on offer, it runs on keyboard controls rather than on the mouse. The opening scenes are rigidly organized and, if you do not choose correctly, your character is blown up very quickly. On the other hand, most of the eighth-graders who looked at this game were familiar with the movie and indeed had just seen the opening credits as part of the video collection, so some questions of salience were straightforward.

Anita rejected the CD-ROM because of the violence, though she had enjoyed the movie. She also disliked the keyboard control. Catherine also rejected it, but more for the absence of action combined with the cumbersome quality of the keyboard controls: 'It's pretty complicated and you just get to walk around and that.' Madeleine was another player who rejected the game; she likes action games but only if they are easy to play and this one was too complicated for her – a textbook case of balancing salience and fluency.

In this case, Jack proved that gender stereotypes can sometimes ring true. He knew the movie well and had actually played a demo version of the computer game of *Men in Black*. The issue of fluency played itself out differently for him: 'I like the keyboard because you, it's – because I think you have more control. You know where you're going; you can't skip.' Possessing a set of skills more appropriate to the requirements of the game, he was able to comment, 'I like it. I think it's easy to navigate and it makes sense. There's a story that begins to develop and ah, yeah, it's more fun!' Again, it is possible to see him weighing the trade-off between interest and accessibility.

Choosing among media

Asked a general question about which of the fifteen texts they had seen they would most like to take home, the students came up with varied answers. Six said they would take a book. Three opted for video and two for a CD-ROM. Three added a qualifier that they would not really like to choose between one and another, that they have different preferences at different times of day, and so forth. Whatever the effects of easy access to different media upon these students, it is clear that the book continues to be a meaningful choice for them.

Asked to make comparisons among the different texts on offer, the main consideration of most of the students seemed to be, 'Is it a good story? Will I be able to make sense of it? Will I enjoy it?' There was no sign of media bias in these questions; the students took for granted that you could process a story in a variety of ways and the story was the major element to be considered. The only text that received a nearly universal thumbs-down was a text-based CD-ROM (of *Anne of Green Gables*) with very limited interactive and animated elements. The general view on this product was that if you wanted to read a story that was based largely in words you would naturally turn to the book.

Different students described the potential for frustration in varying terms. One student used a clear criterion that any book she chose must not be full of big words. Many baulked when a CD-ROM did not lead clearly from one point to another, though they often expressed confidence that with more time and access to the help manual they would be able to make progress. The frustration threshold with the interactive software clearly varied from student to student, and I suspect this was partly based on their skill and experience with such games and partly on their own personal predilections: levels of dexterity, powers of observation, mental adroitness and also patience clearly differed. There was a general consensus that video was the least demanding of the media on offer, a factor which many students described as positive, though one or two did mention that video therefore invited a more lazy response. There were one or two interesting examples of students who had specific behaviour for each medium; one boy absolutely never re-reads a book but often watches a video over and over again, for example. For the most part, however, the students expressed their preferences more on the basis of genre of story rather by choosing one medium over another.

Nasrin, a Grade 8 student, spoke for many when she articulated the idea that different media simply offer different pleasures, rather than one being preferable to another:

> I like computer games because you can be in control of them and they're pretty colourful and the sounds are really good and you can listen to a book. In a movie, see, there's no imagination or thinking whatsoever involved. You kind

of sit there and just watch it. And this [the computer game], it gives you a change to kind of explore for yourself by controlling it, but the book you can't control, but you can use your imagination. So each one makes you having to do different things.

Text processing in a multimedia environment

How can we think about reading in terms that take useful account of the many text processing skills of today's young people? I want to suggest a few pointers based on what I have learned from these students and drawing on insights developed in the field of reading.

I particularly want to explore the major elements of text selection that arose in this stage of the project: the issue of fluency and the issue of salience. How does a reader or viewer or player gain a sense of how straightforward the access to a particular text will be? How does exposure to a small opening sample of a text provide enough of a sense to enable a person to decide whether it is worthwhile to continue? What criteria of judgement fuel the assessment of how much interpretive effort a text may justify in terms of that person's balance of interests?

The comments of the students as they reached conclusions about each of the sample texts they were offered provide some windows into a process that all readers are familiar with, yet that is often swift and nearly always transparent.

Fluency

We know of print processing that a highly important step in the acquisition of skills and abilities is the development of automaticity. We need to be able to recognize almost every word, effortlessly and instantly. As long as our attention is focused on decoding individual words, we do not have attention to spare to be able to make meaning of the text as a whole. If you have ever heard a beginning reader laboriously process even a short passage of text, stopping every word or two to decipher what on earth could be coming next, you will know how meaning-deficient the final result can be.

Some information we use to decode comes from the bottom up; we use the information of the letters, the spaces, the capitalization and so forth. Some of it comes from the top down; we use our general knowledge of the world and of the way stories usually work in order to rule out some options and highlight particular possibilities. We weave information from the page together with information from the world and from experience with other texts. Colin, for example, decided, on the strength of a single page of *My Teacher is an Alien*, that he would choose not to read more of this story because he was pretty sure it was going to be about bullying and he didn't like to read about bullying. It is not difficult to see various kinds of real and virtual experience informing that decision. Possibly he has a full repertoire of top-down understanding about bullying situations that could actually have eased his access to this story, but his response suggests that other, possibly affective, factors were also at work.

We know that interweaving of bottom-up and top-down information happens in print processing and it is relatively straightforward to observe similar processes at work in the other media. Students watching the videos had to take note of the elements made visible on the screen, interpreting the nuances of the actors' expressions, observing the details of the setting and processing the dialogue. They also clearly made use of expectations drawn from experience of other movies and of the world at large and could not have made the predictions they did about the likely development of the story without calling on both sources of information.

All the students in this project are clearly very experienced video watchers and the majority are also highly skilful and strategic readers. The CD-ROM games elicited a broader range of response. All of the young people in this study have a certain amount of experience in dealing with multimedia texts but they varied substantially both in the automaticity with which they tried out particular options and in their ensuing confidence that they would be able to carry on and enjoy the challenge of the game. In the case of both the reading and the viewing, their interpretive activities had to be inferred from what they said; with the CD-ROMs, because I handed over the mouse, their interpretive operations were made active and visible.

Operating at a level of fluency and automaticity requires practice and this is as true in playing computer games as in any other form of text processing. These students took over the mouse in a reasonably confident way but the controls of the game clearly functioned more transparently for some users than for others. Only one of them could use keyboard controls with any skill, and all the others rejected the game of *Men in Black*, in many cases as a direct consequence of the struggle for fluency.

Although specific print and video texts may present particular roadblocks to comprehension, in general it is possible to adopt a few general processing strategies for all of such texts and then to apply these strategies to particular cases. With the CD-ROMs it was much more necessary for the students to establish the particular rules for each game. I did not supply any rulebooks and most students made little use of the help screens. This approach, the *medias res* or deep-end route into a text, is only one way of proceeding, of course, and in some cases it led to interesting discussions on the acquisition of fluency in the processing of different computer texts.

Angela, for example, if she were playing on her own, would opt to read the rulebook before she even began the game. But her preference is clearly to find a more knowledgeable partner:

> Well, sometimes it's harder to learn by yourself just with the instructions because you may not understand such and such, or you might not know the little tricks that other people have found out, so in some ways I think it would be better to play it with a partner who knows what it's about.

I asked her about any drawbacks of working with a partner. 'Well, sometimes you don't get a turn. They just know what to do and they just go ahead and play the game.'

Claire, Megan, Colin and Janice would all start by fooling around on the screen but would want ready recourse to the guidebook at the first sign of trouble. Lisa and Anita would start with the rulebook until they had a feel for the game, and then would return to it at the first sign of trouble. Kelly uses the rulebook to install the game but rarely reads directions after that. Madeleine, on the other hand, would invest time with the guidebook rather than be frustrated by the screen; she would start with the screen but 'just try it once and then, if I don't get it, I'd go right to the rulebook'. Or as an alternative strategy, one that combines the virtues of more than one approach, she would 'probably get my brother to come and help me. I'll let him read the book!' Lisa also likes this social approach:

> I kind of like learning how to play it at other people's houses because I don't have to read the instructions, but, if I don't know how to play it, my dad reads the instructions, or I do, or my brother, or somebody, whoever plays it first.

Angela drew attention to another resource that is often available: related texts in book form or on television. She would read the book of *My Teacher is an Alien* as part of learning how to play the computer game, for example, and she draws regular connections between her *Carmen Sandiego* CD-ROMs and the television series of the same name.

One or two students mentioned the idea of looking for help on the web, but they generally scorned the idea of turning to a cheat-sheet or a walk-through, at least until they had wrestled with the game on its own terms. In some cases they would look up a particular stumbling-block, rather than accept help for the whole game.

In all of these responses, it is clear that the students regard fluent access to a particular game as something that has to be actively built, by some form of interaction among the game, the guidebook and the help screens, related texts and other more skilled players. This is a topic to which we will return in more detail in the discussion of *Starship Titanic*. In many cases, the students explicitly referred to issues of salience as they discussed how much effort they would be prepared to invest in learning how to manage one game or another. The question of salience was germane to all three platforms, and we will turn to that issue next.

Salience

Salience involves issues of what matters right now and what is likely to matter as the story progresses. To reach a conclusion on the basis of very limited access to a text, the students had to reach rapid decisions about what was likely to develop in one text or another.

As Peter Rabinowitz (1987) suggests, we do direct our attention according to particular expectations about stories: for example, we are aware, as we read a story, that the status quo is unlikely to be maintained from start to finish. Our expectation is that something will happen. And yet our sense of the conventions of how stories work is that, while something will happen, not just anything can happen (1987: 117). We expect the story to follow the rules of its genre.

As you look at the opening page of a book, one of the things you are trying to do is eliminate some of all the possibilities in the universe. In a surprisingly short time, an experienced reader will at least have some idea of things that are unlikely to happen in a story. These students, looking at the first pages of the different novels I gave them, swiftly reached shrewd conclusions about possible and likely developments in each plot. Their grasp of which details in the opening text were most likely to be salient in determining a possible outcome were clear – and clearly based on experience with different kinds of convention. Even if it was a story they personally thought they would not like to read, they were relatively clear, on the evidence of a single page of print, about what was likely or unlikely to follow.

It is not surprising that the students applied the same kinds of perceptive powers to the texts in other media. They know how to watch videos and are aware, for example, that, when a mean and horrible clown shows up in the opening scenes of the movie *Air Bud*, he is likely to play an important role throughout the movie and not disappear without trace. Their observations dealt not only with plot structure but also with questions of emotional weight and force. An orphan who antagonizes the person who has power over her is an orphan whose subsequent story has the potential to be harrowing; it takes a very short scene to set the players in place and establish an emotional connection with viewers.

With the computer games, the question of salience worked out in slightly different ways. Students appeared to attend rather less to questions of emotional import and rather more to issues that were likely to affect the workings out of the plot. Given that the emotions of the characters were indeed less salient in the game-oriented texts of these particular narratives, such a response was appropriate. The CD-ROMs were the most convention-bound of all the texts the students explored and their reactions showed that they are aware of the need to observe these conventions in their processing.

There were other questions involving fluency and salience with the CD-ROMs. The issue of how readily and how quickly readers made use of the tool bar to check options, look for help and explore alternative strategies was interesting even at the preliminary level of initial response. All of the students automatically checked over the screen with the mouse, searching for hidden hot spots, but they varied in how methodically their search was organized. One or two of the games call for information to be typed in and students varied in the quickness of their response to such a different demand.

Students also responded to the content of the CD-ROMs, as well as ease of handling. In some cases they were clear that the game was not worth the candle to them. *Virtual Springfield*, for example, includes a tour of the home town of the Simpsons. Players can enter particular houses and rummage through doors and cupboards but there is not a lot of real action in the initial stages. Furthermore, in order to find these buildings that can be entered, players must navigate around the town with a map and a compass, an exercise that can be very frustrating until you get the hang of it. Simpson fans, not surprisingly, found the returns rather more worth the investment of time and patience, but even some who admire the cartoon found the content of the CD-ROM disappointing. On the other hand, I saw players who found the whole exercise funny enough to be completely rewarding, and one who was skilful and lucky enough to discover short cuts on her very first sally and who therefore experienced no frustration at all. In a similar way, the ritual violence at the start of the *Men in Black* game elicited very different responses from different users.

Some of these students also have relatively strong views on how much a computer game should bend the rules. *Discworld II* is based on the Terry Pratchett fantasy novels which none of these particular students had read. They responded more to the length and elaboration of the introduction, which rolls on for many minutes before any form of interactivity is permitted, than to the actual content. Some were confident enough to press the 'Escape' button and leap over some of this introductory indulgence and some just sat it out, but all were critical of the lapse of time before they could start to make an impact by interacting with the screen. Clearly they have their own ideas of propriety in game design, ideas which do not include such a leisurely start.

Different media have different points of rigidity and flexibility. Video is inexorably linear, for example, and the CD-ROMs we explored are highly rigid in the options open to users, at least in the preliminary stages. Students varied in how relaxed they were in dealing with these particular limitations but it is hard to say how much of this particular form of response relates to their experience and expectations with and of the medium and how much is a factor of their own innate patience.

Conclusions

These young people are clearly very accustomed to making judgements about whether a text is worth the investment of their time and were able to articulate their reasoning in a very informative way. It is very clear from the transcripts that these students are very used to having a broad range of texts to choose from. They did not express any great commitment to persevering with a story that struck them as dull, regardless of the medium, although one or two did mention that they might expect a text to get better after the first confusing stages.

Weighing the balance between personal salience and fluency of access was a strategy that manifested itself across all three media and for many different texts. Different students used specific criteria (long words, black and white pictures, etc.) as cues for decision-making in particular media. The students explicitly worked on a kind of trade-off: the more salient the story, the more prepared they were to invest time and effort into reading or viewing or playing. It is worth noting that there were some examples where students rejected texts because they seemed too simple, either in terms of access or in terms of content.

Students were clear that some stories work better in one format than in another, but at all times it appeared to be the story they were judging; the platform was an issue only as it provided appropriate access to the story in question. All students testified to enjoying stories in each of the three media we were discussing.

If a single sentence could sum up this part of the project, it would be that these young people demonstrated a predilection not for 'either/or' when it comes to media but rather for 'both/and'. They were interested in and also selective about all forms of media. They were able to discriminate in meaningful ways among texts and to articulate the reasons for their choices. They were neither overly dazzled by bells and whistles, nor dismissive of print. They confounded many stereotypes about their generation and perhaps about the nature of the communications revolution.

Questions of salience and fluency continued to be of primary importance throughout the study. Over and over again, the students weighed up the balance between the personal interest and appeal of a text versus issues concerning its ease of access. The judgement of what constituted a favourable trade-off was very personal and worked differently according to which reader, which medium and which story were involved.

Afterword: new literacy ecologies of the twenty-first century

In this chapter I have talked about a balancing point between salience and fluency, in the contexts of novels, films and games. Can this concept be transferred usefully to the idea of online reading? Do readers exploring online sites engage in similar trade-offs?

With online reading, very often the balance point seems rather more like a flash point. Decisions about salience are rendered very quickly indeed; assessments of fluency of access seem often to be achieved on a simple yes/no basis; in other words, if the site is not instantly seen as readable a reader moves elsewhere. To an onlooker it is often remarkable how quickly a young reader can reject a book, but a book generally calls for at least a minimum of physical engagement – pick up, turn over, put down. A website can be dismissed by a single click and in many cases easy come inexorably leads to easy go.

Ease of use, paradoxically, may actually be harder to ascertain on a website than on the page of a book. The book runs on very strict conventions. The number of ways in which words and pictures can relate to each other is limited although the 'rules' about those relations may change over time. A contemporary child who confidently explores the complex layout of an informational double-page spread, loaded with images, tables and graphs, different font sizes, box colours and typefaces, and a distribution of information across different channels, might well be baffled by the now-obsolete convention of the old illustrated book with its frontispiece and its tipped-in colour plates offering pictures that illustrate action points in the story that are many pages away. But some things about the book remain constant – a Western book is generally bound on the left-hand side, the pages turn in reliable order, the page numbers offer guidance to location, and so forth.

Conventions of the web are still establishing themselves. We may hope that a good website will offer usable forms of tracking progress but it is by no means a given, and even experts disagree about whether the organizational apparatus of a site belongs on the left-hand side, across the top or elsewhere. We may prefer it if exit routes are clearly flagged but many websites are retrospectively navigable only by means of the 'Back' key.

Furthermore, online reading is much less likely than print reading (or film viewing or, to a lesser extent, embarking on a game) to offer the compensation of swift absorption. Absorption is often an aspect of salience, but it is easy to overlook the ways in which it acts as a kind of tool for ease of access as well. An engrossed reader, following the content of a printed page with great interest, is likely to solve problems of access with less rather than more conscious attention, which is a surprisingly helpful approach. Online, where continuous absorbed attention is less likely to be part of the reading package, such obliviousness to roadblocks is harder to achieve. Problems look and feel more like problems when forward momentum does not pull a reader past the sticking point. In assessing ease of access online, readers may be warier about obstacles, and more likely to abandon the project at an early stage – especially when the Internet abounds with alternative prospects.

While salience and fluency thus remain important issues for making decisions about whether to read further in online situations, they change shape and significance. Fluency in particular means something quite different in online reading. Flying through a number of links because none leads to completely satisfying options may look like a kind of fluent behaviour on the surface, but it may actually be an activity that represents a series of fast rejections and an accumulating dissatisfaction.

'Sticky' sites cause viewers to linger and to return. Young readers may indeed be faster than older readers in assessing the value of a website in terms of its personal value and its ease of use, but high-speed surfing may represent something more perfunctory. There is a great deal more work to be done before we understand the processes by which young readers make decisions about their online reading.

Chapter 7

'Remediation'

E-books and DVDs

'Remediation'

Jay David Bolter and Richard Grusin have written an account of new media entitled *Remediation*, a term they define as 'the formal logic by which new media refashion prior media forms' (1999: 273). Remediation works through two contradictory styles: hypermediacy, defined as 'a style of visual representation whose goal is to remind the viewer of the medium' (1999: 272), and immediacy, 'a style of visual representation whose goal is to make the viewer forget the presence of the medium (canvas, photographic film, cinema, and so on) and believe that he is in the presence of the objects of representation' (1999: 272–3). The tension between these two forms of re-working creates some of the energy of new media, yet the process is not exclusive to new digital forms and has a history of its own.

Bolter and Grusin helpfully summarize their argument in the following terms:

> Like other media since the Renaissance – in particular, perspective painting, photography, film, and television – new digital media oscillate between immediacy and hypermediacy, between transparency and opacity. This oscillation is the key to understanding how a medium refashions its predecessors and other contemporary media. Although each medium promises to reform its predecessors by offering a more immediate or authentic experience, the promise of reform inevitably leads us to become aware of the new medium as a medium. Thus, immediacy leads to hypermediacy. The process of remediation makes us aware that all media are at one level a 'play of signs,' which is a lesson that we take from poststructuralist literary theory.
>
> (Bolter and Grusin 1999: 19)

Bolter and Grusin go on to explore the impact of new media in terms that can be described as ecological:

> Furthermore, media technologies constitute networks or hybrids that can be expressed in physical, social, aesthetic, and economic terms. Introducing a new media technology does not mean simply inventing new hardware and

software, but rather fashioning or refashioning such a network. The World Wide Web is not merely a software protocol and text and data files. It is also the sum of the uses to which this protocol is now being put: for marketing and advertising, scholarship, personal expression, and so on. These uses are as much a part of the technology as the software itself. For this reason, we can say that media technologies are agents in our culture without falling into the trap of technological determinism. New digital media are not external agents that come to disrupt an unsuspecting culture. They emerge from within cultural contexts, and they refashion other media, which are embedded in the same or similar contexts.

(Bolter and Grusin 1999: 19)

The electronic book

One example of 'remediation' that seems straightforward at first glance is the electronic book, which takes the very old technology of the book and re-works it in digital form. Yet the responses of the students to this new technology demonstrate both that the role of this gadget is not yet clear cut and also that the students are at least implicitly aware of some of the issues outlined by Bolter and Grusin.

The Rocket e-book, which was the version of electronic book I showed to the participants, appears to have been designed to resemble a book as closely as possible. It is the approximate size of a paperback, and is created with a curved bulge on the left-hand side that is supposed to remind the reader of a folded-back paperback. It weighs 20 ounces and provides a single screen with a button that refreshes the screen (no scrolling: a 'page' is replaced at a time, wrapping down the screen). On its own, it looks like a high-tech Etch-a-Sketch; alternatively, it can be wrapped in a rather cumbersome leather jacket, which is designed to exude 'the primordial odor of bookishness' (Silberman 1998: 101). It hooks, via a cradle, to the computer to download books from a website based at the online site of Barnes and Noble. Books purchased by the individual are maintained on this website and can be downloaded into the e-book, deleted and then downloaded again if desired. The e-book will hold the equivalent of about ten paperback books at a time.

The features of this early incarnation of the e-book are fairly restricted. Working on a tiny keyboard, either with the stylus that slots into the casing or with very delicate use of the fingers, it is possible to add notes to the text. Readers can underline words and phrases, and can look up words in an attached dictionary, either by highlighting them in the text with stylus or finger, or by typing them on to the little keyboard. It is possible to search the text for particular words or phrases, for underlined sections or for notes. In other words, some home-grown and relatively primitive hyperlinking is possible with this machine.

The screen is backlit, and there is a choice of large or small font, although none of the fonts available through the website at the time I was organizing this part of the project was particularly attractive to my eye. One of the texts I had loaded on to my e-book, *Alice in Wonderland*, contained black and white illustrations (the original Tenniel drawings).

At the time that I showed the e-book to the students, the list of available titles was fairly restricted. I tried to offer a range of materials, but there was little for sale that offered any obvious appeal to adolescents. Different students chose to look at the following titles: *Alice in Wonderland*, *The Secret Garden*, *Unleashing the Killer App* (a book about computer applications), *The Age of Innocence* and a couple of issues of the *Wall Street Journal*. They made it clear that this list lacked appeal, and there seems little doubt that this absence of appeal contributed to the 'tinkering' approach they took to the whole project. On the other hand, there was no doubt that all of them appreciated the fact that this technology was still in a fairly early stage and they could easily imagine future developments that would make the gadget more appealing to them.

'Remediating' the book

Steve Silberman, writing in *Wired* magazine just before three different electronic books first became available on the market, provides a clear account of the perceived qualities of remediation that attended the production of this new format:

> The book made of paper, bound in sturdy vellum covers, is an icon of permanence, of thoughts deemed worthy enough to be fixed in a form designed to endure. In the digital era, however, we've come to think of texts as fluid resources, circulating through the watercourse of the Net and pouring themselves into convenient forms in our browsers. With three electronic reading devices coming to market this fall billing themselves as 'books,' it seems the time to ask, What does it mean to take the beech tree out of the book?
>
> The assumption behind these new devices is a contemporary one: Divorce the content (bits) from the container (atoms) and you no longer have to schlep the atoms around . . .
>
> To streamline the delivery of content, the creators of the new digital readers propose a new model of publishing. The digital 'book' you carry in your purse or briefcase is an empty vessel. A text inhabits the book for as long as you care to store it, before reading and deleting it to make room for more texts, or offloading it to an online 'bookshelf' for later . . .
>
> Gadgets fail when we don't understand them, but also when they don't understand us. The measure of success for the makers of electronic books will be how much they comprehend why we pick up a book in the first place.
>
> (Silberman 1998: 100)

Jim Sachs, the chief executive officer of SoftBook, also makes comparisons between electronic books and paper books:

'We're not out to replace books,' he said. 'I tell people, if there's a book in the bookstore, buy the book. Books are wonderful until they gang up on you. If you're an elementary student with a backpack of 20-pound books, there is a good reason not to have that many and replace it with one 2.9 pound book.'

(Mandel 1998: C10)

Martin Eberhard, the chief executive officer of NuvoMedia, the makers of the Rocket e-book, also stresses the issue of convenience:

Ultimately, reading isn't about feel and smell and the sound of pages turning. Reading is about the words, the content. While I'm in my living room, it's nice to read a book. But otherwise it's not always the most convenient way.

(Mandel 1998: C1)

These comments suggest that the electronic book may be more an example of reformatting rather than remediating in the terms described by Bolter and Grusin. In contrast, it may be useful to look at some alternative ways that digitization remediates the impact of the print book. Direct publication on the Internet occurs in a variety of ways. Douglas Cooper published *Delirium* in serial form on the web before it appeared in print (Renzetti 1998: C8). Coach House Books in Toronto now publish all their authors directly on the Internet and have set up new ways of making payment. In at least one case, they invite readers to vote on whether a book should be republished: 'Though this book is not currently available in print, there are rumours of a possible reprint. To help us decide, cast your vote for a reprint by tipping the author's estate' (http://www.chbooks.corn/news/index.html, 30 November 1999).

The Internet sometimes affects the actual writing of a story, as in this example from 1998: 'Last summer, noted technophobe John Updike wrote the first paragraph in a short story sponsored by the on-line book retailer Amazon.com. It was completed in a series of paragraphs written by Web dwellers, 140,000 of whom submitted entries' (Renzetti 1998: C8).

The web can also offer ways of expanding on the fictional world of the print book, as in the website for Philip Pullman's *The Golden Compass*. Here, enthusiasts can locate a more detailed explanation of the symbols on the eponymous compass than the book itself contains (http://www.randomhouse.com/features/goldencompass/goldencompass/aleth.html, 30 November 1999). The site also provided an advance opportunity to sample a chapter of the long-awaited third volume of the trilogy.

Or readers can interact with some authors by way of the Internet. Mary Doria Russell, author of *The Sparrow*, includes her e-mail address on her website and encourages correspondence with readers (McKeen 1999: C1).

All of these forms of expansion on the print book take some account of the interactivity made possible by digitization without even branching into questions of hyperlinking or of involving additional forms such as audio or video connections. Janet Murray (1997) explores some of the issues involved in making the step from simple expansion on print to more elaborate re-working in her book on new forms of narrative; the chapter is tellingly entitled 'From Additive to Expressive Form'. Murray suggests that there are four essential properties of digital environments: they are procedural, they are participatory, they are spatial and they are encyclopedic (1997: 71–90).

Judged alongside any of these examples of remediations of what Coach House Press calls 'the fetish item formerly known as the book' (Renzetti 1998: C8), the electronic book looks very tame. In its effort to capture the qualities that keep book lovers happy, the early incarnation of the electronic book can fairly be described as an unadventurous option. It will be interesting to see how it develops over the next decade.

Alan Kay says, 'World-changing inventions are so different that they initially have to masquerade as "better old things" rather than "completely new things"' (Geirland and Sonesh-Kedar 1999: 124). In the early stages of new technologies, it can be difficult to establish how radical their impact is going to be. Interestingly, the students picked up on this difficulty in their responses to the electronic book.

The students' responses to the e-book

In the early months of 1999, students looking at the Rocket e-book for the first time expressed many of the questions raised above, although in indirect ways. My motive for acquiring an electronic book to show to them was to capture their responses to a form of technology they were not likely to have encountered before. I did not anticipate the degree to which they would ask, 'So what exactly is so new about this?' Nor did I predict that some form of this question would be asked both by those who liked what they saw and by those who did not.

Some participants were cool to the whole idea of an electronic book. Megan said, 'I think that ordinary books are just good enough.' Janice agreed: 'It's kind of dumb though because it's so much work. I'd just rather have a book . . . This is fun to play with, but after a while it kind of gets boring.' Jack, the ninth-grader we have already seen exploring this technology, said, 'I think that I prefer to sit down with a book. Like, a book.' His classmate Jeff said, 'Right now with this sort of thing, it's kind of limited as to what you can do.' Even Kyle and Leonard, two ninth-graders who were highly enthusiastic, lost their commitment somewhat when asked to consider what price would be low enough to tempt them to purchase an e-book. Leonard said:

> Well, I'd start to think, is this just another piece of electronic equipment to carry around? And I'd wonder if it was really worth it or if I could just take the one book I needed. Rather than carry around ten books because I wouldn't read ten books of course.

Madeleine expected more bells and whistles, asking in some surprise, 'The pictures don't do anything? It's just, like, the storybook on the computer?' Anita similarly expected more interactivity. 'Are there any pictures?' she asked. 'If you touch it do you get a picture?'

In general, Kyle and Leonard were enthusiastic, as were Tom and Jordan, the sixth-grade boys. Like their less committed peers, however, they all had suggestions for how to make the e-book more desirable, and it is interesting to see how many of these suggestions involve some kind of remediation in the sense described by Bolter and Grusin.

Tom and Jordan wanted to add plug-ins to make it easier to use a keyboard and a printer, 'because the typing was a little bit awkward because you had to type it really small'. They would like to see the addition of colour and audio. They might like an audio dictionary but would still want to be able to see the words. Angela was leery about even adding audio: 'Except for the voice, because I get really annoyed with computer voices. Unless it was, like, a nice voice.' Madeleine and Janice also voted for an audio component; Madeleine in particular was enthusiastic about having the text read to her.

Kyle and Leonard threw themselves into suggesting improvements, even though their enthusiasm for the e-book as it stood was already considerable. They admired the dictionary component and they greatly liked the idea of having any book you wanted at your fingertips. In terms of improvements, they liked the idea of colour and of a bigger screen (or two screens) so you could see diagrams more clearly. They also liked the ability to add notes but wanted it made easier to do, and they suggested that a maths version might have a built-in calculator or even (Leonard's suggestion) 'a built-in auto-solve!'

Gregory and Jack, as we have already seen, produced a substantial list of improvements: a better font, a higher pixel count, colour, better menus and a larger screen. Greg said:

> One that I prefer in a book as well is you can see pages at the same time and especially when it comes to, like, larger size books. You can see so much at the same time instead of just having a little bit and having to keep flipping back.

Jeff asked if the texts on the e-book had been specially produced or if anything could be loaded. He and Anita also argued strongly for a larger keyboard. They were less committed to the idea of colour, saying it depended on the audience: 'If it's, like, for a little kid maybe for the colour because kids like colour and everything', said Anita.

These suggestions can be divided into two categories: those that express an urge to find a more user-friendly way of operating the tools already available in the e-book and those that call for extra facilities such as audio links and interactive pictures. The observations on the virtues of the e-book largely focus on the convenience factor.

Issues of transparency and opacity

How do these comments relate to questions of hypermediacy and immediacy or, to use Bolter and Grusin's alternative terms, to questions of opacity and transparency? The students addressed these questions in a variety of ways, never raising anything like these issues in any explicit sense, but drawing on tacit assumptions that can be teased out in the terms of remediation.

For example, it seems clear that one of the virtues of the online dictionary, in the eyes of many participants, is its capacity to increase the transparency of the reading process. Establishing an unknown meaning becomes a much more automatic process and reading can continue with less of an interruption than would be caused by a trip to a print dictionary. On the other hand, the smallness of the keyboard is clearly a factor leading to opacity; it is impossible to overlook the presence of the medium itself as you pick out the letters with the little stylus.

Many of the activities involved in organizing text on the e-book can be managed in two ways: by using the stylus or by using a finger. I rapidly found that using a finger felt much more natural to me, less intrusively different. I liked the e-book better the minute I switched to a two-handed arrangement. We are perhaps not aware of how much we use our hands in reading. It may be that someone who habitually reads with a pen in hand would be more comfortable with the stylus, although it is much more slender than the average pen and it would probably take some time for most people to develop automaticity in its manipulation. A number of the students (though not all) also preferred a manual approach, but nearly everyone found the stylus essential when using the keyboard.

Automaticity is an important factor in the perception of transparency, and those factors that interfere with automaticity draw attention to the opacity particularly of an unfamiliar medium. There are many examples of student comments in this regard. A number of them commented on the font and in particular on the fact that the p and the f were 'broken', that is, the shape was not fully closed. Some disliked the glare on the glass of the screen and/or the inadequate pixel count of the letters, both of which contribute to a less than crisp letter quality, certainly inferior to what we expect in print on paper. One or two students experimented with the large and small versions of the font and observed that the advantages of the larger print are somewhat undermined by the fact that correspondingly fewer words appear on the screen when the large font is engaged. How much exposure to the e-book it would take to reduce or eliminate their awareness of some or all of these factors is a question to which I cannot provide an answer.

It should be noted that most of these points involve issues of fluency or accessibility, and that the highly restricted list of titles meant that there was almost no opportunity for the advantages of salience to restore any balance and to increase the perception of transparency. The priorities of readers play more of a part in the evolution of new media than Bolter and Grusin really acknowledge. Many new media involve questions of old wine in new bottles. When we come to explore the responses of the students to the DVD, a form of remediated video, it will be clear that the greatly increased salience of the contents to these particular readers plays an important role in their comfort level with a new medium. It is not the only issue at work, but it is one that matters a great deal.

Much of the discussion concerning the e-book centred on the practical advantages of not hefting a stack of books around; comments on the actual quality of the reading experience were limited to some extent by the content that was available. It is not surprising that this limitation increased the quantity of tinkering that was done and virtually eliminated any potential invitation to become engrossed that could be expressed by the text itself. This fact both represents a limitation to the study and also testifies to the complexity of what is involved with the introduction of a new medium.

If the e-book catches on enough to bring the price down to a more mass-market level, it will be fascinating to see whether writers begin to compose specifically to take account of its potential and limits. At present the e-book is focusing on replacing a conventional print text. If and when the producers begin to think in terms of remediating *computer* texts into a portable form that eliminates the drawbacks of reading from a monitor, we may enter entirely new aesthetic territory.

'Remediating' the video

A second new medium was much more popular with the students who participated in this study: the DVD or digital video disc. In the early months of 1999, domestic DVD was still relatively rare, though it has gained substantially in popularity since that date. Again, it is necessary to describe the specific example that the students used: the DVDs were loaded in a drive of an IBM ThinkPad laptop computer. It is possible to link this computer to a television screen and play the DVDs directly on the TV, but the students and I did all our exploring of this format on the monitor of the laptop.

This fact matters because it affected the quality of the experience to a surprising extent. The laptop operates on a different scale from the television; the focal distance is different and the sense of intimacy is correspondingly greater. My initial response to the very first DVD I played on this computer surprised me by its powerful affective charge. The initial image I called up happened to be Bugs Bunny welcoming me to a Warner Brothers movie, nothing that I had not seen many times before. But I was caught by surprise by the impact of this familiar figure moving and speaking on a screen designed to be literally within arms' reach (again that manual connection seems meaningful). Similarly, when I spent a decadent morning in bed watching *Bonnie and Clyde* on my laptop (curled up with a good movie, so to speak), the effect was quite different from watching a movie on a bedroom television set (though the moral turpitude involved was probably identical!). It is now possible to purchase a DVD Discman, with a five-inch screen, and the affective charge of watching a movie in miniature is presumably different again from what I have experienced with the laptop.

I am not the only person to notice this effect. Geirland and Sonesh-Kedar, in their account of media convergence and new story-telling media, reflect on the difference between a television screen and a computer screen in related terms:

> [Some people] believe that the desktop variety of the Internet is in fact an interactive storytelling medium in a way that television could never be. [Thomas] Lakeman referred to the desktop as the 'ten-inch experience' as opposed to television, which was a 'ten-foot' experience. The ten-inch distance between the user and the screen was approximately the same as the distance between an individual and an intimate friend. The desktop offered a level of intimacy and solitude necessary for interactivity that the television couldn't deliver – even with Web-browsing capability.
>
> (Geirland and Sonesh-Kedar 1999: 256–7)

The DVD remediates two related forms, film and video. (It also, in different guise, remediates the even newer technology of the CD-ROM, but that is not an issue to be addressed here.) I found that a first glance at the new format confirmed the power of Bolter and Grusin's account of the oscillation between immediacy and hypermediacy created by remediation. With the DVD, the quality of the digitally produced picture is so spectacularly clear that it simultaneously pulls you into the visual experience of the movie and draws attention to its own remarkable clarity in a way that distracts you from the story. It is as if the more granular effect of the lower pixel count we take for granted in film and video actually makes more space for the viewer; the glossy surface of the DVD image almost repels involvement. Undoubtedly, we will develop forms of automaticity for processing DVD images that take less and less account of a feature that presently strikes us as unusual.

Like the electronic book, film-based DVDs basically give us old wine in new bottles. Like the early print books that attempted to reproduce the effects of manuscript, the initial DVD takes a familiar vehicle and recasts it. Unlike the e-book, however, the DVD does (at least in some cases) take advantage of its digital capacities in ways that would be difficult or impossible to achieve in the original format.

One major advantage of a digital movie is that it is browsable, without all the drawbacks of fast-forwarding and rewinding. A second plus is that the user can make many of the decisions about how it will be broadcast: what language will be supplied for the soundtrack and for the subtitles, whether or not to switch right out of the diegetic dialogue of the movie itself into an extradiegetic commentary from the director, the producer and the special effects personnel. The capacity to move back and forth between the created fictional universe of the movie and the motives and explanations of the creators is not unprecedented, but the simplicity with which it can be achieved marks a major break with the more cumbersome arrangements of the past.

The students' responses to the DVD

The participants were familiar with many forms of extradiegetic commentary on 'how the movie was made'; many television shows, magazines and books, and websites are devoted to background information about one movie or another. At least one student, Jordan, had visited Universal Studios and seen some examples of the technology of movie-making at work.

The students differed in the degree to which they valued and enjoyed such information. Several of them expressed some version of the view that they might want to know some things about the movie-making process but certainly wouldn't be interested in every detail – and many of them wouldn't want to watch any of it until they had seen and enjoyed the movie itself. Having the background information assembled with the movie itself all in one DVD package would probably give them rather more control over organizing their viewing of the different components. With television programmes and newspaper articles particularly, the chances of seeing the 'making of' sequences before you have actually seen the film are considerable. The haphazard nature of public exposure probably means that our viewing habits are relatively flexible at present; it may be that the DVD package will enable many movie watchers to become more systematic and methodical in how they approach a film.

One of the students, Jeff, had had a DVD drive attached to his television at home for some months at the time of our meeting. He was eloquent about the drawbacks of the little laptop:

> It's a bit more fuzzy on this because it's a laptop as opposed to, ah, an actual television set . . . Also we have the, ah, surround-sound speaker system so it enhances the sound a lot more than this . . . So it's fifty times or a hundred times better than this . . . We also have the surround [sound] with videos. It really enhances the effects and stuff and things like that.

Jeff was already showing signs that he had effectively transferred his visual and aural allegiance to DVD quality. 'The graphics and the visual effects with the DVD kind of make it a bit more real, like, it's kind of hard to get into the movie when it's sort of all grainy and a little, like, fuzzy.'

Anita, who was Jeff's partner on this occasion, was not familiar with the DVD, but was quick to ask questions that illustrate how expectations can be developed in a more general way. The following exchange is instructive:

JEFF: I found that you can also play music CDs on the actual DVD.
ANITA: Can you?
JEFF: Yeah, it doesn't give, ah, special features, it's just kind of like, it's like a blue screen. At the top it says, like, Track One.
MARGARET: Oh yeah? This is on your television?
JEFF: Yeah.

ANITA: Can you get the lyrics, like?
JEFF: No, I don't think so. Maybe if they kind of enhanced some of the CDs.
ANITA: Yeah, I guess so.

Anita, as became clear in her session of playing *Starship Titanic* with Jack, has had relatively little experience with computers. Yet her response to Jeff's description of a piece of media convergence he had discovered by exploring his new machinery was not to be overwhelmed by the expansion of the television's powers; it was to ask for more – in this case, lyrics to go with the music. Who actually expects more of the digital revolution – those who are familiar with the powers and limits of computers or those with less exposure and experience – is an interesting question.

Kyle and Leonard were very enthusiastic about the DVD, as this sample exchange demonstrates. They were not even trying to be 'cool' about what it would offer:

LEONARD: So they're talking in Spanish now? Listen to it.
KYLE: Si, they're talking in Spanish.
LEONARD: Wow! Neat!
KYLE: That's neat.
LEONARD: What a great little feature.
KYLE: You can, like, this is –
LEONARD: So if I have Spanish people coming over today, I'll just set it on Spanish.
MARGARET: You can have it in Spanish with English subtitles, or English with
    Spanish subtitles, or French with Spanish subtitles.
KYLE: So you can have any combination then?
LEONARD: Spanish and English.
MARGARET: Yeah, and in this one, this one offers you any combination.
KYLE: So it's on the DVD then, not in the machine.
LEONARD: This is amazing.
KYLE: That's neat.

Jack and Gregory, who were so suspicious of the electronic book, were much more interested by the potential of the DVD. Gregory showed more interest than any of the others in the technological aspects of the drive, and kept returning to the question of whether a fast computer would produce a better image than a slow one. Jack, though he baulked at the price of a DVD drive, was much more impressed by the quality of the product. He kept producing involuntary exclamations:

'Oh, ooh, it's got an index thing. Contents.'
'Wow!' (as the DVD began to play).
'The quality is amazing. Extreme movie. That's very very clear. Oooh!'
'[The ability to browse] is great. That's really great.'

On the other hand, Jack was lukewarm about the additional commentaries. He thought you could find them elsewhere in a less expensive form, and was not convinced he would find them generally of interest.

Janice, opting for the conservative response as she did on more than one occasion, suggested that she would prefer video to DVD. She did not make her reasoning completely clear, but seemed to be responding in this way because she was simply more familiar with video and did not find enough added value in the DVD to be worth the effort of getting to know how to use it. As also happened more than once, Madeleine did not appear to agree completely with her friend but did not advance any serious argument.

Angela and Megan were even more tepid in their response. They were moderately interested in the background information but thought it was as likely to interfere with their enjoyment of a movie as to enhance it. 'If it was really good', said Megan, 'I'd probably want to know how they made it, but not like the *whole* thing, how they made every little thing.' They both professed to be uninterested in background information about the actors. Yet both said they would be happy to own a DVD if money were no object. Megan admired the small discs and Angela added, 'And you can kinda explore what you want to do.'

Tom and Jordan were much more enthusiastic, though at least some of their engagement was fuelled by their evident affection for *Ace Ventura – Pet Detective*, which they chose to explore on the DVD. They moved on to *Contact*, which has a much fuller set of backup information, and I asked them if they watched a movie differently after they had seen the analysis of the special effects:

TOM: Like, when I just looked at that, I just looked at all the little splashes and how they were placed.
MARGARET: Does that distract you from the story?
TOM: Not real . . . sort of. Not that much though.
JORDAN: I don't know. I guess I kind of want to watch a movie first . . .
MARGARET: So you want to have the story first and then pick it apart.
JORDAN: Yeah. But still, I don't think it really affects the story.
MARGARET: You think you could watch that final disc and then go back and watch all the rest and get caught up in it again.
JORDAN: No, I'd rather watch the movie first, but in that, I don't know, I think it would kind of distract me a bit because I try and look for that. Like, I tried to look for the people laughing [extras in the pod explosion scene in *Contact*].
TOM: Yeah, that's exact – I was looking for this one lady who went back and then forward and then back.

Changing the experience of film

Tom and Jordan provide a textbook example of viewers whose attention has been drawn to the constructed nature of the text. In Richard Lanham's terms, they are oscillating between looking through and looking at the textual surface (1994: 5), another way of talking about transparency and opacity. Jordan is explicit: he would rather watch the movie first (looking through) because keeping an eye out for the effects he had just seen layered into the film (looking at) would be a distraction if he were simultaneously trying to process the story. But in the final analysis, he doesn't think it really affects how the story works.

The DVD does offer some re-working of the material offered in the film itself, but generally it works on a fairly superficial level. *Contact* offers a range of information about the creation of special effects but does not open up the story to deeper exploration. Other DVDs offer other insights, but the movie itself remains sealed. For example, there is a soundtrack for the film *Pleasantville* that provides the director's commentary on what he was trying to achieve in each scene, what the symbols represent, and so forth. The film appears, frame for frame, exactly as it does with the diegetic soundtrack, but the director's voiceover is added: the linear world of the story is undisturbed.

Similarly, browsing is possible with a DVD disc, but the film simply runs forward or backward from wherever you join it in its usual order of frames. The fictional universe is not opened up; current film productions do not take imaginative advantage of the enormous capacity of the DVD.

Conclusions

There are many ways of describing the current situation where so many new technologies strive to represent 'better old things' rather than moving into new creative modes straight away. Janet Murray talks about the incunabular stage of a technology in its infancy, and says it is too soon to make artistic judgements about what is happening with digital texts of various kinds (1997: 28). The electronic book and the DVD may seem like extremely primitive prototypes in a very short time indeed, as media convergence accelerates. The question of how our stories will be delivered in a generation's time will be answered as a result of a combination of artistic, technological and commercial factors.

Meanwhile, market and cultural forces continue to affect developments. For a long time through the late 1990s, the question of whether DVDs would take off continued to be unresolved. My own feeling that the die had finally been cast came late in 1999: I went into my local media store and discovered that, for the first time, the DVDs had been moved to the prime selling location at the top of the escalator, and the videos had been relegated to the back wall. For the moment at least, the DVD appears to be securely on an upward ramp.

Questions about the e-book are nowhere near being answered. Early in 2000, there was much excitement about Stephen King's novella, *Riding the Bullet*, which was published only in electronic form. As Charles Mann reports, 'The results amazed the book industry: Within 24 hours, about 400,000 people downloaded the text, even though most of them also had to download and install the bulky software required to read it on their computer monitors' (2000: 115). Mann's account of the fate of the e-book, however, suggests that proponents of paper may win the day in the end – except that it will be electronic paper. The e-book of the future, he suggests, may resemble a paper book much more closely than my Etch-a-Sketch tablet now does, with the electronic information downloaded on to special pages that can be turned and manipulated in the way we use paper today.

The role of such manipulation as part of the reading process is not a topic that even occurred to me when I began this study. However, the considerations that arose in the readings of a picture book foregrounded that issue in surprising ways. It may be that the students who were perturbed by the e-book were drawing more deeply on their tactile experiences of reading than any of us realized – a topic to which I will turn in the next chapter.

Questions of salience were important in the students' responses to the e-book texts in particular. What the text is about seemed to matter to them rather more than the medium through which it is presented. The very newness of the electronic book in the winter of 1999 caused some problems of its reception, in that it was almost impossible to locate titles that would engage school students in any genuine way. It is not completely clear to what extent this caused them to treat the e-book as a curiosity rather than a genuine vehicle allowing entrance to a textual world.

Another issue that came up in the responses to both e-book and DVD was the variation between 'looking through' and 'looking at', immediacy and hyper-mediacy in Bolter and Grusin's terms. This question of oscillating between these two kinds of attending featured in different ways in just about all the textual encounters.

Afterword: new literacy ecologies of the twenty-first century

Contrasting attitudes towards the DVD and the e-book were manifest at the time I wrote this chapter in 2001, and the intervening five years have confirmed the success of the DVD, while the marketing of different incarnations of the e-book continues to flounder. Clearly the DVD manufacturers found a way to offer a 'better old thing' that struck a significant chord with buyers; the DVD player was adopted more rapidly than most other household electronic devices. In 1998, when I was first introducing my DVD player to the participants in my project, 1 per cent of Canadian households owned a DVD player. By 2003, that percentage was up to 48. 'In comparison, it took the personal computer, the CD player and the VCR about 12 years each to reach comparable penetration levels' (Damsell 2003: B4). Meanwhile, the e-book industry endured takeover turmoil, raised false hopes about rapid development, lost support from retailers (Barnes and Noble have ceased their website backup for the Rocket e-book) and suffered from a nearly terminal vagueness of marketing strategy.

As I write, the Sony® Reader is advertised as coming soon to North America. This new product offers a form of electronic paper (though the display system is still a rigid tablet). 'It's the way on-screen reading was always meant to be – book-like', says the Sony website. But the Sony® Reader will tackle more than books:

'It also displays Adobe® PDFs, personal documents, blogs, newsfeeds, and JPEGs with the same amazing readability, so you can take your favourite blogs and online newspapers with you. It even plays audio files.' A footnote adds that some of these formats require file conversion using applied software, but even so it is clear that Sony are paying attention to the virtues of flexibility (http://products.sel.sony.com/pa/prs/reader_features.html, accessed 17 April 2006).

It remains to be seen how successful the Sony® Reader will be, but e-reading is changing in other ways as well. A different electronic competitor is the digital calendar, the PDA, some of which feature software that will present complete novels for those who are happy to read on a very tiny screen. A few of the more expensive digital gadgets combine calendar with telephone, and of course texters are by now long accustomed to reading words on their cellphones.

Essentially, the challenge for all forms of e-reading is to establish a definitive way of being 'better' than that old survivor, the paper book. The current thinking about e-books still requires a computer link where batteries can be charged and book texts stored and loaded. Whether the market ever strengthens to support a form of wireless e-book remains to be seen, but, as long as connectivity on the fly is not possible, the e-book will in some substantial ways remain in competition with the most durable and successful artefact of them all. You can read your blogs and online newspapers on your new Sony® Reader but you need to load them from your computer first – a two-step process that may or may not strike users as an improvement.

Meanwhile, the DVD goes from strength to strength. Having marketed various deluxe versions of movies with large quantities of backup material, manufacturers are now turning their attention to complete television series (Mackey 2006). Whereas in 1999 only one of the sixteen students in my study had a DVD player at home and many of the others had never seen a DVD, today I would expect many of them to have several DVD players in their households: at least one formal single-use DVD player attached to a television screen, a DVD-playing game console such as PlayStation II, and DVD capacity in every household desktop and laptop computer.

Yet, while the immediate history of the DVD is startling in the speed and ubiquity of its adoption, the future is by no means as clear. The ability to download watchable video is accelerating, and all systems of capturing and viewing moving images are in flux.

It is not impossible that the possibilities represented by the e-book and the DVD will eventually merge in some new portable, possibly wireless, electronic device that allows users to move between print and video and games at will. A computer allows such transfers even now, as does a PDA in more limited forms, and the cellphone is morphing before our eyes. The Sony® Reader specs suggest that the manufacturer is moving towards taking advantage of the flexibility of digital materials. It is a good time to be paying attention.

Chapter 8

Handling the text
Picture books and CD-ROMs

Hands

Ideas have their own ecological roots. Over the Christmas of 1998, I played with my newly purchased electronic book, trying out different kinds of reading. I discovered I had a strong preference for using my fingers rather than the stylus to manoeuvre as many of the controlling operations as possible. The e-book was easy to hold, but as soon as I switched to a 'hands-on' mode, using both hands to make contact with the print as I read, I felt my comfort level rise immediately – enough that I noticed it consciously as well as unconsciously and began to wonder about the role of the hands in reading.

The e-book is designed to be read one-handed. You can hold it in either your left or your right hand (the text can be re-oriented on the screen) and click to scroll down with the same thumb. Technically, I had no problem with this approach; in terms of habit and comfort, I was much happier using both hands.

Spurred by the question of the role of the hands in reading, I read Frank R. Wilson's *The Hand: How Its Use Shapes the Brain, Language, and Human Culture*. 'Where *would* we be without our hands?' asks Wilson. 'Our lives are so full of commonplace experience in which the hands are so skillfully and silently involved that we rarely consider how dependent upon them we actually are' (1998: 3). Wilson, alas, does not address the role of the hands in reading behaviour but it is not difficult to begin to amass a list of how our hands help us read. In a nutshell, hands and the areas in the brain that control the hands are engaged in organizing the text optimally for the eye. Hands adjust focal distance and turn the book, sometimes by subtle degrees, to catch the light most effectively. Hands prevent pages from flipping and slipping. If the book is ill designed and words are disappearing into the gutters, hands will turn the page for maximum value. Fingers sometimes run under important phrases, or mark the last read word if attention is turned elsewhere for a moment. Fingers can search for and hold down a previous page that suddenly seems important. In short, hands assist, direct and sustain attention, that vital yet often fragile element of reading.

Although most people do read one-handed in bed from time to time, the normal arrangement is for the left hand to hold the book and the right hand to turn the pages. Wilson addresses the question of the two hands acting in partnership, drawing on the work of French psychologist Yves Guiard:

> The question should not be which hand is dominant, but how the two hands interact, or complement each other's action in a given task to achieve an objective . . . In writing – as consistent a unilateral skill as is known – Guiard showed that the nondominant hand plays a complementary, though largely covert, role by continuously repositioning the paper in anticipation of pen movement. Even when *no* movement seems needed (as in dart throwing), the passive hand and arm are probably crucial in counterbalancing the move of the active arm and hand.
>
> (Wilson 1998: 159)

The nondominant hand tends to move on a larger spatial and temporal scale than the dominant hand, and tends to 'frame' the movement of the dominant hand: 'it sets and confines the spatial context in which the "skilled" movement will take place' (Wilson 1998: 160). Wilson sums up this coordination as follows (his italics): *'the left hand knows what the right hand is planning and the right hand knows what the left hand just did'* (Wilson 1998: 160). In normal reading of left-to-right languages, the left hand holds the book at an appropriate distance, adjusts the face of the page for best optics, and presents the bottom right-hand corner for page turning. The right hand performs the grasp and turn.

At the same time, there are questions of aesthetic engagement that are processed exclusively through the hands. When I picked up Wilson's book to look at it again, I paid conscious attention to the way my hands engaged with the smoothness of the paper and the bulk of the hardback covers. I was skimming rather than reading in depth, and my hands flipped the pages in a practised choreography that both followed and sometimes directed the work of my eyes. The weight of the book registered in my hands, and I varied my grasp of it, both for comfort and for convenience.

Elaine Scarry (1999) says hands affect reading in shaping how we develop the sense of the words. Exploring how the mind engenders moving images under the relatively abstract direction of printed words, she describes the bodily effort of reading:

> The imaginer, although almost wholly immobilized in the process of reading, is still performing sustained actions with her eyes (moving across all the words) and hands (turning the pages) . . . [F]irst, the fingers must discriminate the delicate edge of the page from the full array stacked in the book, and then they must lift or flip it away from the others. Often the fingers are engaged in this act during the whole time that the left and right pages are being read: while the left-hand page is read, the right-hand fingers find the upper right-hand edge of the page that must eventually turn; then, as the right-hand page is read, the fingers move down along the page edge to the bottom corner, where, once

the reading of the two pages is complete, the turning motion will be carried out; the right-hand page will be folded over and smoothed into place where it now becomes a left-hand page, and the hand moves back across the two-page surface and up to the upper right-hand edge to prepare for the next turn. Meanwhile, new worlds keep swimming into view.

Reaching, stretching, and folding are the actual motions the hand carries out – like a spell of hand motions performed over the book – as one reads.

(Scarry 1999: 147)

Scarry's 'spell of hand motions' is a romantic image, but her detailed account of how hands participate in the rhythm of reading a print book is clear and convincing.

Designers of tools attend to the hands and bodies of users as well as to their more cerebral needs. Alan Powers, in a book about the organization of bookshelves and libraries, says, 'Reading is not just an activity of the mind, but of the whole body' (1999: 15). Jan Tschichold, famous as a designer of books and typefaces, makes a more complex comment on the role of the hand in reading:

Two constants reign over the proportions of a well-made book: the hand and the eye. A healthy eye is always about two spans away from the book page, and all people hold a book in the same manner.

The format of a book is determined by its purpose. It relates to the average size and the hands of an adult . . . A high degree or at least a sufficient degree of handiness has to be expected.

(Tschichold 1991: 36)

The opening pages of Alberto Manguel's fascinating *History of Reading* (1996) contain eighteen images of people reading; six more adorn the cover. These images cross centuries and continents. Of these twenty-four pictures, twenty-one show the reader's hands in control of the text in different ways. Another two indicate that the hands' job is to support the head of the reader at an appropriate distance from the book, which is laid on a flat surface. Only one image shows a 'reader' who is not using his hands, a head shot described by Manguel as follows: 'The blind Jorge Luis Borges screws up his eyes the better to hear the words of an unseen reader' (1996: 5). Offstage, Borges's reader is almost certainly connecting with the text by some use of his or her hands. The unusual effect of the image – a reader without a book – in itself reminds us of the tactile elements of reading that are so easy to overlook.

Our very schema of 'reading' involves tool use, the tool in question being some kind of text. Visual logos for literacy schemes almost invariably involve some depiction of a book, simply to communicate the meaning of reading, and usually that book is being held by a pair of schematic hands. The standard icon includes a head and a book grasped by two hands, all stylized but unmistakable. Even our language confirms that relationship; we speak naturally of the right-hand, rather than the right-side, page.

Yet it is rare to find a study of reading processes that takes full account of what the hands are doing as the reader comprehends the text. We need to ask whether the activity of the hands is simply a superficial accompaniment of our current arrangements for reading, whether the role of the hands is confined to the aesthetics of the tactile elements of reading, or whether the use of the hands engages the brain in ways that play a constitutive role in the reading processes. I shall not answer that question completely, but I want to tease out the implications of asking such a question at all.

Reading the picture book

Shortcut by David Macaulay is a frivolous and funny picture book. It is tempting to describe it as inconsequential, but since it is a book all about consequences this adjective is not quite appropriate. Stripped to a linear plot line, it tells of Albert the farmer and June his horse, who take melons to market once a week. On the way, they adhere to their usual routines, but their activities accidentally set a number of events in train, with disproportionate consequences for a variety of people and animals unknown to them and to each other. This simple story is split up into nine chapters and an epilogue, which tell the story out of sequence and require the reader to assemble the original chronology. The longest chapter is thirteen pages long; the shortest is three pages. Most pages contain somewhere between one and four lines of print. Five of the first seven chapters introduce completely new characters. The prose is deadpan and a great deal of the information is contained only in the pictures. For most readers, at least two readings are essential in order to make the plot connections clear.

The sessions that included the reading of this picture book ran through the winter of 1999. As with the computer game, we kept the video camera trained on the texts as the students explored the e-book, the DVDs, the picture book and one or two CD-ROMs. When I made my preliminary viewing of some of these videos, the idea of how we handle books was rather more prominent in my mind than it might have been without my earlier personal experience with the e-book. However, I was not deliberately exploring the role of hands in reading. When I first looked at the tapes I was rather more interested in finding material that would usefully coalesce with the work of a colleague, Jill McClay, who had done a study of readers of a different Macaulay picture book; we wanted to do a joint presentation (see Mackey and McClay 2000). Looking closely at the video of Lisa and Claire reading *Shortcut*, I got my first glimmering of a highly manual activity taking place. Witness, for example, the following sequence.

The video shows the girls' second reading of the book. Lisa is sitting to the left of the book and Claire to the right, but their hands often cross over as they explore and point. The following transcript provides only a fraction of the information in the video but does give some sense of the very tactile approach to meaning-making adopted by both girls:

LISA: [reading] Chapter Seven. Bob sleeps all day. He loves the peace and quiet of the river. In his favourite dream, he is the admiral of the fleet.

Lisa points to the words 'admiral of the fleet', mispronouncing 'admiral'.

And here come all the bags, and knocking him –

Lisa points and traces the flight of the bag on the right-hand page.

CLAIRE: And yeah, and when they, when they stand, right at the beginning, here you can see that –

Claire points to the left-hand page, her hand crossing over Lisa's. She points to the symbol engraved on the bridge.

– then right here, it's the same one –

Both girls turn back, flipping pages between their four hands. Claire points to the same bridge on an earlier page, indicating the emblem on the side.

– and the professor flies over top –

Claire traces a line with her finger from left to right, above the top of the pages.

– and drops all the things that rock the boat –

Claire moves her hand down the page to follow the path of the ballast weights dropping, and then traces Bob's trajectory under the bridge to his present position in the picture.

– and he goes down and finds all this gold because of Albert dropping it.
LISA: Yeah.

Claire turns the page. Both girls hold the new page open.

CLAIRE: [reading] Suddenly he – you see that all comes –

Claire traces the movement of the ballast dropping into the boat on the left-hand page.

[reading] Suddenly he is thrown from his boat. Fortunately he sinks to the bottom which is how he makes his dream come true.

Lisa reaches to turn the page, and holds the new page open.

Because, um, every single time that Albert and June go past the bridge they make a wish and they drop gold down there.

In this session, we can see the development of what is literally a 'felt meaning'. Lisa reaches for the text to place her finger under the word 'admiral' as she struggles to pronounce it. Claire sorts out plot movements by tracing trajectories of the hot air balloon, the ballast and the boat. Both girls turn pages and point to the engraved emblem on the side of the bridge in two different chapters. The video provides a strong image of them both creating a sense of control out of their ability to *handle* the book as they sort out a confusing text.

'The most thinking book'

Eight pairs of students read *Shortcut* aloud together, alternating page and page about, and commenting as they went along. Most of the pairs read the story a second time, or at least returned to particular sections for clarification. Jack and Gregory were so quick to make connections in a single reading that they alone did not return to the book for a second run-through.

A number of the students were surprised by this book, which looks so simple but which actually challenges their powers of observation and intuition. The most telling comment came from Tom, a sixth-grader, who read 'The end' and immediately observed, 'I enjoyed the book. Probably the most educational kids' book I've ever read.' 'Is that right?' I said, and he expanded, 'Well, as the most thinking book.'

The videotapes of the readings of *Shortcut* testify with considerable vividness that all of the students made use of their hands to help them with the 'thinking' challenge that Tom described. Their handling of the book is similar in a general kind of way, but they manifest different strategies at the micro-level. One sixth-grade reader, Jordan, consistently ran his finger under the words as he read them aloud. Kyle 'performed' the movement of the railway switch as June inadvertently altered it. Leonard 'drew' the pig's profile with a hand in the air. Almost everybody flipped pages and pointed, often with considerable enthusiasm.

This particular reading task might have been (though it wasn't) designed to highlight how readers may make use of their hands in reading. If there is a continuum running from routine to constitutive or generative hand use in reading, the task of reading *Shortcut* clearly belongs at the latter end of the scale. The readers were both solving and performing the book as they read it, and they used their hands to help with both purposes. Furthermore, they were not only reading for themselves, but also coordinating the reading of a second person. They co-orchestrated a complex tune as they sorted out the information in the words and in the pictures, both on the page currently presented to them and as they recalled it from previous pages.

From babyhood, we use our hands to direct and coordinate the attention of another. We also use hands to *elicit* performance, as anyone who has ever worked with a musical conductor will testify. It is not surprising that these students made maximum use of the assistance of their hands in this complex yet quite ordinary task of reading a picture book together. Two questions of interest are immediately striking. To what degree does this particular reading activity represent a special case when considered in the broad range of normal daily reading? And what is changed when readers encounter a text of equivalent text/graphic balance on the screen instead of in print?

Hands at work

Only once did a pair of readers make it from beginning to end of the book while using their hands simply and exclusively to hold the book open and turn pages: Kelly and Catherine in their first reading. They paid fairly perfunctory attention to the words and more or less ignored the pictures, and at the end of that first reading they were quite confused. In their second reading, prompted to look at both text and pictures for clues about how the story worked out, they too pointed and gestured, though rather less than some other readers. Their comprehension of the story improved considerably with this second reading.

Kyle and Leonard, in contrast, used their hands fluently. Leonard was quicker to grasp how much content lies in the illustrations of this particular book. Here is their initial reading of the first pages:

KYLE: Okay. [reading] Chapter One. Albert and June are up early.

Kyle gestures vaguely at picture.

It is market day.
LEONARD: You have to look at the pictures.
KYLE: Oh, okay. Um –
LEONARD: It's a horse.
KYLE: Yeah, it's a horse/cow typish kind of –
LEONARD: Okay, okay. [reading] Once a week, they take their ripest melons into town. As they cross the bridge, Albert and June always make a wish.
KYLE: Oh, I take it June is the horse.

Kyle points to June.

LEONARD: Yeah.
KYLE: Okay, and they're throwing the coin down into the –

Kyle points to the coin.

LEONARD: And there's a shield of some sort on the bridge.

Leonard points to the shield.

KYLE: Mmm. [reading] To save time they will take the shortcut. Albert removes his coat and helps June up the hill. And this is the shortcut.

Kyle gestures in the directions of the arrows on the sign.

LEONARD: [laughs]
KYLE: Oh, look at all the little eyeballs.

Kyle and Leonard manipulate the right-hand page to the light so that the eyeballs of the animals (in the bottom corner) are most prominent.

LEONARD: They've got really detailed pictures. [reading] When they reach the top, Albert –

Leonard points to Albert.

– gets his coat and they're off again. In a little while they stop to eat at the Railway Café.

KYLE: I take it the Railway Café is the grass next to the railway. [laughter]

MARGARET: I think it is for June, isn't it?

LEONARD: Tying the horse to it, yeah.

Leonard points to the switch.

KYLE: Yeah. Isn't that kind of, ah –

LEONARD: Railway Café [chuckles].

KYLE: [reading] June is very hungry. She stretches to reach some tasty clover. After lunch they continue toward town (it should be 'towards' town), crooning their favourite songs, and there's the birds –

Kyle points to the birds.

– and they're kind of annoyed I see.

LEONARD: Annoyed by the songs? Yeah, look at all the notes floating upwards.

Leonard waves upwards over the musical notes.

KYLE: Oh, yeah.

LEONARD: Hold on. Wait a second. Did he just turn some sort of train lever by accident? Oh, he may have.

KYLE: Oh, maybe he pulled the rail towards the –

Kyle gestures in a 'switching' motion.

LEONARD: [reading] A rope blocks their path, but not for long. Oh, what's going on here, this – they're just untying a rope.

Leonard points to the rope.

It looks as though they're setting themselves up for something here.

KYLE: [reading] Their melons are very popular and their wagon is soon empty. Once again Albert and June get their wish. They are home before dark. So people are buying all their melons.

LEONARD: And there's all their money they earned.

Leonard points to the money.

There's the melon.

Leonard points to a picture of a melon on Albert's wall.

KYLE: And they're watching TV.

LEONARD: Playing horseshoes.

KYLE: Are you sure that, um, June just didn't take them off?

Kyle points to June's feet and horseshoes.

LEONARD: Well, maybe she did except they're nailed to her foot.
MARGARET: Look, Albert has taken his shoes off, so maybe June did too.
KYLE: Oh, yeah.

Kyle and Leonard use their hands to interpret and understand the book, just as Lisa and Claire did, but at this stage they do rather less in the way of demonstrating and performing with their hands. Later on, however, as they return to the book to point out parts they had particularly enjoyed (the sub-plot of the pig especially appealed to them), their gestures become more performative.

Bodies at work

The other noteworthy element in the video of Leonard and Kyle's reading of *Shortcut* is the constant intrusion of the back of their heads into the frame. Normally, the participants in this study (Kyle and Leonard included) were careful to keep out of range of the camera as they knew that our intention was to record the text. However, in this case, each boy often moved into camera range to scrutinize the details of a picture.

The old phrase 'Sit up and pay attention' crossed my mind as I watched this video. With 20/20 hindsight, I regret that I did not use a second video camera to record the demeanour of the readers in their encounters with the different materials. The record of the text as read is highly valuable and informative, but it would be useful and very interesting also to have a record of the extra information conveyed by the posture and expression of the readers. In this stretch of video of Kyle and Leonard, however, some of their body language got recorded inadvertently from behind, and it is highly persuasive to marry their alert heads and shoulders with their evident engagement with and enjoyment of the book. The audiotape of this session is riddled with laughter and exclamations of pleasure, a response also expressed by their bodies as they hover attentively over each page.

Does posture affect the quality of attention, or vice versa, or both? Do we associate particular body arrangements with certain kinds of reading pleasures? The constant lament about screen reading – 'you can't curl up with a computer' – would suggest that many readers make some connection, however vague. A young reader described Philip Pullman's complex novel *The Amber Spyglass* to me as 'the kind of book you have to sit up to read', a description that ought to be meaningless but is not.

Certain physical qualities of a book lead to certain requirements of a reader. A thick and heavy book cannot be balanced in one hand as the reader lies in bed. Reading a book in which the spine requires some extra support rules out some reading positions. Does this limitation affect the quality of the reading experience? Posture affects breathing; it affects balance. What is its relation to alertness and attention? Can an experienced reader render almost any posture transparent, or is the physical relationship with the book, the specific distance and orientation between eyes and page, an irreducible and ineradicable element of the reading experience? What is the role of habit in the development of possible transparency? And is my young friend correct that a book as challenging as *The Amber Spyglass* cannot be read properly while slouching in bed? Such questions seldom arise since we usually forget that reading is a physical as well as an intellectual activity. But as our reading tools change, the implications of how we engage physically with a text become more important.

The question of hands' and bodies' role in reading would be of general, perhaps largely abstract, interest in this study except for one factor that suddenly renders the question more immediately important. With many of the new media, we are changing the role of the hands. A mouse is run by a single hand; there is little, even in the way of counterbalancing, for the left hand to do. The electronic book, as I have already suggested, appears to be designed for one-handed use. The screen is generally not as receptive to the laying on of pointing fingers as is a page of paper, and it requires a certain posture of attention. If the role of our physical interaction with text is changing, we need to be alert to the implications. (The role of our hands in other text processing activities may also be worth considering. Control of the television remote is clearly an issue of domestic power politics, but does the remote also have a role in focusing attention? What is the significance of the contrast between the one-handed mouse of the computer game and the two-handed controls of the Nintendo game? Does that difference bear affective and/or cognitive consequences?)

Other questions arise from the physicality of reading. The students reading *Shortcut* took it in turn, page and page about, to read aloud. Jordan (Grade 6) seemed to find this task relatively difficult; he used his finger to underline the words and hesitated often. Some readers read flatly and hastily, but many invested their reading with more and more expression as they became involved in the story. To speak of the verbal music of *Shortcut* is a little pretentious, but the phrase raises more body-related questions: the physical production of our voices, through breath and muscle, and the impact on our attention of rhythm and cadence.

The affect of hands together

Touch matters to people, and hands are primary agents of touching. We shake hands; we hold hands; we clap to show approval, or pat somebody on the back. The affective power of touch can work between hands and words too, at least in extreme cases: people at tombstones or at war memorials often brush the name of their loved ones with their hands. Images and photos are often stroked in much the same way. Hands are used in many ways to establish an emotional connection.

It is not too much of an extrapolation to raise the question of the affective pleasure involved when two people use their hands together to coordinate an activity. The kinds of connection established are not quite so direct as in a hearty handshake, but there is still active linking going on. There is no example among the eight tapes of pairs of readers with *Shortcut* where the enjoyment is not achieved jointly and, in each case, the hands of each student work hard to bring the other reader along. This element of connecting with hands may be one of the specific pleasures of reading graphic texts together and one reason why picture books are so often cited as creating bonds between the adult and child who read them together. (Whether similar questions arise in, say, coordinated Nintendo games is worth considering as well.)

Lulu's Enchanted Book

With the Grade 6 cohort, there was a chance to make some direct comparisons between the reading of the picture book and the students' responses to a CD-ROM interactive picture story. *Lulu's Enchanted Book* makes some interesting use of the potential of its digital format, although overall I would not describe it as a completely successful story.

Lulu's Enchanted Book tells the story of a bored princess who is visited by a space alien. I found the story not particularly well written and the images not particularly well drawn or animated; however, the CD-ROM does make some interesting and creative use of the conventions of its genre.

The 'standard' kind of story CD-ROM has developed fairly widespread conventions in its short life. It generally works with changeable images that animate or alter when the mouse is clicked on a particular hot spot in the picture. *Lulu's Enchanted Book* has many such examples but the pictures can also be changed by clicking on the *words* and the changes in the images are actively linked to what the words are saying. Sometimes the images perform the movements described by the words that have just been clicked by the reader.

The Grade 6 students moved directly from reading *Shortcut* to looking at *Lulu's Enchanted Book* and some changes in the quality of experience are vivid on the video. The most dramatic difference is the immediate alteration in pacing. The CD-ROM activates a narrator reading aloud, so the students immediately lost control of the pace of the telling of the story. It is not an exaggeration to describe much of their reading and exploration of *Shortcut* as joyous; that quality of feeling evaporates at once as they turn to the CD-ROM and their role in working out the story becomes rather more passive. I do not think I am reading my own prejudices into the case when I say that I can clearly discern a quality of retreat in the level of engagement as the video record moves from the book reading to the CD-ROM story. It is impossible to cite the transcripts in support of this observation; I am interpreting intangibles such as tone of voice. But to ignore the change of atmosphere as the students moved from *Shortcut* to *Lulu* would be reductive.

The audio narration is reasonably well done and the impact of the voice on the experience as a whole is not negligible. Listening to a story read aloud is quite a different physical experience from reading it yourself. In both cases, the words are interpreted as meaningful in the brain and the sound reverberates in your body; but the impact is quite different if the sound is being produced in your own throat. Furthermore, if you are listening in the clear understanding that you can interrupt with questions, your posture and consequent attention are probably different as well.

The politics of mouse control are visible in some exchanges with this story. Each student had access to a mouse but one had the regular external mouse and the other had the internal mouse of the laptop keyboard, a control with which they were much less familiar. The students traded places from time to time, so each had access to both types of mouse at different points in the readings. The most extreme conflicts came between Lisa and Claire, who invariably cooperated much better when the mouse was not an issue. Lisa was very anxious to dominate the mouse decisions; Claire occasionally got annoyed but, perhaps in deference to our presence, she did not often tackle Lisa directly. Lisa was one of a very small minority of students who often took charge even when she was using the internal mouse.

The picture-book transcript above shows Lisa and Claire cooperating harmoniously as they develop the meaning of the story in *Shortcut*. As the girls read the beginning of *Lulu's Enchanted Book*, Lisa had the internal mouse (which all the students used less skilfully and often), and the dialogue was constantly interrupted by Lisa's attempts to control the cursor. The following comments are extracted from a single page of twenty short lines of conversation; Claire made no reply to any of these instructions: 'Claire, use the mouse. I don't see the mouse; oh, I got it, Claire. You want me to click on it? There, I did. Do you have to double-click? Claire, let me. Claire, I had it!' The atmosphere of the session was radically different from that of the *Shortcut* episode that immediately preceded it.

In the case of *Lulu's Enchanted Book*, all the students interrupted the reading with mouse play, but for the most part these actions occurred only after the full segment of text on screen had been read. Yet because these activities slowed down the 'page' turns, and because in many cases they were only trivially related to the story, they radically affected the potential for linear plot development. Rebecca James, in describing how four children of different ages (4, 6, 9 and 14) responded to *Lulu's Enchanted Book*, uses playful terms to describe these interactive interruptions:

> Consciously or otherwise, the children *allowed* themselves to be diverted from the basic plot to explore certain aspects in more depth . . . The reader is offered numerous opportunities to equivocate, to play with the pictures . . . Unusually for a CD-ROM narrative, *every* page of *Lulu* gives the reader the option of exploring the written text as well as experimenting with areas of the illustrations as hot-spots; yet the reader can choose whether to 'stand and stare' at the fascinating details or move through the story from start to finish, in the manner of readers of complex, postmodern picture books . . . or lift-the-flap and pop-up books.
>
> (James 1999: 54–5)

James and I disagree about the execution of this interactive story. She talks about 'its highly artistic illustrations and background music' (1999: 52), whereas I found the illustrations unremarkable, the animation primitive and the music downright annoying. Nevertheless, she draws attention to many positive qualities of the relationship between her young readers and this text:

> They became increasingly willing to click on areas at random, sometimes laughing with astonishment. Their enjoyment seemed to prevent them from being fazed by the diversity and amount of material available or the fact that combinations of different media (such as video, text, graphics, and sound) were on screen simultaneously. They were apparently able to absorb the visual and aural surprises and novelties, even if this did mean they noticed the details of the written text less. They gained obvious pleasure from the degree of freedom provided by the highly interactive nature of this text.
>
> (James 1999: 55–6)

James compares the experience of her readers with that of reading a postmodern picture book. My readers, of course, had just finished a version of that very activity before they looked at *Lulu's Enchanted Book*, and their responses to questions of comparison are extremely interesting.

Here are Angela and Megan on the subject of the differences between *Shortcut* and *Myst*, a conversation that occurred just before they looked at *Lulu's Enchanted Book*. This extract of transcript is long because the girls were teasing out some very complex questions:

MARGARET: This is a detailed kind of book. Which do you prefer, looking in detail at it? Still pictures like this or pictures that you can move around with or interact with like in *Myst*?

MEGAN: Probably ones you can interact with.

ANGELA: Yeah.

MEGAN: 'Cause the things kind of like, a puzzle you can sort of figure it out.

ANGELA: Except when you get lost. It's harder to get lost in a book . . . It doesn't really come down to much in the end other than when you're on the computer you can use your mouse and go where you want to, like, you're walking in there, and here you just have to visualize yourself and flip the pages. It is a bit different.

MEGAN: Yeah, and, like, in games where you like interact, the things are like, they could be hidden more. Like, you need to unlock the door sometimes to find them.

ANGELA: And the key to unlock the door, put notes together to find the key to unlock the door to get whatever you need.

MEGAN: In a book though, you can't really, like, look around the tree to see what's there . . .

MARGARET: Which do you like better?

MEGAN: A game probably.

ANGELA: Yeah, I guess so. I haven't read a book like this though.

MEGAN: But I wouldn't always want to be, like, playing games.

ANGELA: This book is good.

MARGARET: Would you recommend this book to somebody else to have a look at?

MEGAN: Yeah, to puzzle them.

The girls' ambivalence, in part at least, arises from the either/or nature of my question. In effect I was asking them to make a distinction that they might not have made on their own, 'both/and' being their preferred mode of judgement (notice how Angela is reluctant to rule out a book like *Shortcut* and how Megan wouldn't want just to play games). In the course of discussing this distinction, however, they raise a number of questions about how each medium can develop the enigma of the plot, postponing the conclusion and engaging the reader's attention with both distractions and solutions. The appeal of how the interactive qualities of the computer screen can complicate the puzzle are clear in Megan's line: 'In a book though, you can't really, like, look around the tree to see what's there.'

However, both girls agreed that, compared to *Lulu's Enchanted Book*, *Shortcut* was more challenging and less dull *as a story*. On the other hand, if *Shortcut* were to be turned into a CD-ROM story, it would need to be expanded, possibly with the addition of some games.

Their general observations on *Lulu's Enchanted Book* are quite clear and completely in line with many other assessments of value and quality made by this group in different ways and different circumstances. Format is not enough on its own; it must serve content. *Shortcut* is the more interesting text of the two, but if it were to be turned into a CD-ROM it would not work as it stands and would need to be adapted so that format and content again worked well together. But as a book, even though it is shorter than *Lulu*, it is 'more interesting' and 'more busy'.

It could very well be that, if we had had more time so these girls and the other Grade 6 students could have read more of *Lulu's Enchanted Book*, they would have discovered more narrative complexity to engage them. As with most of these engagements, there is always a sense of not having been fair to the text, of having moved the readers on far too quickly. The readers reached judgement on partial exposure to a text and, in any given case, they might have been more positive in their specific assessments if they had been allowed more time. What I find fascinating, despite these caveats, is that, given the texts available to them, these students consistently applied a kind of gold standard. The story has to work as a story and it has to work in the format chosen for it. Partial measures are not good enough. Technology by itself is not sufficient and indeed, given the responses to *Shortcut* and to the short story 'Tunnel', not even necessary.

When Jill McClay and I made our initial assessments of the videos of the young people reading *Shortcut*, we were impressed by the way the readers made use of the stability of print, pinning down meanings with their hands. We quoted Derrick de Kerckhove's thought-provoking description of print. He called the book:

a resting place for words. It sounds trite, but in fact the printed page is the only place where words do have a rest. Everywhere else, they are moving: when you speak, when you see them on a screen, when you see them on the Net, words are moving. But a book is a restful place. The printed word is, and always was, still.

(de Kerckhove 1997: 107)

I still find that quote a powerful, if partial, explanation of some virtues of print. Yet at the same time, I cannot help being engaged by Megan's observation, 'In a book though, you can't really, like, look around the tree to see what's there.'

Deictics and graphics

Texts based on graphics as well as words abound in our culture, and the impact of the graphics works through our culture in sometimes unexpected ways. The ability, actual or virtual, to point to a graphic alters the way we use language.

The impact of this alteration is particularly striking in our use of a small class of words called deictic. Deictic words, or shifters, are words that can be fully defined only in context. There are not very many of them, and they take part of their meaning from the specific situation in which they are uttered. 'Here' and 'there' are deictic, as are 'today', 'tomorrow' and 'yesterday'. 'I' and 'you' are deictics whose specific identification alters throughout a dialogue between two people. Tense markers can also function deictically; Jerry Palmer gives the following example:

The difference between 'I saw him' and 'I have seen him', for example, lies not in the time in question (since both could easily refer to the same moment in time), but to a difference in the relationship between then and the moment of speaking.

(Palmer 1991: 70)

Take a simple sentence: 'I'll come here tomorrow.' This sentence is grammatically coherent as it stands, but its contents must be defined in context. Who is 'I'? Where is 'here'? When is 'tomorrow'? If the message is a spoken one, all of those meanings will be clear to the receiver from the context of the surroundings. If the message is contained in a text, then the text must contain supplementary information if the contents of the sentence are to make more than notional sense.

It is easy enough for a text to add words to fill out the meanings of the deictic signifiers. However, words are not the only available backup; more and more contemporary texts use graphics and they too can supply the context for deictics. Indeed, there are those who argue that our use of graphics is actually making some changes in the development of the language.

In a fascinating article on the language of live action sportscasts, Russell Smith draws our attention to a reduction in the use of the conditional mood and an increase in the use of a (perhaps deceptively) simple present tense as commentators call games. The construction 'If he comes down the sideline, he catches up with his opponent' is now probably more common than the technically more correct 'If he had come down the sideline, he would have caught up with his opponent.'

> In describing a failed field goal attempt, the hip announcer will now say, 'He angles that just to the right and he has three points on the board.' Or even for a future tense, to predict what a referee will rule after a replay analysis: 'I don't think he changes the call' (meaning *will change*).
>
> (Smith 2000: R4)

Smith has a persuasive explanation for this language shift:

> The all-purpose present probably came about as a result of the instant replay. In describing a play that is in the past, the televisor merely recalls the image, via replay, to the present, and starts again, drawing little arrows on the screen: 'You see here, if he dekes left, he finds a seam.' It makes sense while the replay is actually rolling, but the announcers have grown so used to the ease and simplicity of the present tense that they are using it even when not explicating a replay.
>
> (Smith 2000: R4)

As Palmer suggests, tense is a deictic marker, denoting the relationship between the speaker and the action described. In Smith's example of the sports commentary, that marker has been replaced by the ability to point to the graphic and express the relationships visually rather than verbally. His is perhaps an extreme example, but there are many more mundane examples. If you can point to an illustration as you say 'He went *there*', you are released from the responsibility for accounting verbally for the specific content of 'there'. It is perhaps not surprising if the backwash of this effect then reduces the need to use the tense marker as well, and the phrase becomes 'He goes there'.

'The present tense is the tense in which pictures happen', says Philip Pullman (2000: n.p.). The impact on our language as our communications grow more visual will be profound in many different ways.

The Way Things Work

A CD-ROM such as *The Way Things Work*, with its animated sequences exploring the workings of different machines, might be seen as a kind of action replay machine. There is no limit to the number of times a sequence can be replayed (though it is always the same; it does not have the live-action addition of explanatory arrows and commentary on any re-run as a sports clip may do).

It is perhaps not surprising, therefore, that at one level the written transcripts of the reading of the CD-ROM of *The Way Things Work* are extremely uninformative.

Without the visual content of the video, the transcripts are flat and lifeless, full of unexplained deictics. Witness, for example, Jeff and Anita (Grade 9) investigating how they can go about exploring the CD:

JEFF: Principles of Science. Okay, we've got a lot of choices here. I guess we'll go – electricity.
ANITA: Sure.
JEFF: Electricity is the most –
ANITA: You touch one of those.
JEFF: Let's see –
ANITA: You touch the word.
JEFF: It gives you a little –
ANITA: And if you touch the highlighted word there? It just gives you a little –
JEFF: Glossary of definition.
ANITA: Yeah.
JEFF: Let's try 'What is electricity'.
ANITA: Okay, you could try one of those.
JEFF: It's mainly just definition.

With the 'action replay' of the video record of this dull-sounding conversation, it is easy to see that Anita and Jeff are actually working quite hard, checking possibilities, exploring the apparatus of the encyclopedia, drawing connections to their work in science classes, and analysing the utility and effectiveness of the animated graphics of the disc. Much of this work is not verbalized, nor, in context, is there any reason why it should be.

It may very well be that the understanding conveyed through Macaulay's lively animations and clever organization in this CD-ROM is greater and more precise than what could be clearly articulated by Jeff or Anita if they tried to express their new comprehension verbally. Or it may be that they would more truly understand what they put into their own words. What is clear is that our ability to reproduce by pointing is increasing very rapidly. In more and more cases it is possible for us to say 'I mean *this*', and to create a reproduction by pointing (and, in many cases, clicking). The still graphic has been accessible to this treatment for centuries; recently we have acquired equivalent power over the moving graphic in routine domestic settings.

A large percentage of the information conveyed in *The Way Things Work* is more precisely represented with a moving graphic than with a very large number of words. Jeff and Anita are actually responding appropriately with their economical use of speech in the passage above. Nevertheless, this little piece of transcript, in its modest way, provides a hint of a substantial change in how we address many forms of text.

The Way Things Work offers a variety of approaches. Explanations are conveyed in print, still graphic and animation. In a major change of register, fictional 'Mammoth Movies' illustrate challenges that machines have been invented to meet.

Macaulay himself appears in both video and audio, and moves around the screen changing size and scale as he goes. The CD-ROM offers a complex and very lively route to understanding, but it is clear throughout that understanding is the main aim of all the textual approaches.

Handling the CD-ROM

In the picture-book tapes, it is possible to see the readers' hands actively engaged in what we might call 'deictic work', pointing and directing. The manual engagement with the CD-ROM worked differently. The students sat side by side in front of the computer. As with all their computer engagements, one person had access to an ordinary mouse; the other one could use the little mouse button on the ThinkPad keyboard. Students swapped places from time to time, so each had access to the more familiar mouse at different stages of the interview. A few students used the little red keyboard button, but for the most part it was clear that they were much more comfortable with the regular mouse. It was commonplace for the person with the keyboard button to ask the other student to make a move with the ordinary mouse.

The readers' use of their hands altered quite radically when they turned from the picture book to the CD-ROM. In general, the person in control of the regular mouse ceased to intervene in the reading with any hand gestures at all; all hand activity was transferred to the mouse. The person using the less familiar mouse (which in some cases effectively translated to no mouse access) did occasionally still point or gesture towards the screen, but it was much more unusual than with the picture book.

The hand motions in the picture-book video are purposeful, easy to describe and to 'read'. With the virtual pointing and tracing done with the mouse, it is much harder to establish a clear-cut interpretation of the reader's intent. Often the reader would move the cursor around the screen, sometimes underlining or specifically pointing to an individual item but often simply skimming over the screen in a circular or random pattern. The role of this skimming in the direction and maintenance of attention is very difficult to ascertain.

I did a detailed assessment of Jeff and Anita's readings of *Shortcut* and *The Way Things Work*. Tallying the hand motions in the picture book was easy. During their complete reading of the book and their return to particular chapters to work out plot details, they made fifty-seven hand movements, excluding page turning. These motions were more or less equally divided between them, and it did not matter which one of them was actually reading the page in question.

When they shifted to the CD-ROM, some points became clear very quickly and some were difficult to be sure about. Jeff was in charge of the external mouse at this point, and he made no hand gestures of any kind. Anita made three over the course of the session, all relatively vague pointing gestures; and when Jeff failed to grasp her point she clarified it with words rather than with further gestures. 'Click the word', she said and, when that didn't lead to action, 'Click the highlighted word'. She made no use whatever of her internal mouse.

Jeff clearly used the cursor in lieu of his hand, and I tallied forty-four moves that appeared to be of some significance. I do not feel I can support this number with any real conviction; it was not at all clear cut when he was using the cursor to direct his sightlines or to check for hot spots (i.e. pointing) and when he was simply swivelling around the screen in a relatively idle way. However, the imbalance in real and/or virtual gesturing between the two participants is quite conclusive (forty-four to three is fairly overwhelming even factoring in some margin for error in my interpretation), even though the transcript shows the verbal exchanges to be more or less equal. If the role of pointing in the reading of *Shortcut* helped in the creation of a shared construction of meaning, it might be useful to explore more fully the effects of real and virtual pointing in joint computer use.

Conclusions

All the students used their hands to direct attention – their own and their partner's – when they read the picture book. It did not appear to be an issue of control, since either reader could and did turn back or point without interfering in any way with the other's access. Use of the mouse to read the CD-ROMs was more ambiguous and, in the case of two readers at least, consistently fraught with questions of power and control. Readers pointed at the screen but did not manipulate or touch it directly, and the movements of the cursor were much vaguer and more difficult to interpret than their actions when they were handling a page.

Whether four hands or two are available, the mouse works most successfully under the control of a single hand. A lone screen reader is not hampered by political quarrels over mouse power; does this reader still miss something by using one hand instead of two to make the connections with the words? Is it simply a question of having our brains get used to the dominance of one hand in this different kind of text processing, or is something of major significance being lost? Alternatively, will technology bow to our determination to keep both hands 'on' our reading material? Resistance to the electronic book in tablet form and enthusiasm for electronic paper in its stead (Mann 2000: 118) suggest that resolute readers may still succeed in forcing the market to sustain their preferred manual form of reading print.

In any case, the role of hands in reading print and in directing attention between print and graphics is clearly significant for these readers of *Shortcut*. The ability to point at action replays on the CD-ROM of *The Way Things Work* also affects how these students use language to direct a joint reading. The politics of who can point may become an issue when the mouse serves as intermediary between hands and page. The changing role of hands in text processing is clearly a topic worth more consideration.

Katherine Hayles suggests that we need to attend to how hands work effectively in conjunction with computer screens and keyboards, and it is possible to use her own words to shed light on how we actually deal with books as well. She says:

it is a *historical construction* to believe that computer media are disembodying technologies, not an obvious truth. In fact, this belief requires systematic erasure of many significant aspects of our interactions with computers. It is almost never used as a working hypothesis by the people who are engaged in developing the technologies, for they cannot afford to ignore the materiality of the interfaces they create or the effects of these interfaces on their customers.

(Hayles 2000: 93–4)

The materiality of interfaces is a major issue of this project, but it is too simplistic to consider that only new media present such questions of materiality. The materiality of the book is a major component in our experience of reading. If we render the tactile elements of book reading transparent, we run exactly the risk Hayles describes in terms of computers: 'If we accept that the materiality of the world is immaterial to our concerns, we are likely to miss the very complexities that theory at its best tries to excavate and understand' (2000: 94).

The question that arose in the processing of the DVD and the electronic book – the oscillation between 'looking through' and 'looking at' the book – was also a factor in the picture-book readings, though I have not directly addressed it in this chapter. The postmodernism of *Shortcut* does what the newness of the medium does in other examples: it foregrounds the textual construction. Readers who were proceeding effortlessly through the story of Albert and his horse June were thrown back to the surface of the story when they hit Chapter 2 and discovered what appeared to be an entirely new story. Their sudden oscillation between depth and surface is probably more persuasively communicated on the video where tone of voice adds to the evidence suggesting shifts of attention between *what* is happening and *how* the story is constructed. It is possible to argue that *Shortcut* represents an old medium, but it is also arguable that such a story would have been far less likely to be written and published in the era before film and video were readily accessible to very young readers. *Shortcut* is, in many ways, a cinematic book remediated back into print.

In a different way, the students also oscillated as they looked at *The Way Things Work*, attending differently as they discovered items like the fictional Mammoth Movies compared to how they responded to items they had recently covered in their science classes. Often they were concerned with the surface of the text, looking at what would animate on a click and so forth, but from time to time they looked 'through' the text to see how a particular machine actually worked.

The videos (and, to a lesser extent, the transcripts) of the readings of *Shortcut* also reveal the students changing their minds about questions of salience and access. In terms of interest, it is possible to observe that, when they perceived unexpected difficulties of access, their view of the salience of the story also changed. The tone of voice in a number of readings indicates that many of the students began the story by paying fairly perfunctory attention to what they saw as an extremely simple and not very interesting story. Discovering that access was more of a challenge than they had anticipated also changed their minds about the interest level of the story.

In short, although I am separating elements of processing activities, such as salience, fluency, oscillation, etc., into distinct chapters, it is not very difficult to reassemble these diverse elements in any one kind of reading activity. In actuality, of course, all these different factors worked together and can be seen in most of the interpretive activities of this project, regardless of which medium is involved.

Afterword: new literacy ecologies of the twenty-first century

I began this chapter by thinking about hands and I will conclude it by thinking about ears. A picture book is a polysemic work, with meaning conveyed through words, pictures, and design elements such as font, colour, white space and so on. In the years since this project was completed, I have begun to pay more attention to the kind of picture-book 'package' that includes an accompanying CD.

Picture books marketed with accompanying records, audiocassettes and other forms of old technology are, almost by definition, not new. In many cases, what these packages offer is an audio channel that more or less replicates the verbal channel of the printed text – a read-aloud of the story, with or without an audible prompt to turn the page.

I am more interested in those picture books that offer an audio component as a further channel for meaning. At present such books are relatively rare but they are certainly interesting, and as electronic forms of story-telling become more common we may find them multiplying.

Two fascinating examples of such books offer a complete contrast to each other. *Yellow Umbrella* by Jae Soo Liu, with music by Dong Il Sheen (2002), originally published in Korea, has no words at all, except in an appendix. The CD that comes packaged into its cover offers an audio track to accompany the pages of pictures of umbrellas in the rain. The piano music fades to indicate a page turn and it is quite obvious which notes accompany which page. In this case, the polysemy is between pictures and music, with words almost entirely eliminated, yet the book tells a slight but meaningful story.

The serene world of *Yellow Umbrella* could hardly be more different from the world represented in Sandra Boynton's *Philadelphia Chickens* (2002). In this book–CD package, the printed pages offer words, pictures and musical notation for a set of songs created for an imaginary musical revue. The CD provides the songs (no longer imaginary, though the stage revue remains virtual) as performed by real stars such as Meryl Streep and Kevin Kline. These songs are as rowdy and silly as the crowded and lively pictures.

In both cases of book–CD combination, the audio component makes an active contribution to the creation of meaning, rather than recreating an element already present in the print text. At present such multifaceted materials are rare, but we are not short of potential formats that could make such polysemic formats more commonplace. Any form of electronic story-telling would have the potential to incorporate music or other forms of 'soundtrack' to what we currently think of as the picture-book category. A CD-ROM, a website, any form of electronic reader – including a reader built into a PDA or a cellphone – all have the potential to make the incorporation of a soundtrack something much less exceptional than it is today.

If we move into a new kind of polysemy where the audio component has to be factored into the final production of meaning, will we see changes of posture, of physical attitude in our 'reading' of such materials? Music can alter breathing, even pulse; to what extent will the physicality of our reading habits change if we add associated soundtracks to our reading? We use our hands to organize what we are bringing to the attention of our eyes, but I am not sure that hearing works on the same basis. We do not normally use our hands to align our ears with what we are listening to, though it is not true that there is no relationship at all; think of the hard-of-hearing listener who cups a hand behind an ear or the resistant listener who claps both hands firmly over both ears. In general, however, if we want to hear better we turn our heads to maximize reception.

Whatever the changes that may possibly be contributed by new uses of audio as part of our reading experience, the physicality of the experience will remain a significant factor and one that should not be overlooked when we come to explore the whole of this complex activity.

Chapter 9

Narrative strategies

Playing *Starship Titanic*

Recording the game

In the autumn of 1998, five pairs of Grade 9 students played the computer game *Starship Titanic*. In order to preserve a complete record of the game as played, we videotaped the screen from behind their shoulders and audiotaped all the conversation as the students explored the game. After forty-five minutes or so, we stopped and replayed the video so that students could comment retrospectively on the decisions and responses they had made while playing. This second, retrospective commentary was also audiotaped, and the two parallel transcripts were later aligned in two columns, using the audio cues from the videotaped game to make the connections.

Thus the record now includes the original videotape of the played game and a set of transcripts that shows both what the students said at the time and their later reflections on particular points in the game. Most of the students talked with gusto, both as they played and later, as they reflected on their strategies.

Starship Titanic

Starship Titanic opens with a domestic scene: a peaceful study with classical music playing. There is no indication of what to do until you range the cursor over the screen and it enlarges at certain directional points, suggesting to the initiated that it is possible to look around the study. In one corner of the room is a computer, with some CDs lying beside it. After you click to open the CD holder and insert the most gaudily coloured of these CDs by clicking and dragging, the game begins. A spaceship crashes through the roof of the study, and a robot descends to invite you aboard the Starship Titanic. To agree, you have to type in the word 'yes' and the robot then shows you how to acquire items for your 'personal electronic thing' or PET. As you ascend in the starship's elevator, Fintible, the robot, explains that the ship is careering out of control through space. All the bots on board have also been damaged and may be unreliable. You are invited to help save the ship. Having set up a kind of 'YOU ARE HERE' introduction to the story world, the robot takes you as far as the embarkation lobby of the ship and disappears again. You are on your own.

Up to this point, the story is fixed. From this moment onwards, every session of the game is different. At different stages, you are helped or hindered by a variety of 'bots' who are sullen, sarcastic, indifferent to your needs, or all three. You communicate with these bots by typing in your observations and questions, and, thanks to the game's language parser, their replies are germane, if not always helpful. Their responses appear in two forms: you hear them speak and all conversations appear in print on the bottom of the screen where you type in your part of the dialogue.

The geography of Starship Titanic is labyrinthine, and there is no real assistance for you as you grope your way around. One chamber contains a noisy and insolent parrot; another holds a bomb that you set into countdown mode if you innocently click on the button saying 'Press here to disarm bomb'. The elevators to take you to your stateroom are fiendishly difficult to locate. A mysterious succ-u-bus appears to be a message-distribution system for the starship, but seems more adept at losing your messages than at anything else. If you complain when something is lost, you are referred to 'mother', apparently a giant succ-u-bus in the bilge. In other words, the general impact of the early stages of the game is surreal and incoherent.

Analysing the transcripts

The game-playing sessions were fascinating and it was clear to me from the earliest stages that the transcripts would be full of potential insight. It took rather longer to find an analytical framework that would allow me to explore these transcripts in a manageable yet useful way. The key came from Peter Rabinowitz's study of conventional prose reading, *Before Reading: Narrative Conventions and the Politics of Interpretation* (1987). Rabinowitz posits a set of 'rules of reading' (1987: 42), which I have often used as part of my exploration of the processes of print reading. I have referred briefly to these 'rules' earlier in this book, but here I want to expand on their definition and usage. These 'rules' are drawn from the conventions we make use of as we seek to interpret a piece of prose narrative, and I wondered if they would apply usefully to a different form of highly conventionalized narrative.

Rabinowitz comments on the general applicability of his rules as follows:

> Specifically, the system sets out four types of rules. These rules govern operations or activities that, from the author's perspective, it is appropriate for the reader to perform when transforming texts – and indeed, that it is even necessary for the reader to perform if he or she is to end up with the expected meaning . . . The rules, in other words, serve as a kind of assumed contract between author and reader – they specify the grounds on which the intended reading should take place. They are, of course, socially constructed – and they can vary with genre, culture, history, and text. And readers do not always apply them as authors hope they will – even if they are trying to do so, which they sometimes are not . . . But even when readers do not apply the *specific* rules

the author had in mind, in our culture virtually *all* readers apply *some* rules in each of the four categories whenever they approach a text.

(Rabinowitz 1987: 43)

The four sets of rules of reading work as follows:

- *Rules of notice.* We cannot pay equal attention to every detail in a novel, so we learn to give priority to certain points, sorting out figure from ground. To do this, we must decide what needs to have particular attention paid to it. We use a variety of clues: a book or chapter title can point to what is significant, for example. We also tend to pay more attention to something mentioned in the first or last sentence of a paragraph, or a chapter. A very short sentence, a single-sentence paragraph, the use of typographical cues such as a line of asterisks – these and many more signals attract our attention.
- *Rules of signification.* These conventions help us to decide how to pay attention to what we have decided is notice-worthy. How realistic is a story? How believable is a character or a narrator? How and to what extent should we draw on our own daily psychology to understand the situations in a story? What is the symbolic importance of particular details?
- *Rules of configuration.* These rules govern how we assemble disparate elements into patterns. They lead us to develop certain expectations of the outcome, often based on our previous experiences of the genre or the author. Rules of configuration help us to recognize the shaping of a story. They also govern our general expectations of how a story works.
- *Rules of coherence.* These rules, in Rabinowitz's words, help us to 'read a text in such a way that it becomes the best text possible' (1987: 45). They enable us, for example, to find ways to deal with textual disjunctures (perhaps treating them as symbolic or ironic). They make room for us reassess our initial reactions to early details, folding them into a new understanding of the story as a whole.

Rabinowitz is careful to say that this set of rules is not a recipe for how to go about reading. We do not apply them sequentially or separately:

Reading is a more complex holistic process in which various rules interact with one another in ways that we may never understand, even though we seem to have little difficulty putting them into practice intuitively . . .

In addition, a given convention may well be capable of reformulation so that it fits into more than one of the four categories . . . The division of conventions into these four types, therefore, is intended neither as a descriptive model of the way the human mind actually reads nor as an absolute and exhaustive classification. It is, rather, a practical analytic device, of value to the extent that it is useful for answering particular questions.

(Rabinowitz 1987: 46)

I was looking for a 'practical analytic device' that would enable me to explore examples of ongoing text processing activities. Rabinowitz is talking about conventional prose narrative, but it seemed arguable to me that such a bizarre story as *Starship Titanic* would also have to make very careful use of conventions in order to allow readers to navigate its confusing territory at all.

I addressed the transcripts through Rabinowitz's codes, and found that they worked very helpfully to illuminate principles on which the students drew to tackle the game at all. With some allowance for the porousness between categories that he describes, the rules accounted for much of the dialogue between the players and also the retrospective commentary that followed. I added a fifth category – explicit remarks about strategy – and found that I had a tool that enabled me to move around the transcripts in suggestive and illuminating ways. The players did engage in noticing, signifying and configuring. They also moved outside the story world to discuss strategies with each other, a process that was clearly an essential element in their engagement with the game. The role of the rules of coherence was rather more academic in this particular project since the players came nowhere close to the end of the game, but it is easy to see how these rules could also apply. Taken as a set, these five markers enabled me to analyse patterns in the game playing in a very useful way.

One note about the observations that follow: the transcript of Kelly and Catherine caused some problems. The two girls were not very talkative and they often spoke in low voices that were difficult to distinguish over the sound effects from the computer. Although I have drawn some quotes from their observations, I did not do a full coding of their transcript and they are omitted from the few tallies and totals I refer to later on.

Playing *Starship Titanic*

There are many, many things to notice in *Starship Titanic*. At the very beginning, the music plays over a still picture of the study until you start to move the cursor and observe the first change as the arrow enlarges and points to the edge of the screen. The game does not begin until you select the multicoloured CD from the silver ones and insert it in the computer after opening the tray. Your tool kit, the personal electronic thing (PET), is a band at the bottom of the screen, and it is helpful if you notice that it has a set of five icons that give you some limited control. Certain visual motifs are repeated (in some cases a symbol appears both within the game and in the PET), and alert players may try to draw out the significance.

Given the way they were asked to play this game, with no preliminary reading of the instruction book, the students had to operate two sets of rules of notice: those which would help them make sense of the storyline and those that would provide them with some strategies for playing. For the most part, they seemed comfortable with this double requirement, and drew as effectively as they could upon their previous experiences of playing computer games and of processing science fiction in different media. The rules of notice operate very intertextually in such circumstances.

Thus we have Gregory and Kyle explaining how they chose the correct CD-ROM to start the game:

GREGORY: You can tell, like, it's the same with animation, like, if you look at something you can see what fits, and then at the character. You can immediately see the environment; it's always a different colour than something and that seems a little more vibrant than everything else.
KYLE: Yeah, it's brighter.
GREGORY: So it sort of sticks out.

Leonard and Jeff describe the need for close attention as one of the attractions of a computer game. 'Because this [CD-ROM], you can't actually flip back a page like you could with a book', said Jeff. 'Once you make one decision it kind of sticks.'

Jeff and Leonard also pointed out that it is not enough to notice; you have to be in the right place when you do notice. Describing how they had moved past the elevators they were seeking, Jeff said, 'I saw that [the picture of the elevator] and I was looking for it, but by then we were already past it. When we clicked on it, it didn't say elevator.' 'If we had been in front of the elevator and pushed on it . . .', said Leonard.

Alertness, even to the point of obsessiveness, is compulsory in this game. Sorting out the problem of the succ-u-bus, which constantly refers to 'mother', students had a head start if they had noticed that the succ-u-bus in the bilge was larger than the others. Making this connection did one or both of two things: it helped them make sense of even a tiny bit of the story and/or it gave them enough of a sense of progress to be able to avoid complete frustration for a bit longer. As a non-game player, I take that second alternative as a fairly unattractive description of a textual encounter, but the expectations of the students that they would be extensively frustrated appeared to be part of their game-playing experience. Witness Janice and Madeleine, also talking about the succ-u-bus:

MADELEINE: One way I was thinking about is, I think the little guy was, like . . .
JANICE: With the little thing on his head.
MADELEINE: Yeah, like a little microphone.
JANICE: Yeah, he had to do something. He symbolizes something, but we didn't know what he was.
MADELEINE: Because he's in every room.
JANICE: So –
MADELEINE: We didn't know what he was doing. He's like –
JANICE: And he kept telling us stuff, 'Nice to make your acquaintance' and stuff, and we didn't know what he was.
MADELEINE: He seemed, like, sarcastic.
JANICE: Yeah.

Here we see a textbook case of two readers taking note and then trying to decide how to attend to what they have noticed, exactly the situation Rabinowitz describes as signification. They reached no conclusions but did not appear impatient.

Similarly, Leonard and Jeff, trying to make sense of the role of the succ-u-bus, applied all the evidence they could muster. They put their photograph from 'home' into the maw of the succ-u-bus and clicked 'Send'; it instantly announced that the photo was lost and that they would have to see 'mother'. This is what they said as they played:

JEFF: Oh, no! See what?
LEONARD: Mother. It must be the big one.
JEFF: The big one.
LEONARD: Okay, so we know he's on the second floor, right?
JEFF: Yeah.
LEONARD: Should we just see if there's anything else?

And this is what they said retrospectively, as they watched the video of this segment:

JEFF: Like, right here, we were trying to, like, get anything out of what he said, like, we were trying to, like, look at what he said and see if it, like, had a special meaning.
MARGARET: Right. You are looking for all the clues you can get at this point, you mean?
LEONARD: Here there was something we could pick up.

Video playing – photo is lost.

LEONARD: That was a bad decision.
JEFF: Yeah.

Video playing – succ-u-bus refers them to mother.

LEONARD: Here we go.
JEFF: You had to listen to me, Leonard! [laughter] That was really interesting. There he gave you some clues as to, ah, when he says 'mother' you kind of, like, self-explanatory if you went back to the main –

At the heart of this discussion are questions of what to notice and how to pay attention to it and assess its significance, once it has been focused on. It is interesting that Jeff considers it 'self-explanatory' that the larger succ-u-bus is 'mother'. If he had not noticed and attached significance to the different size of one succ-u-bus, he would have had no grounds on which to proceed further. The information he needs is not on the screen at this moment, and he really has no way of hunting for it; he cannot thumb back through the pages of a book, and he has no 'Back' key for retracing his path. He needs to have observed and remembered prior to developing any link or even any reason to pay heed. At this early stage in the game, his only real tools are observation, memory and a kind of general genre awareness.

At play on the borders of the diegetic

It was clear that most of the students were immersed in the game as they played it, but it was a kind of hybrid immersion that partially reflected the fact that they were playing publicly with a partner, and partially reflected the nature of this kind of game. Their comments on what they noticed and what their observations might signify were interspersed with strategic comments on what tactics to follow to make more headway. To use Genette's terms, their game moved between diegetic levels (1986: 228).

The Concise Oxford Dictionary of Literary Terms defines diegesis as follows:

> an analytic term used in modern narratology to designate the narrated events or story (French, *Histoire*) as a 'level' distinct from that of the narration. The diegetic level of a narrative is that of the main story, whereas the 'higher' level at which the story is told is extradiegetic (i.e. standing outside the sphere of the main story).
>
> (Baldick 1990: 57)

The students plunged into the story but also moved outside it to make strategic decisions. Although they were not always inside the story, it is clear that they were always inside the game. When they were not engaged with sorting out a potential plot, they were still immersed in issues of how the story was to be told, how the game was to be played.

Even with those students (namely Kelly and Catherine) who never did become really engaged by the game, it is possible to see them working the diegetic borders. In this stretch of conversation, the two girls are retrospectively discussing the point in the video of their game where they have located the parrot and discovered that the cursor changes to a hand as it passes over the parrot's body:

MARGARET: What do you make of the parrot?

KELLY: He's annoying.

CATHERINE: Yeah. It's probably not as annoying as the other ones because he seems to be able to do something, since there's a hand. He's more, like, interesting.

MARGARET: Any idea what's happening there?

BOTH: No.

MARGARET: I mean, clearly you achieved something there.

KELLY: Yeah.

CATHERINE: Like, that stick thing had something to do with the bird. It has a perch. It never worked, we tried it, so –

MARGARET: But at this point you thought you might have a chance of sorting out something with the parrot?

CATHERINE: Yeah.

The change of the cursor into a hand is a strategic hint that further elucidation of the story may be possible at this point. The girls' discussion involves both strategy and plot. They are baffled by the events of the story world, but use the cues of the telling – the changing cursor – to direct their attention. They were the least engaged of all the players, but they still operated across the boundary between story and telling.

Such diegetic border-play may be part of the way the game is played, but other issues also affect our movement between diegetic levels in the early stages of engaging with any story. Hugh Crago, writing about the process of becoming immersed in a print book, describes the early stages of reading as a time when readers are more likely to dip in and out of the text. He is not talking about moving between levels of diegesis; but he addresses related questions as he considers how readers attempt to make sense of the new imagined world of the book by referring to their understanding of the world outside the book:

> Indeed, it would be surprising if both adults and children did not evidence this process of active grappling with the opening stages of a new aesthetic experience before becoming more completely absorbed. A common-sense explanation would be that we need to establish our points of reference before we can expect to understand the rest of a tale. A less obvious and by no means contradictory explanation (since the cognitive and emotional are so often two sides of the one coin) is that all readers of whatever age need a *defence* against the emotional impact of the new imaginative experience provided by a novel (or picture book or movie) [or computer game], and that they defend themselves by moving in and out of the world of the novel, asking questions about it, comparing it with their own world – being very *rational* simply because they are under *emotional* threat.
>
> (Crago 1982: 179)

It is clear that all the players of *Starship Titanic* were in the early stages that Crago describes. They were attempting to establish points of reference in a very confusing fictional universe. At the same time, they were dealing with a number of emotional question marks. Within the context of the story world, there was an evident shortage of allies; the few characters of the story are unfailingly sarcastic and unhelpful, at least in the preliminary stages. In terms of working out the game strategies, the early parts of the text offer little material to work with, and the parameters of success and failure appear to be fairly ruthlessly drawn. Finally, of course, there was the fact that they were playing in public and for a video camera. It is astonishing that they perceived any promise in the game at all; the potential to feel threatened at every level seems very great.

On the other hand, computer games are designed to be played more than once, and this knowledge was part of the emotional equipment the students brought to the game. Witness this exchange between Janice and Madeleine, as they clicked on the button that says 'Press here to disarm bomb', and discovered that they had set the bomb off instead:

MADELEINE: Mmm . . . where are we?
JANICE: Click on it to push button –
BOTH: To disarm bomb.
MADELEINE: There is a bomb!

Voice announces bomb is about to explode.

MADELEINE: Oh, no, turn off, turn off!! Maybe we just set off the bomb!
JANICE: Oh, my gosh, look what we did!
MADELEINE: What are we supposed to do? Type in a password or something.
JANICE: Yeah, probably.
MADELEINE: Mmmm.
JANICE: Push the button.
MADELEINE: Oh, man, look what we did! I think we're going to explode!
JANICE: We'd better go away. We'd better go far away.
MADELEINE: We have to be twenty-two miles away. All we want to do is find the
    elevator. We didn't mean it to happen. We have to disarm the bomb.
JANICE: I know that. Man!
MADELEINE: It's going to go off sometime during the game. He has to count down
    from a hundred, right, nine hundred and thousand. We have a thousand seconds.
JANICE: Yeah. At least we have to be on the Titanic.
MADELEINE: It said to disarm bomb, but then it really armed the bomb.
JANICE: Yeah.
MADELEINE: Oh, well, if we die we can start again.
JANICE: Yeah.

Janice and Madeleine are noticing, signifying and configuring; but as they engage
in their dramatic expostulations, they also appear to console themselves with the
option of the replay. They are moving in and out of the world of the story, and this
movement appears to be part of the pleasure they find in the game. It might be fair
to say that in this early stage of the game the knowledge of an exit route to the replay
is the clearest kind of emotional security on offer in such a confusing environment.

In their secondary commentary on this scene, as they watched the videotape,
Madeleine and Janice relived their surprise but drew on what they understood of
the game's overall pattern (using rules of configuration and coherence) to make
some sense of the experience:

JANICE: It was just so bad –
MARGARET: Did you feel the game was going to stop?
JANICE: We thought that the bomb was going to explode and blow up the Titanic
    or something because remember how they said at the beginning how –
MADELEINE: Something would go wrong – we kept on trying to touch that button
    to disarm it, but it's like 'No, no – stop it!' and then it would start again. It
    would recount. I lost count and we'd start again.
JANICE: It was hard to get out.

Later again, in the final stages of videotape viewing, the two girls returned to the subject of the bomb in an interesting way. I asked them when they had begun to use the icons in the PET and they replied that the bomb had been the trigger that made them attend much more closely to their strategic options. What they seemed to be arguing was that a jolt in affect within the diegetic world led them to pay more careful attention to their strategic options within the extradiegetic world of the game controls.

Such border-play is relatively common in many cultures (see Goldman 1998). Small children do it all the time in their imaginative play, as they regularly alternate strategic discussion and diegetic immersion: 'No, you be the daddy and you go to work. Bye-bye, daddy. Now, say I'm the mummy and you're the baby. Here, baby, come to mummy.'

Similarly, much movie and television culture operates in a constant state of diegetic border-crossing. Magazines, websites and television programmes regularly engage in such activity and viewers are very sophisticated in their applications of extradiegetic information. To take a single example, my daughter and I watched a particularly harrowing edition of the television programme *ER*, which orphaned two small children, killed off a nice old lady, and concluded with two of the major characters being knifed by a psychotic patient. As John Carter and Lucy Knight lay critically wounded on the hospital floor, the credits rolled. My daughter, devastated by this carnage, made a remark about Lucy's upcoming death, and I said, 'Maybe it's Carter who will die.' 'No, that actor's staying with the show', she replied instantly, and the diegetic borders lost their integrity for a moment, even at a point of considerable emotional intensity. She left the world of the story but remained within the world of the show – and at all times she remained comfortable in her role as viewer.

Steven Poole expresses this dichotomy very delicately: 'The purpose of a videogame, then, is never to simulate real life, but to offer the gift of play. In a videogame, we are citizens of an invisible city where there is no danger, only challenge' (2000: 77).

The 'gift of play' comes in many fictional forms and formats, and sometimes, as in these examples, the 'play' quotient is more visible or more complex or more multifaceted. It is clear that Janice and Madeleine relish their commitment to the idea of the bomb as dangerous, but they step out of that commitment very readily with their recurring references to the replay. At that level, they are clearly thinking in terms of challenge more than danger.

Another way of describing this movement between diegetic levels is to return to the distinction between 'looking through' the text into the story world and 'looking at' the text to see how to manipulate it to advantage – the oscillation that Bolter and Grusin describe as part of remediation. In this case, however, we are not exploring a text that has been 'repurposed' from another medium, but rather a text that has been designed to foster a similar form of oscillation within the terms of its own play.

'Soft mastery'

Another issue in text processing involves a more general question of strategic approaches and preferences. Sherry Turkle, in her landmark study of computer users, *Life on the Screen* (1995), uses the term 'soft mastery' to describe the experimental and bottom-up approach taken to computer programs by some users. Such users assemble their concepts and understandings about a program from bits and pieces of experience. Turkle refers to these users as bricoleurs.

The Concise Oxford Dictionary of Literary Terms defines bricolage as follows:

> a French term for improvisation or a piece of makeshift handiwork. It is sometimes applied to artistic works in a sense similar to collage: an assemblage improvised from materials ready to hand, or the practice of transforming 'found' materials by incorporating them in a new work.
>
> (Baldick 1990: 26)

Turkle applies this improvisatory motif to questions of information processing in computer simulations:

> As the computer culture's center of gravity has shifted from programming to dealing with screen simulations, the intellectual values of bricolage have become far more important. In the 1970s and 1980s, computing served as an initiation into the formal values of hard mastery. Now, playing with simulation encourages people to develop the skills of the more informal soft mastery because it is so easy to run 'What if?' scenarios and tinker with the outcome.
>
> The revaluation of bricolage in the culture of simulation includes a new emphasis on visualization and the development of intuition through the manipulation of virtual objects. Instead of having to follow a set of rules laid down in advance, computer users are encouraged to tinker in simulated microworlds. There, they learn about how things work by interacting with them. One can see evidence of this change in the way businesses do their financial planning, architects design buildings, and teenagers play with simulation games.
>
> (Turkle 1995: 52)

The teenagers playing *Starship Titanic* were not given the option of starting with the rulebook, but most of them did not appear to be troubled about immersing themselves in a world where they figured out the rules as they explored. Indeed, even the use of the word 'rules' in this context may be overstating their sense of certainty. In many ways their experience of the game was more passive and submissive than my account of it so far perhaps makes room for. They could not cheat or take short cuts, or even often return the way they came. They had to submit to the apparent anarchy of the setting, with only the generic tools of alertness, memory and some sense of story schema as their main tools. When the different bots refused to help them, they had no recourse but to tinker and to pay attention to what discoveries they could make, always on the watch for potential patterns and predictions.

To explore the issues of hard and soft mastery of this intricate game, the partnership of Jack and Anita is illuminating. Their game-playing strategies, for different reasons, drew less on the general power of the story schema, or the Rabinowitz rules of reading, than those of any other pair. The descriptors of hard and soft mastery are much more helpful when it comes to analysing their game.

Anita and Jack, who were set together for this occasion by the school, appeared to be friendly enough but they certainly had no history of computer playing together. Anita, indeed, had almost no history of playing with computers in any form. Over and over again, she referred to her lack of experience. Jack, on the other hand, was one of the computer veterans in the group. Against all the gender stereotypes associated with such a partnership, he went out of his way to acknowledge Anita's help on many occasions. More than once he observed that her different way of thinking made a valuable contribution to their partnership, and that she was good at noticing things that had escaped him.

Jack was clearly of the 'old school' of hard mastery as described by Turkle. He was anxious to establish rules and apply them in an algorithmic approach. When asked about his favourite activity on the computer, he said:

> It's not really games. I don't really know. In my, we had our old computer, there was, and it's got BASIC programs and so I like playing with them and see what I can do. Just fooling around, sitting there, and seeing what it can do.

He is tinkering but his tinkering has a structural focus.

Jack and Anita took a long time to get the game started, and Jack was somewhat annoyed even before the spaceship crashed into his 'house' on the screen. It took them some time to realize that they had to make a move before the game would be activated, and the computer had already said 'Get on with it – don't just sit there!' when they got the CD-ROM inserted into the computer to trigger the start of the game. 'I was very frustrated here', said Jack, reviewing the video.

> There was obviously some point, and that's when I started pushing F1 and stuff to try and get the, what we're supposed to do . . . Well, 'Help' and the buttons there to see if there was something that we were supposed to find out before.

He was more inclined to find the rules than to 'tinker in simulated microworlds' (Turkle 1995: 52).

Jack liked the combination of graphics and typing in responses but said, 'It's hard talking to people when you don't know what you're supposed to do.' His general approach was to test as he went along; he paid much more early and methodical attention to the tool kit of the PET than most other players, observing, 'Well, we would have been forced to click on those anyway, later.' It is clear that he is accomplishing as much through the use of top-down logic at the outset as he can.

Jack relied extensively on the 'save' mechanism, so that any mistake could be readily undone. It is probably fair to say that he was tactically the most systematic and careful of all the players and the one who made the most moves that I labelled as strategic.

Anita, in contrast, with so little experience to draw on, was operating more than most on simple powers of observation. Her repertoire of the conventions of such a game was quite limited, and so she often perceived only confusion where other players might at least have seen the option of some strategic way forward. She made very few explicitly strategic moves and she also said little that could be ascribed to the Rabinowitz paradigm of story schema.

Paradoxically, Anita and Jack made substantial progress in the game, partly as a consequence of Jack's time-saving 'save' strategy, but simultaneously they were probably the most frustrated of all the players of *Starship Titanic* – perhaps because they failed overall to establish much narrative logic to their game. Jack was working to some extent on a 'hard mastery' top-down approach; Anita had less recourse than many other players to the rules of reading such texts, simply because her repertoire was so limited, and so she augmented Jack's rule-directed approach with observations on the graphic patterning on the screen. She was actually quite good at making these connections, and Jack had the expertise to follow up on her hints. Nevertheless, both were unsatisfied; neither approach engaged them as most other players were engaged. They 'looked at' the screen but almost never seemed to be 'looking through' it into the world of the story. The impact of the mismatch between these two players must be taken into account, and so must Jack's understandable frustration at being so slow to get started, which probably tinged the rest of his game with a negative affect. His systematic approach to the logic of the game perhaps failed him right from the outset. He was expecting the game to take over and it did not occur to him for a long time to look for images on the screen that might hold narrative significance (in this case the computer and the CDs that trigger the start of the game). Jack and Anita's contrasting game styles were strategically effective but Jack was clearly troubled by feeling a lack of control and Anita's humble approach lowered her expectations.

Anita made very few observations that I could code under the headings of the four sets of 'rules'. In some ways, she may well have been the player operating on the purest sense of bricolage, the *ad hoc* assembling of whatever bits and pieces are to hand. But, in acting with very little in the way of repertoire, she could not ascribe any kind of narrative shape to her assembled fragments, and her game suffered as a consequence.

Turkle suggests that players engaged in a simulation game do resort to bricolage either out of initial preference or because they discover that a top-down strategy is not helpful. Jack was clearly attempting such a top-down strategy; Anita was simply putting bits together. What were the other players doing? It seems as if they were operating somewhere in a middle territory – not operating solely on strategic experience but not simply assembling either. They were using their story schema to moderate the kinds of bricolage they would attempt. The idea of a bounded bricolage is so paradoxical that I am not sure it is worth pursuing very far, but it does raise the idea of a hybrid text, and a set of readers responding with a complex and sometimes contradictory range of interpretive operations, according to their grasp of the conventions and of the specific details of the scene before them. Neither the algorithms of hard mastery nor the bit-by-bit assemblage of details is a sufficient approach to the narrative content of this game. Jack's strategic experience and Anita's sharp powers of observation took them a long way, but they wound up more frustrated by the story side of the game than any other players. Their experience raises questions about how important it is to begin a game as complex as this one with a general narrative schema that will be helpful – and about the role of luck in instantiating a useful schema on the basis of very little information at the outset of the game.

Conclusions

Over and over again, the transcripts make the point that *Starship Titanic* is a game and a game is different from a story. Yet those students who drew on story conventions as well as game conventions had a more successful experience, even though nobody came close to making sense of the story overall. In a way, their conversations about *strategy* acted almost as a kind of safety valve for some frustrations of their experience with the *story*. When they reached a dead end with a plot thread, which happened often, they could revert to talking about tactics and different ways of approaching the problem. Their understanding of narrative rules fuelled much of their strategic thinking and seemed to be a robust element in their game-playing tool kit.

Obviously, these transcripts record five short and very idiosyncratic experiences with a complex game that nobody could expect to interpret in less than an hour, which is all the time these players were given. It is perhaps all the more striking that the conventions described by Rabinowitz in his rules of reading should be evoked so continuously by nearly all of these students. It seemed as if Fintible the robot's initial explanation of the situation on board the starship triggered a general story schema that students reliably made use of, even as the details of their individual performances failed to cohere in any way. They appeared to be comfortable with the idea that such a game is a long-term operation and, for the most part, displayed considerable patience when very little of it made sense at once; the lack of immediate gratification did not stop them applying the conventions.

In short, the transcripts show the students using a hybrid approach to a hybrid text. They drew on a great deal of relevant intertextual experience, from other game playing, from other encounters with science fiction plots in different media, and from other exposure to the kind of taunting, sarcastic and ironic tone displayed in this story. The quality of their engagement with the game varied, I suspect partly according to the adequacy of their repertoires in these three areas (though Janice and Madeleine, who seemed unaware that such games even existed, thoroughly enjoyed themselves, so that is not a complete explanation either). Madeleine and Janice and the two all-boy teams had the most successful encounters in terms of engagement; it is difficult to quantify achievement in what amounts to a small fragment of the complete text. It is easy, however, to see issues of salience and fluency at work once again. Those players who perceived some salience to the puzzles posed by the robot made use of that response as they worked on ways of establishing access to a complex text.

With regard to 'looking through' and 'looking at', it is clear that this story kept the players on the surface of the text for much of the time. They did not really have long enough to move 'into' the story world in any way that might have felt organic to them. Even at the level at which this game was played, however, there are interesting questions about whether the shift from the story world to the extradiegetic strategy world is one form of oscillation between immediacy and hypermediacy.

As usual, I wound up wanting more. I wanted to pair Jack and Anita with different partners and let them try again. I wanted to see what everyone did on a second exposure to the game. Even within the limitations of what was possible within the school's schedule, however, I found myself once again admiring the ability of the students to draw on their narrative and procedural competences in order to begin the processing of a large and often overwhelming text.

Afterword: new literacy ecologies of the twenty-first century

In the years since these data were collected and this book was first published, a great debate has arisen over narrative computer games and whether their first and determinant identity is that of story or of game. The way I found it necessary to add a fifth category of strategy calculations to Rabinowitz's four rules of reading in order to interpret the conversations between participants that arose around the game playing suggests to me that, in fact, a narrative game is actually a kind of hybrid. Jordon Mechner has expressed this hybridity in very economical terms: 'In a movie, the story is what the characters do. In a game, the story is what the *player* does' (2006: 145).

In short, there is no story until the player starts noticing, signifying and configuring. The same can be argued in an abstract way about reading a print story; in Rosenblatt's terms there is no 'poem' until the transaction of reader meeting text gets under way (1994: 14). But the playing of the game is not simply a case of a reader bringing a pre-existing text to a form of cognitive and affective life. In a game, the text does not begin to take its particular shape until the player-protagonist starts making decisions. The game played by each of my five pairs of students was different from all the others, in ways far more extreme and far more constitutive than the differences recorded in the readings of the short story 'Tunnel', which are presented in the next chapter.

Janet Murray, in what she calls the 'last word' on the debate over whether games are stories, says 'Those interested in both games and stories see game elements in stories and story elements in games: interpenetrating sibling categories, neither of which completely subsumes the other' (2005: n.p.).

The participants in this study used their knowledge of stories and story schemas, their experience with digital games (which was highly variable) and their more generic understanding of games as more broadly defined, in order to help them bring some kind of coherence to a complex and bewildering text. It is very clear in the transcripts that each pair drew on all these different forms of tacit and articulated awareness in order to assist them in a very messy enterprise.

How might an equivalent set of 14-year-olds tackle such a challenge today? Although digital games are evolving very rapidly, my strong suspicion is that they would be more likely to find *Starship Titanic* dated in its surface features (quality of graphic imagery, fluidity of interaction) than in its presentation of story. I suspect that rather more of them would have some superficial awareness of game play, both through exposure to games themselves and through a broader awareness of the elements of gamesmanship in the general culture.

I am very unlikely, however, to attempt to replicate any work with *Starship Titanic*. The study of game playing will for the foreseeable future face an element of time-boundedness that does not afflict other forms of culture to the same degree, though any text can become dated. A study of *Starship Titanic* will not be easily mounted today because of the technological requirements and limitations of that particular set of discs. In my teaching, I can introduce my students to all the other texts used in earlier research, but the CD-ROMs and computer games rapidly become inaccessible because I do not keep an archival set of old game-playing equipment.

It is important for us to remember that our evolving research with digital games involves a moving target. Gamers may well be becoming more sophisticated but it is very difficult to assess such a possibility against a static set of texts. It is important to register the implications of this fact. A story schema may be well established and reliable; a game schema may be far more tentative and exploratory – and these differences will have little to do with some kind of balance of story and game within a hybrid text, but rather more to do with the differential stability of the two formats and their consequent conventions.

Chapter 10

The complexity of deixis

Reading 'Tunnel'

The double deictic of writing and reading

Where is meaning located? How much does it matter? Is there a right interpretation of a story? Is there a wrong one? How much is created by the author and how much by the reader? To whom does it matter *what* or *how* someone reads?

Janice Radway (1994) says that we have lost our way, that our culture over-values the text and underestimates the creative force of the reading process. She speaks of the:

> habitual erasure [of reading] as a process, an erasure that results in the elevation of the object that usually gives rise to it, that is, the book itself. Part of the reason we know so little about the complexities of reading, it seems to me, is that our culture both fetishizes visible objects like the book, the observable product of the writing and publication process, and deeply fears the intersubjective, imaginary act of engaging with the fantasies and subjectivities of others.
>
> (Radway 1994: 276)

Radway suggests that reading processes are not only vital but also variable:

> Reading is itself constituted by a set of variable strategies and procedures that change from situation to situation. As an act and event like any other, it is an activity that takes place always within a specific social context. To think of reading in this context-specific way is to stress its hybrid nature as well as its social character and to render it eminently visible as a practice, that is, an activity, a set of deliberate and complex strategies engaged in by communities of people.
>
> (Radway 1994: 276)

Radway argues against overvaluing the text as the sole and reified source of knowledge and insight. Yet the text is a specific and important part of the social nexus of reading. The social, historical and political relations of the reader are significant, but to erase the writer from the equation seems to be as one-sided as to rub out the actions of the reader. The text may, of course, simply be subsumed as part of the context of the reading situation. Such an approach seems to me to undervalue the non-accidental nature of the text. It is not just 'there'; it was created to develop responses. It seems more useful to find a way of addressing this question directly.

I quote Radway, not simply to disagree with her (in fact, I think she raises a valid and important point) but to emphasize the complexity of reading, an activity in which a dynamic process operates in conjunction with a fixed artefact. This paradox, which is at the heart of interpretation, makes any description of reading processes very challenging.

In fact, there is a grammatical convention at our disposal that gives us a way to talk much more precisely about the complexities of author, reader and text: that way is the already familiar territory of deictics or deixis. As well as helping us to point, deictics offer a linguistic means of changing places.

Deicitic shifters are the words that have a conventional grammatical role, but have an actual content only in each specific use: words like 'here' and 'there', 'now' and 'then', 'you' and 'I'. Readers are accustomed to the complex mental and emotional adjustment needed to align their contemporary reading selves with the *I* or the *now* of a narrative, to submerge their own personal identity into the present tense of another. Yet theirs is only half of the deictic relationship established in the text; the author has also and already created that alignment from the other side of the equation. The paradox of the subsequent relationship between author and reader is delicately expressed in E.D. Blodgett's title for the second volume of poems in his *Apostrophe* series: *Through You I*. Through you the author, I the reader become another *I*; through you the reader, I the author speak my words in another's voice. I as author write *now*; I as reader read *now*; yet we meet in a third space that is a different *now* for both of us. The dust jacket of Blodgett's book says, 'The act of apostrophe continues to bring what is addressed into light.' Radway has expressed her concern that 'reading' needs to be seen as a verb. This little phrase about the apostrophe from Blodgett's dust jacket that describes the 'addressing' affirms the corresponding need to perceive 'writing' as a verb also, a verb with similar concatenations of social and historical pressures. The written words, though their usual place is inert on the page, have to be doubly activated in this way – have to be doubly breathed – by both writer and reader, though not at the same time.

Breathing and attention

I think this factor may be one of the criteria that separate reading from other forms of text processing. That double breathing is more intimate than the multiply voiced and incarnated forms of other kinds of text. No consensus of directors, producers and actors, no team of animators, no budget committee or publicity team impinges on the imaginative experience. 'Reading is an intimate act', says

Harold Brodkey, 'perhaps more intimate than any other human act. I say that because of the prolonged (or intense) exposure of one mind to another' (quoted in Booth 1988: 168). The contingent, socially and politically located reader meets the contingent, socially and politically located author; the finality of the printed text and the evanescence of the reader's reactions create a chemistry of something new.

Elaine Scarry expresses the same idea in different words:

> [T]he material on which a writer works is not, as with other artists, paint or wood or stone or canvas or paper or strings or reeds . . . but something alive: the tissue of the writer's own mind on which he or she practices mental composition, and the live tissue of the many other minds that will mentally recompose the pictures as they read. The writer is composing instructions for motions that will themselves take place on a surface – the quick of the human mind – that is already, always itself in motion.
>
> (Scarry 1999: 241)

The enigma of how the words reach and affect 'the quick of the human mind' is an endlessly fascinating question. Clearly this operation involves issues of attention. The physiology of silent reading is livelier than we assume. Reading a short story for me, the students held a pencil and occasionally checked a point that struck them as worth noticing – useful activity in the focusing of attention. Their hands were undoubtedly also occupied in the usual ways of adjusting the page, maintaining a viable focal distance, and so forth. But the writer's body is also engaged. Poet Dennis Lee, talking about the writer's side of this deictic relationship, also registers the manual elements of writing, as he speaks of 'hearing the music in your forearms and trying not to muff it' (1998: 59).

Reading 'Tunnel'

In May 1999, I spent an hour with each of the Grade 9 students individually. During that time, each of them silently read a copy of the same short story: 'Tunnel', by Sarah Ellis, the first story from a collection with a supernatural edge, *Back of Beyond*, published in 1996. As with all the other encounters, of course, this engagement represented only a sampling of students' reading lives.

I chose this story deliberately. Sarah Ellis is a contemporary Canadian writer. *Back of Beyond* is aimed at young adults and I calculated that my group of Canadian 14-year-olds would be as close to the implied reader as it is possible to get. The textual *I* of Sarah Ellis's narrator should speak fairly directly to the *you* of these young readers, without calling on repertoires beyond their likely experience. The setting of the story, at least initially, would be highly familiar to these suburban young people: the narrator begins the story by talking about babysitting jobs, work experience, Barbie dolls and anxiety about the future. Not only the topics but also the vernacular tone and contemporary vocabulary would be intimately recognizable. Another helpful quality of this particular text is that the opening stages of the story are quite funny.

The story is not completely straightforward, however, and it was in the twists and turns that I saw potential for exploring how readers react to the unexpected. Initially, the narrator's gender is not revealed, although there is much talk of babysitting; it is only when the story is well under way that he is identified as a 16-year-old boy. The sentence that reveals his gender conclusively was one that appealed to the students on more than one level: 'When you have sixteen-year-old guy hands, there is no way to hold a nude Barbie without violating her personal space' (Ellis 1996: 12).

More substantially, the story moves away from the recognizable, if boring, life of a babysitter's long summer day into a world where something strange is going on. The story ends happily but not before something undefined but sinister happens to the child and her babysitter. A supernatural explanation accounts for the details most satisfactorily, but it is not an obligatory reading of the story.

'Tunnel' opens on an ordinary day with Ken, the babysitter, and Ib, his 6-year-old charge, climbing up to a local culvert. He begins to be haunted by unwanted memories of a time when he was much younger and he and his friends also played in the culvert. Flashbacks alternate with the present-day account and we learn that something terrifying happened to Ken there, in the past.

Ib climbs into the culvert and disappears. Ken calls her frantically, 'Come back, Elizabeth', and she reappears. She has been playing with some mysterious girls who have offered her cake, but she doesn't really think she likes them after all. The final pieces of Ken's memory slide into place: he too was tempted by these girls and returned to the ordinary world only when his friends called him by his full name, Kenton.

The story ends with Ken and Ib climbing back into the sunshine, and the strange girls are never explained.

Although they also saw a copy of Ellis's book, the students actually read a photocopy of 'Tunnel', made with large margins for annotating if they chose. They read the story silently, ticking anything that struck their attention and jotting swift notes in some cases. After they had finished, they went through the story again, mentioning anything they had particularly noticed on their first reading, producing a retrospective think-aloud protocol. Inevitably, some made new discoveries on looking through the story for the second time, but for the most part, as I requested, they worked to recreate their first assessment of the story. Their accounts of the story, not surprisingly, included many points of agreement, but no two readings matched in every particular.

Redescribing the deictics of 'Tunnel'

We may speak of the deictics of the *I* and the *now* of the story, which undergo subtle changes throughout this text, or we may talk about a shifting demand on the repertoire of the implied reader. However we label the changing patterning of this text, it is clear that this story plays games with the apparent contract with readers that is established in the first few pages. All the students were fully familiar with the range of background experience and knowledge required of the reader in the opening of this story. As the story progressed, they were invited to recognize the shift to a different register, one where daily life is not so recognizable and transparent. They were given the opportunity to change their reading stance, to enlarge the imaginary world of this little text to include supernatural and sinister elements. At the point of their reading, Sarah Ellis's role was completed; the readers were the ones 'breathing' the story, and some chose to refuse that invitation.

Before moving on to these readings, however, I would like to turn briefly to the deictic composition of the story itself. The relationship between author and text, and between reader and text, is deictic in the way I have described above. Within the words of the story are also deictic directions.

We step into the fictional world of a story with a change of *mood*, in the technical sense of that word, meaning the 'form of a verb serving to indicate whether it is to express fact, command, permission, wish, etc.' (*Oxford Guide* 1984: xx). Stories, in Jerome Bruner's terms, operate in the subjunctive mood or mode. 'To be in the subjunctive mode is, then, to be trafficking in human possibilities rather than in settled certainties' (1986: 26). Given that we are dealing with possibilities, we are set into a world with a future. In Torben Grodal's words:

> In standard fictions, as in real life, the future has not yet taken place, therefore it activates the wish for or an option of future mediation between the different registers of sensation . . . To participate at this level of meaning when consuming fiction, the viewer or reader must identify with some protagonists' capabilities for subjectivity and action within the fictive world.
>
> (Grodal 1999: 47)

Thus readers move into the subjunctive mode where they must participate 'as if' there is a future tense available, despite their real-world knowledge that the story they encounter in these conditions is always already written and not, therefore, open to change in the form of an open future. Within the specific fictional world of 'Tunnel', the tense markers become even more complicated, as the story moves from the present of the telling to specific flashbacks, which also operate in the present tense of the narrator's memory at the moment of narration. Finally, towards the end of the story, the layers of conditionalism and contingency become even more complex, as readers are asked to judge the role of the girls in the culvert. Are they real? Are they imaginary? Are they from yet another subjunctive layer of fictional possibility? At what level of reality – within the story and maybe within our familiar world too – should we 'read' these girls?

Gregory and Jack

As with the readings of *Shortcut*, most of the students read the latter part of the story for a second time. Re-reading in full knowledge of the ending is quite a different experience from a first reading, and the students picked up details they had missed or interpreted differently on the first encounter. Two students, however, were completely satisfied with their interpretation by the end of their first reading, and it is to the contradictions of their two interpretations that we will first turn.

Jack immediately assumed that supernatural elements were at work in the lives of Ken and Ib; Gregory rejected that possibility outright, first tacitly and then explicitly. How these two intelligent readers reached such conflicting conclusions is an interesting study.

Jack's reading of 'Tunnel'

Jack was immediately positive about the story:

JACK: Well, at the beginning, the whole first page talked about the kid and his future. It's very accurate and very accurately captured. And it's a well-told story.

MARGARET: Can I just interrupt you and ask you? You talk about the kid and his future. Did you think of him as a boy right from the outset?

JACK: Yes. I thought somebody, like, my age. Somebody who was thinking, like, I really have no idea of what I what to do. I mean, I've thought about law; I just don't know. So it's –

MARGARET: So it rang a bell straight away?

JACK: Yes. And other than accurate and funny, playing with the Barbies trying not to violate her personal space –

MARGARET: You liked that, did you?

JACK: I liked that. And then when he's trying to make Ninja stars, he tries to do what he wants to do and not be this grown-up job guy. And then he tells her, *oh, let's go on an exploration mission*, that's what I want to do. I don't want to play Barbies any more. [chuckling] And I think he was really starting to get, not really worried about, the future, but thinking about how it's not how he imagined it. When, *well once I stop playing with Barbie dolls and practicing making my body into a K.*

There are a number of points to notice in this short stretch of conversation. Jack, as he consistently did throughout the eighteen months of this project, made an early comment on the quality of the writing. Almost instantly, he raised the question of salience and made some observations about his own uncertainty about his future. It is noteworthy that Jack thought of the narrator as male right from the outset (all five male readers made this assumption). When he reproduced Ken's thoughts about his future, he slipped back and forth between third person and first person in his report of the indirect speech.

From this identification with particular aspects of Ken's identity as related in this story, Jack moved immediately into discussion of the flashback scenes, reverting to third person as he did so:

JACK: And then the memories with the woodpecker and stuff. This is obviously something that he remembers vividly, something that has really struck something with him that he remembers everything about it, even the sounds of the woodpecker and he has flashbacks. And then when she wants to go in this tunnel or this area, he says *I don't want to go there* because he's afraid of the memories. He knows that something weird happened, that something bad happened. And then she gets lost and he's really scared. I thought because of his memories, because what he knew could happen or something.

MARGARET: Did you have any idea at this point what it was?

JACK: I thought that Jeff might have died or something. That something bad had happened. And I was really weirded out about here.

Jack did not hesitate to identify the flashbacks, and was quick to comment, at least implicitly, on their foreshadowing potential. When he spoke of the end, he referred to the point 'when we found out it was fairies or spirits or whatever':

JACK: He overcame the fear of whatever could happen to her and he figured she was just tricking him and, um, and then he really got scared and he really got worried that maybe he was right and he needed something to happen and he was worried about it. I think he was worried about his future when he said *Child drowns in four inches of bath water*. I think he was worried that, like, he screwed this up playing with Barbies and that, what's going to happen now? And that he was really worried and just scared when he found, when he found he had her body. He wasn't like, grief stricken, [more] scared that he had screwed up.

MARGARET: Do you think that's reasonable?

JACK: I think that, you know, he's scared that she might be dead. I think he's also scared that, of his future. That's what he was thinking before. And then he finds her and he's relieved and he doesn't believe in fairies any more, I don't think. And then she tells about the fairies and spirits and he remembers his encounter with them until they called his real name, so I think it's like a new world with like, not, it's not this world, it's the opposite. Like, you can't be yourself in this fairy place.

MARGARET: So when you're called by your real name that breaks the spell?

JACK: It breaks the spell because I don't think this is reality. I mean, it's not like; it's a new area and has nothing to do with who you are in real life, yes. And then she says *I don't really like those girls*, so they wouldn't play with her unless she was *fake* and now Ken's like 'oh, this is weird' and so goes home, that's great.

For somebody operating on a single reading of the story, augmented by the fact that he is now browsing through the pages for a second time as he speaks, Jack does an impressive job of merging questions of identity, of future commitments, and of truth and fairyland. He reverts more than once to the theme of anxiety about the future that he has discerned in this story. It is also interesting to analyse his response in terms of the deictic elements: he switches between past and present tense; he uses the word 'now' at one time, and the word 'before' at another, and moves between 'he' and 'I' in his account of the story. He seems to be engaged in the deictic space of the story, but at the same time he is piecing the elements together and making sense of the story as a whole, as in Rabinowitz's rules of configuration and coherence. He is also passing judgement:

MARGARET: What do you think of the ending?
JACK: The ending I think is Ken saying everything is okay and I'm not coming back here, but everything is going to be okay.
MARGARET: Right. So they're going back into the sunshine?
JACK: Yes.
MARGARET: What did you think of the story overall?
JACK: It was a good story. It was interesting.

Jack's reading was noticeable for what it did not say. He did not appear to be confused at any point; he did not say any equivalent of 'Oh, *now* I get it', and he did not change his mind. This reading makes an interesting comparison with that of Gregory, who was also definitive in his interpretations.

Gregory's reading of 'Tunnel'

Gregory referred almost at once to the author and to her deliberate construction of the story with particular motives in mind:

> Okay, like, the first thing I noticed was, in the first part, the author was trying to get your attention. She was trying to get a little comical so you would want to read on. All I notice is that [Ken's previous babysitting charge] *Laurence likes impersonating trucks and being held upside down*, that caught my attention there. And then I really liked the name *Ib* because normally when I'm reading a novel and there are so many characters I keep going back, *who's that, who's that?* and if I've, like, there's a character whose name is sure that you'll remember, then it's easier to get into the story.

Gregory assumed the narrator was male, and spoke of how his ticking of points of interest had tapered off as he got more engrossed with the story. He raised particular details and dwelt on their resonance for him – Ken's dislike of French verbs, and his fantasies about spying, which reminded Gregory of a *Dracula* cartoon.

These recollections are less thematically significant than Jack's question of anxiety about his future. The question of salience may be slightly different for Gregory, therefore, though there certainly seems little problem with fluency of access. Nevertheless, Gregory and Jack parted ways when it came to describing the import of the ending:

MARGARET: Let's start at the end. What do you think happened to them?

GREGORY: When he was looking for her and stuff? When he finally realized that they were there like. I don't think the ending was anything more than what was actually said here about how, you know, the girls aren't nice, let's go, I don't like this.

MARGARET: Who do you think the girls are?

GREGORY: Just girls that just live around the same area that they do. If they have free time, it's kind of like a clubhouse-type thing.

MARGARET: Why do you think he couldn't see her when he was looking through the tunnel?

GREGORY: Oh, it was mentioning his eyes were starting to adjust to the darkness so maybe when he was really looking hard at the very beginning he didn't notice her. That's what I originally thought was just happening and then she was just playing a trick on him at the end of the tunnel and then it explains it near the end that the girls were, she was in a circle, the cake and all that.

MARGARET: Mmm. Why do you think it mattered that he called her by her full name, Elizabeth?

GREGORY: Well, in a lot of TV shows, they touch on this as well. You know, as soon as, um, your parents use your full name, then it's like, 'Listen, I'm getting upset now, come on, enough is enough', so I think it was kind of what they were trying to do.

MARGARET: Right. Then the same thing when Jeff called him back by his full name?

GREGORY: Yeah, to get it back into reality.

Gregory supplies a convincing explanation for every question, but draws on a much more realistic repertoire to back up his conclusions – though there is a hint in his final remark about 'getting it back into reality' that at least part of his mind is registering something else. In light of this overall reading, it is perhaps not surprising that he would have preferred to see the tone of the humorous opening carried on more consistently. He was committed to his realistic reading and refused to consider an alternative:

MARGARET: What do you think of the story as a whole?

GREGORY: It's okay. It could have incorporated a little more humour into it.

MARGARET: Uh-huh. It changes direction somewhat, doesn't it? It starts off funny, but it's not so funny by the end.

GREGORY: No. I think they could have explained the characters a little better as well, but I know it's just a ten-page story and you don't have that much time to do that, but I think that's one of the things the author could have done.

MARGARET: What about if I put up a theory that these girls are some sort of supernatural group like leprechauns or fairies or something like that and that the reason –?

GREGORY: I don't think that will go over.

MARGARET: You don't think that works?

GREGORY: No. No, it wouldn't go over. As soon as I heard that, I'm like *huh?* and I'd probably know that's too much.

Some details in the contrast between Jack's reading and Gregory's reading bear teasing out. It is noticeable that, even at the end, Gregory is still talking about the story as the author's construction, and he also suggests limitations of the short-story form itself as a partial cause of why it is disappointing. Gregory's response offers no hint of the deictic crossover that surfaces in Jack's rendition of the story, and his comparisons consistently provide examples of creators deliberately achieving an effect, for example the use of the full name on television programmes. He shows little sign of identification with any of the characters or the situations described in the story.

In a perfect world, I would have set up an extra session to let Jack and Gregory discuss this story together. Unfortunately, this conversation could not be organized. Instead, we may turn to the other transcripts for further interpretations of the story.

Interpretive moments

There were several points where the story took a turn that most of the students noticed, and in many cases interpreted differently. There is the introductory sequence where the narrator talks about his ambitions and assumptions about what he would be doing at the age of 16. There is the sentence about the Barbie in guy hands where it is clear for the first time that the narrator is male. There is the first flashback, when Ken recalls the woodpecker on his first visit to the culvert. There is the point at which Ib disappears. Finally there is the resolution and conclusion.

So far in this summary, I have generally talked about meaning as residing at least potentially in the text. How these parts of the story were energized by the readers is a different kind of description. Most of the readers mentioned each of these points, although, like the proverbial witnesses to an accident, they often brought different perspectives to bear. They also demonstrated different reading stances: some paid much more attention than others to the role of the author or the constructed nature of the plot.

I tried to do a tally of where students agreed and diverged in their readings, but stopped in some distress. It was clear to me that I was attempting to collapse something that was intrinsically irreducible: turning from the reading to the text itself, in Radway's terms. For example, Janice took in from the start that the narrator was male but struggled with the flashback; Madeleine grasped the implication of the flashback at first sight, but spent the entire story happily assuming the narrator was female. Those reading experiences are so different that no amount of putting a check mark in one column or another will express the qualities of the differences.

Voice and recognition

All the students, in one way or another, acknowledged and enjoyed the recognizability of the story. In the early stages at least, it is clearly set in a contemporary world very similar to the one these students inhabit.

How much does this matter? In earlier stages of the project, these students had happily browsed through texts set in a variety of real, fantastic, local and foreign locations. Yet there is no doubt that they responded to the familiarity of this story in very positive ways. They actively enjoyed the references to Barbies, childish job ambitions, work experience and so forth. Undoubtedly, the readers all drew on copiously stocked repertoires of contemporary Canadian suburban experience to activate these positive responses. Their pleasure was at least partly generated because they found much of their recognizable world represented *in a story*. To what extent is their delight actually in-built into the story as crafted? Certainly Ellis seems to be addressing a reader with the requisite repertoire to make immediate sense of the Barbie issue, and to be drawing on that reader's recognition of this universe to *literary* effect in her later shaking up of the assumptions of that world. This effect is also reinforced by the way that the initial recognition is also threaded with a sense of humour that fades sharply away as the story becomes more menacing.

Gaps and volition

There are other ways of describing the effect of the very familiar world described in the opening stages, and these descriptors also shed light on our processes of reading print. Wolfgang Iser (1978) speaks of the importance of gaps in the text, which allow us to introduce our own schemata into our imagining of the story world. Christopher Collins (1991) goes further in his description of how print differs from, for example, movies, where figure and ground are equally in evidence. Writing does not supply a complete ground; all the background can never be fully described. He refers to this phenomenon as 'nouns situated in a void' (Collins 1991: 151), and says we may supply some background detail from our own experiences.

In earlier work with print reading (Mackey 1995), I drew on David Gelernter's useful concept of affect linking (Gelernter 1994: 28) to describe how we extrapolate from our own emotional experiences to activate and vivify affective moments in a written text. We may not have experienced the exact circumstances described in a story, but we can supply an appropriately nuanced affective charge from a different experience. How we flesh out the affective qualities of a particular fictional moment out of our own repertoire of memories and experiences is one of those relationships that makes reading personal as well as social.

All of these descriptions highlight Mikhael Bakhtin's idea that language always belongs at least half to somebody else (1988: 293). The writer brings the words to the page but it is with our own experiences that we, the readers, flood the words with detail, background, emotion and consequence.

The familiarity of the initial setting of 'Tunnel' leads readers to make a number of easy and automatic inferences right at the outset. None of the readers in this study seems to have read the word 'Barbie' without instantly invoking a rich set of associations, and I suspect it would be impossible for them to read the word otherwise. By the end of the story, Ken's terror about Ib is increased when he spots Wanda the Barbie floating in the culvert, and the doll has been rendered strange to the point that some readers invoke Ib's set of dolls as possibly sinister and connected to the strange girls. In Iser's terms, it seems as if the gaps that must be filled in by the readers have widened. The automatic application of a very familiar schema is no longer sufficient.

Overall, the process of moving from the beginning to the end of this story is not a straightforward operation. Initial assumptions are activated and then dropped. To explore these questions, we can turn once more to Rabinowitz's rules of reading. They were, of course, actually designed in the first place to apply to print reading. In addition, the short-story reading has an advantage over most of the other texts on offer in this study in that students actually read it to the end.

Rules of reading

All the readers noticed that the narrator was their contemporary, talking about a world that they recognized. They differed in their assessment of signification in at least one respect: six of them assumed he was male from the outset, one of them considered the narrator to be female from start to finish, and the remaining three started off thinking of the narrator as female but switched at the sentence about the guy hands. It is a small issue at one level, but it means that three of the ten readers had a fairly substantial surprise built into their reading experience, and had to recast their initial reading in a new light. Already, this is a substantially different literary experience from that of the readers who never questioned the narrator's gender, and responded to the narration as transparent.

Readers had to notice the first flashback and then decide how to interpret it, and again their experiences diverged. Madeleine, Anita, Jeff and Jack all registered it as a flashback immediately. Catherine also mentioned an explicit element of fore-shadowing at the first hint of the flashback, so her experience of the reading may have diverged from the others because of this premonition. Kyle eventually picked up the flashback effect, but not at first appearance. Janice did notice the flashback at first inkling, but was confused by it. Kelly also found the tunnel sequence confusing. We can see rules of signification and configuration being differentially applied by different readers throughout this part of the story. Even if all these readers had eventually worked through to a reasonable consensus on the implications of the story, their experiences of meeting it word by word are clearly quite varied.

Because the students read to the end of the story, there is also an opportunity to explore how they applied Rabinowitz's rules of coherence. Rabinowitz's most general statement of these rules suggests that 'we should read a text in such a way that it becomes the best text possible' (1987: 45). The differing ways in which students aimed to achieve this end are worth teasing out rather more elaborately.

Reading the best text possible

There are numerous ways to read this story coherently. One is to work out a single explanation of the strange events and apply it consistently; different readers might settle for alternative single interpretations. Another way to read this story positively is to accept that the author wants to leave the ending open and unresolved and to consider such openness to be the best rendition of the story.

Of course, readers will naturally diverge when they have variant perspectives on whether the story as it stands is actually a complete unit. Two readers, Madeleine and Anita, assumed they were reading an initial part of a longer story, and this misapprehension naturally affected their approach to the text. Leonard also seems to have been unclear about the genre.

The remaining students knew they were reading a complete short story and responded accordingly at the end. Between them, they came up with a variety of theories to explain the strange girls: they could be Ib's dolls come to life, they could be cult members, they could be ordinary girls or they could be supernatural. Several readers were happy to leave it open that more than one of these alternatives was a possibility. Yet whether or how they chose to make it the best story possible varied in quite distinctive ways.

Some readers were not interested in taking this step. Madeleine was relatively dismissive: reading the story was 'too much work'. Jeff, although he was intrigued with many aspects of the story, found the ending too abrupt, and Gregory found the change of tone disappointing. Several readers (Janice, Kelly, Anita, Leonard) found parts of the story confusing along the way. It is very possible that their acceptance of an open ending reflected an absence of any wish to work on the story in sufficient detail to establish a preferred ending, rather than any more principled attachment to artistic ambiguity. Of this group, Leonard was the most definite about listing possibilities and the most positive about the way the story 'lets you decide for yourself to some degree'. It is much more possible to read into the responses of the three girls an element of that familiar teenage response, 'Whatever'.

Some readers made the story better and fuller for themselves by investing in it at a more emotional level. Leonard, with a 3-year-old sister, was probably the most involved reader in terms of identification. Kyle supplied an interesting example of a reader looking for point-to-point comparisons with a character. He checked the story against his own work experience, and mentioned a discrepancy between himself and the fictional boy: Ken is afraid of the water but Kyle himself loves to swim. Jack interpreted Ken's fears for the future in light of his own experience. The girls, perhaps not surprisingly, made more mention of playing with Barbies, and they also shared Ken's childish enthusiasm for picturing himself as a lifeguard.

There is not enough evidence in the transcripts to point to an affective change in the reading stance of the three girls whose mental image of the narrator shifted from female to male. It seems clear that their inclination to identify wholeheartedly would be reduced, not simply because the narrator had changed sides on them, so to speak, but also because they would not henceforth be able to trust the apparent transparency of any element of the story. Whether this effect was alienating or simply engaged them more closely in the story in a different way is not clear in any case. Catherine's transcript does show the gender misunderstanding lingering, at least in her pronouns, long after she had notionally made the switch to thinking of the narrator as male. Speaking of Ken's claustrophobia, she says, 'That's her, gives her that scary feeling, that something happened and he knows what's going to happen next.' But her most explicit association with Ken's feelings comes in a sentence where the gender is clear cut: 'And then, *a tight heaviness*, you sort of feel like he's scared, how scared he is . . . I sort of relate to it.'

Public, private and shared readings

These readers were reading in a relatively public way, and they made use of formal vocabulary to some extent, especially those who chose to address the question of foreshadowing in the story. At the same time, it is possible to see some more private questions of reading surfacing at different points in their transcripts. One major issue of private reading is the interface between the reading that is 'good enough' (Mackey 1997) and the reading that creates the best text possible. Much private reading settles for the good enough, for whatever suffices to get you to the end of the story to your own satisfaction. Catherine, in the example above, for instance, did not stop to disentangle her apparent confusion about the narrator's gender. It is entirely possible that she read the story with her mental image of the narrator wavering, sometimes remembering that she had decided to treat him as male, and sometimes forgetting. This wavering may have been annoying to her as a reader, or she may have been untroubled by it, focusing instead on the emotional implications of claustrophobia in a way that reduced the importance of the gender question. What is important here is that it is up to Catherine herself, as a private reader, to decide what made this story the best possible text, given this apparently ongoing uncertainty about the narrator's gender. If asked, she could produce the 'correct' answer: at the beginning the story is ambiguous about gender, but it becomes clear that the narrator is male at the sentence about the guy hands. Yet at the much messier level of what she actually experienced as she read, it would seem that the ambiguity continued to activate her interpretation. It is even arguable that this is a more appropriate reading of a story that sets the reader up in this way. If you hear a joke that revolves on a double meaning, you have to retain both meanings to find it funny. If a story sets up ambiguity as part of its initial premise, that ambiguity may appropriately colour the entire reading of that story. And of course, the word that opens reading to many interpretations is that well-known weasel word, 'appropriately' – who is the judge of the appropriate reading anyway? Appropriate to what purpose must be the follow-up question, and the issue of whether reading intent is public or private is part of what we describe as purpose.

Conclusions

It is commonplace to think of authors as enabling us to 'see' new scenes. Christopher Collins (1991) suggests this concept is an overstatement and that the conditions of reading are such that we can never see the *same* complexity as the author sees. Instead, what is set up is a joint space where, at the direction of the writer, we create images that are a hybrid created from materials in both the mind of the author and the mind's eye of the reader. The kinds of convention that govern our capacity to use deictics successfully enable us to share this hybrid space.

The students reading 'Tunnel' responded with pleasure to the fact that their own repertoires were clearly very well stocked to animate or vivify the early stages of the story. Such associations lead to ease and comfort in the activation of the story, and they may also reduce the element of volition required to move into the text in the initial stages. If your mind is stocked with ready associations for the main nouns of the opening pages, you may be fully engaged with little conscious effort. Such a description certainly accounts for many of the responses to the early part of 'Tunnel'.

And yet, for all the commonalities in the responses to the story, what emerged were clearly ten separate and different reading experiences. The moment-to-moment interpretations varied substantially, in a way that would probably never be captured by any summary of the story that the students might give subsequently. Ambiguities were activated or not; initial decisions were sometimes rethought and sometimes taken for granted. The story is short and for several pages almost completely uncomplicated for these readers. Yet the complexity of variation in experience of this imagined world was substantial.

As the story moved into less familiar territory, the reactions of the students began to diverge. Some were intrigued; some were puzzled. Given the size of the group, they came up with a relatively large number of workable hypotheses to make sense of the plot. Most of them readily made suggestions for rendering the story coherent in Rabinowitz's sense of making it the best text possible, given its constraints. To what degree they would have accomplished this task without being asked, to what extent their reading was shaped by being relatively formal and public, it is naturally impossible to be sure. How a reading is retrospectively affected by the simple fact of the reader subsequently talking about it is a question to which there are few clear answers. I suspect that some of these readers would not have paused to speculate very extensively on the identity of the girls in this story without the pressure of talking to me about it. The issue of what passes as a good-enough private reading is never clear cut. It may be that one consequence of these students being accustomed to obligatory reading in their school reading break is that they are content to see a lot of their reading as something that passes the time tolerably without leading to any kind of deep reflection or indeed closure of any kind. 'Whatever' may not always be an intolerable response to a story if your purpose for reading is simply to be reading something.

I do not mean this description to be an attack on the concept of the reading break. Overall, there was no question in my mind that these students benefited from daily exposure to silent reading. In our conversations about texts, they could all talk about reading as effortlessly as about movies or television, and that accomplishment alone – being inside the conversation of readers rather than outside – is very significant.

Be that as it may, the students, asked to speak about the story they had just read, marshalled their responses and read for coherence. The coherence they developed was in many ways local rather than global. We are left, appropriately enough, with the ten transcripts, the ten accounts of separate and individual experiences.

Afterword: new literacy ecologies of the twenty-first century

Many forms of fiction offer the option of stepping into the subjunctive mode of 'human possibilities' (Bruner 1986: 26), of exploring somebody else's potential future. Movies, games, websites and CD-ROMs all offer routes into fictional territory. Reading verbally created fiction, however, remains the most internal, private, intimate step into someone else's world. Only as we bring words to life in our own minds do we create our own very personal instantiations of that world, illuminated by our own experience, vivified by our own emotions and breathed in our own internal voice.

The intense privacy of fiction reading will not necessarily change if we shift our reading from paper to screen. New generations of readers who are accustomed to screen reading from their earliest experience may not ever miss the tangible qualities of paper and may find that their automatic reading processes take over and bring electronic words to life in their minds just as successfully as words on paper. The phrase 'print reading' will not necessarily mean something completely new when readers encounter that print on their portable electronic reader, their PDA or their mobile phone.

What is changing very rapidly, however, is the general ecology within which print reading of any form exists. For many years, the standard defence of book reading has involved the efficiency of the tool: portable, cheap, and accessible to anyone who can read without the need for further technological scaffolding. These are robust virtues and, added to the visual and tactile pleasures of a well-designed and well-produced book and the intimate pleasures of book reading described above, provide a formidable assurance that books are likely to survive.

Yet one of the book's strong points now faces new competition. The portability of the book remains a virtue, at least as long as we are talking about a single book – problems of portability with regard to a whole stack of books may one day provide the opening that a well-marketed electronic book takes advantage of. But other media are fast becoming more portable too. I cannot be the only airline passenger who notices more and more young children travelling with portable DVD players rather than with books. Certainly it is impossible to take a train in Europe without seeing fellow-travellers whose complete entertainment package for a lengthy trip resides in their cellphones. Mizuko Ito talks about 'a broader set of shifts towards intimate and portable technologies that enable lightweight imaginative sharing between people going about their everyday business' (in press: n.p.).

In such a media ecology, finding ways to enable young people to gain sufficient awareness of and experience in the pleasures of reading print fiction takes on new importance. It may be that shifting some of the print from paper to forms of handheld screen may make a difference. For example, iCUE is a system that enables full books to be downloaded on to a cell phone (Poplak 2006: 6–7) and may offer attractive possibilities to some readers.

My own priority is to enable future generations to enjoy the pleasures of extended reading and to understand the deictic relationship that is unique to the verbal form. I want to be alert to changes in a reader's tactile connections with a text when it shifts from paper to screen, but in extended prose reading many of the physical features of the book format (gutter, margins, page-turns, etc.) are of less significance than they are in a picture book, which is designed as a more singular object. The ability to launch the imagination on a stream of words is the key element for reading extended print, and the vehicle matters rather less. If the mutation of the paper book to a variety of electronic formats means the survival of extended reading, it is a price worth paying.

Chapter 11

Playing the text

Conclusions

One historical moment and its general implications

Literacy has never been a completely fixed set of skills. Kathleen Tyner's list of obsolete technologies ('Tallies, hieroglyphics, kinescopes, viewmasters, 78-rpm record players, and 8-track cassette players' (1998: 18)) is a reminder that literacy is always historically contingent. Literacies are grounded in a complex world of social custom and specific technologies, and change in literacy tools and equipment is not new.

This project took place at a particular historical juncture, at a time when technological change was particularly rapid. To what extent do any findings have generalizable implications for the time, maybe only five years away, when the technologies are so different that this account reads like history?

In recording some of the behaviours of the young readers who participated in this study, I have captured not only the technologies of the late 1990s but also some glimpses of how readers respond to change, a topic that is not simply of local or historical interest. The challenge is to explore what useful general implications can be drawn from one specific and grounded set of examples. I want to begin that exploration in a roundabout way by looking at a possible description of text processing activities.

Playing the text

The word *ecology* is resolutely a noun; I can think of no verbal version of the word. Nevertheless, the concept of *ecology* is a shelter for verbs; it represents an idea whose very force is in dynamism. As I reach the conclusion of this study, I am interested in exploring what verbs of text processing make the liveliest connections with our contemporary textual ecology.

I began this project with a bias towards stretching our use of the word *read* to include the interpretation of other kinds of texts as well, texts that are viewed or interacted with. As I worked with my large data set, the problems with this usage continued to bother me and I often lamented the absence in the English language of an all-purpose and unpretentious word that would cover how we understand and respond to texts in many media.

I have not solved the problem of a verb with the specific meaning of cross-media text processing. However, in the course of working on this project, I have come to recognize that there is, after all, a common word that will make room for a variety of activities, with multifaceted and multimedia connotations. That word is *play*. We use it as a verb to talk about music and games: we play the piano or play tag. As a noun, of course, it is a staged drama. But we can also have a play of light (on water, on a screen) or a play on words. The word has a valid function in many of the ways we talk about the arts; in that sense it is multimodal.

So how does the notion of 'playing the text' serve as a metaphor for some of the interpretive elements held in common across many media?

Playing as pretending or imagining

One of the most common and important meanings of the word 'play' involves some kind of make-believe, the shift to the world of 'as if'. We play house; we play doctors. We may talk about the shift into the 'as if' world to distinguish between fiction and non-fiction. Alternatively, we may use the idea of this shift to distinguish between narrative and non-narrative or exposition. Time after time, the students in this project made the choice to consider the implications of the story *as if* they were stepping inside the fictional universe. The essential step into make-believe, the imaginative leap, took place over and over again, in all the media formats on offer.

Richard J. Gerrig (1993) and Jerome Bruner (1986, 1990) both discuss conditions of fiction, and both emphasize the importance of accepting a world where the future is not known within the world of the text, even though that text is always already concluded before the reader picks it up. Bruner speaks of moving into such a world where the future is still open as 'subjunctivizing reality' (1986: 26) and speaks of it as a way in which 'discourse keeps meaning open or "performable" by the reader' (1986: 26). Gerrig, describing anomalous suspense, suggests that at least some of our ability to suspend the fact that we know the outcome may be predicated on our assumption that every performance is unique (1993: 170). Either of these approaches leads to interesting questions about the 'as if' switch. How do we learn about stepping into a world with an imaginary and still-open future? How do we learn to apply this switch to a new text, or a new format? How do we re-apply it to a text already known, so that we can participate in the subjunctive understandings of the characters inside that world?

Playing as performing

We not only pretend, but we perform our pretending when we play. We play the fool or play the king. The issue of performance is one that is generally undervalued when it comes to many forms of text processing, particularly to reading. Though an oral, choral or dramatic reading may be acknowledged as a performance, silent and/or private reading is far less often viewed through this lens. It is useful in this context to compare and contrast the students' readings of *Shortcut* and of 'Tunnel'. *Shortcut* evoked something much closer to our conventional idea of a 'performance', with voice, gesture, posture and attention all serving the cause of rendering the story coherent. The students were asked to read aloud, to attend to words and graphics, and to coordinate relevant information from both sources even when it appeared on different page openings – and to tie it all in with their general knowledge of the world. They produced a public manifestation of these processes that it is relatively easy to describe as performance. Yet the mental activities were not so very different when they turned to the short story and read it silently. They had to associate information from different parts of the text, and to assemble a useful working repertoire to make sense of the setting and context. They did not point for the benefit of another reader, but they did use their hands to mark places on the page with their pencils. They turned the paper to catch the light most usefully, they held a page in their right hand before flipping it over, and so forth. Small, habitual gestures, but all part of organizing their attention towards the text.

Performing involves some kind of bodily immersion in the activity. In many cases, the relationship between a text and a body is so subtle, so imperceptible and so taken for granted that we overlook it. Is it possible to think of a person sprawled on the sofa with a paperback thriller in hand, or hunched over a joystick making only tiny movements for hours at a stretch, or sagging in front of the television clutching a remote, as in any way *performing* the text under scrutiny? I think we must, even if much of the performance is interior and invisible and the self is the only audience. The body (hands, eyes, balance, breath) is engaged in directing and maintaining attention, often through a set of tiny, subliminal and habitual actions. The connection between body and text may be conventional and taken for granted, but it is real. The mind is hard at work, even if we call it play.

Playing as engaging with the rules of the game

'Play ball', says the umpire, and his words are performative: the time-out is over; the rules of the game are now in force. Actions now have legal consequences within the framework of the rulebook, though few in the 'real' world. Obviously, engagement with a text of any kind entails accepting and working with the rules and conventions in some way or other.

Humans appear to have a profound affinity for conventions of various kinds. Once, as an adult, I tried to remember a game I had played as a child, for the benefit of some neighbourhood children who were bored with all their own games. I could summon up only a fragment of the constituting rules that governed the game of my youth, but, like palaeontologists working with a scrap of bone, the local kids quickly fleshed out a set of living rules that reinvigorated the game in fully playable glory. I don't know if it matched my childhood game completely, but it worked, and it worked because of the children's intuitive respect for conventions and their ingenuity and speed in creating a set of meaningful rules.

And when their newly constituted framework failed them, they were adroit at stepping outside the game to discuss alternatives. Disengaging the rules temporarily in order to play the game better is an activity that comes easily to quite young children.

All these activities are visible in every one of the transcripts. In their engagements with all the different media, the participants set up working conventions, open to change if they did not succeed in making the text operable. They renegotiated readily when it seemed appropriate, stepping outside the interior world of the story but not completely outside the textual world of engagement. They commented explicitly when they did not have enough information about the text to make working assumptions. Part of their judgement on fluency of access was based on whether they could provide or develop an adequate set of conventions to make progress readily.

Playing as strategizing

We talk about game play in strategic terms; we 'play deep', or 'play the line'. We 'play it cool'. The transcripts are simply full of talk about strategy, again across all the media. How to make progress through the set alternatives of the CD-ROM game *My Teacher is an Alien*. How to use the hyperlinks to expand the very terse story of the CD-ROM *Anne of Green Gables*. How on earth to find the crucial stateroom in *Starship Titanic*. How to attend to the sudden and brief appearance of Johnny Depp in the opening scenes of *Benny and Joon*. How to 'read' the map and Pathé News tone of *Casablanca*. What balance to achieve between the diegesis of the film story and the DVD analysis of 'how we made this movie'. How to use the index in *The Way Things Work*. How to make connections between the untied rope and the subsequent adventures of the balloon-riding professor in *Shortcut*. What elements in the story 'Tunnel' to invoke in order to make sense of the strange girls in the culvert. Partly because the students were consistently asked to articulate their approaches to different texts and partly because the activity of strategizing is inherently important, their conversations were full of strategic evaluations.

It is important to remember that one major role of all this strategic analysis is to enable the performance of the story as an engageable if not necessarily believable world. Steven Poole, talking about video games, makes a useful distinction between 'imagining into' and 'imagining how'. Imagining how involves a strategic sense of how to make progress; imagining into enables us to 'understand the rules of the semiotic system presented, and act as if those rules and not the rules of the real world applied to oneself' (2000: 197). He says the game requires us to 'project the active (rather than just the spectating) consciousness into the semiotic realm' (2000: 197). The children who fleshed out the bare bones of my remembered game into a playable version for themselves almost certainly alternated between both activities – working out ways to imagine how so that they could get the game started, but then imagining into the game in order to find out how else to imagine how. It is a complex process to describe in such laborious terms but the activity itself was (there is no other precise word for it) playful.

The strategic necessity to be able to imagine how in order to be able to imagine into is perhaps another way of describing some of the issues of fluency and salience that students manifested in their assessment of the variety of text openings. Imagining how is a prerequisite for imagining into – except that sometimes we imagine into so successfully that imagining how follows without much need for attention. Often we call the narratives that overwhelm us in this way the texts that readers/viewers/players can 'grow' on. Witness Megan, ignoring the hard words on the first page of *The Golden Compass* because her attention was so thoroughly caught, despite her strategic caution about avoiding big words in other books. Most people have experienced something similar in playing a new game, reaching a point where the flow of activity mostly carries them past their inadequate understanding of the finer points of the strategy guide. Most of us know a child who reads way above his or her normal reading level when the topic is of passionate interest. Salience then governs fluency, not the other way around; 'imagining into' leads to 'imagining how'.

Playing as orchestrating

Sometimes we use the word *play* to indicate something more like orchestrating, as in 'play percussion'. The percussion player must produce the drum roll, the cymbal clash and the triangle tinkle in appropriate combinations, a case of managing attention and automatic behaviours to maximize complexity. It is a rare usage for the word *play* perhaps, but it is a crucial connotation for the approach to texts of any kind. We orchestrate many activities for even the simplest form of text interpretation, and we must manage our affairs so that many of these activities can be conducted automatically. The more automatic the procedure, the more invisible; and so much of what we do when we read or watch a movie or play a computer game is unrecognized most of the time.

Some of the judgements made by the students on their way through the collection of texts involved how readily they could move to a state of automaticity. The most visible example of such automatizing in all the tapes and transcripts probably involves the game of *Myst* played by Megan and Angela. Without necessarily gaining a much greater understanding of the game itself, they became more and more adept at moving around the island, retracing their steps and setting out purposefully for particular destinations. Their command of the local environment became automatic, even though their understanding of the nature and purpose of the game remained vague. With their control over negotiation of the local geography requiring less conscious attention, they freed attention to improve their understanding of other elements of the game. Their activity could become more complexly orchestrated, so to speak, because they no longer had to attend directly and consciously to every single element at once.

There are many examples of students realizing the need for orchestrating different kinds of information. Just about everyone, at some stage, consciously noted the necessity to pay attention to information carried in both the words and the pictures of *Shortcut*, rather than just in the words. The tapes show them adjusting their mental focus and also their bodily activities as a result. Students mentioned using cues from both the pictures and the accompanying music in *Casablanca* and *Benny and Joon*. At least some of them learned to use not only the information from the streets of *Virtual Springfield* but also that of the map and compass. Again and again, there is a palpable sense of activities and strands of attention being orchestrated in the cause of a more complete understanding.

Playing as interpreting

Implicit in some connotations of performance is the idea of interpretation; you play the sonata to present your own rendition of its complexities. Interpretation is a major element of all kinds of text processing except the most idle. (Just as a child may *play* idly with her hair, so it is tempting to posit a description, for example, of Madeleine sampling short snatches of movies she has seen before without any real attempt to engage any interpretive attention.) For the most part, however, these students were engaged in at least preliminary interpretive activities in all media. Much interpretation takes place after the encounter with the text is concluded and these students were given few opportunities to finish a text. Nevertheless, we can see their wits flexing, and in the two complete texts, *Shortcut* and 'Tunnel', there is considerable activity at the end of the reading to check any loose ends and sort out an interpretation that allows for balance and pattern as well as specific plot tidiness.

A different study would have evoked different forms of interpretive activity. By and large, either the texts encountered did not tap into any deep anxieties or interests or the students were not given the opportunity to pursue their personal emotional connections in any depth. The emphasis on sampling throughout this project means that we catch only glimpses in the transcripts of those kinds of interpretations that draw on deep personal concerns. But we do see a few examples: Colin tapping into fears about bullying in response to the book *My Teacher is an Alien*; Nasrin musing on the emotional perils of being an orphan as she looked at *Anne of Green Gables*; Jack pondering his own unknown future as he responded to 'Tunnel'. A different selection of texts and a different methodology might have evoked more of such deep connections. Even this very brief list gives some indication of how the individual's own private agenda may set up the warp of an interpretation so that the final texture can be woven using the specifics of the story as weft.

Playing as fooling around

We know what it is to play around with an idea or a suggestion. It is an exploration of possibilities without commitment. We try one option in our minds, mentally extend our understanding of possible outcomes and weigh our views of potential consequences. Free of commitment, we then do exactly the same thing (or something a little different) with an alternative – and maybe another.

Play in this incarnation is a set of trial experiments: what would happen if –? For all its inconsequential appearance, it is also a form of rehearsal, and its application to the activities of text processing is obvious and important. Fluency requires practice and, in many cases of textual interpretation, one goal is fluency to the point of transparency in many elements of the task. Practice can be forced and laborious, but, in most of the cases I recorded, the text tinkering was easy and playful, only turning into something more unpleasant when frustration superseded curiosity.

Providing an environment for safe fooling around does not sound like a grand curricular initiative (or alternatively sounds like a recipe for Internet filters, V-chips and witch-free libraries). Yet the capacity to experiment with texts, to fail sometimes, to try again without recrimination or penalty, and/or to abandon them, is an important part of mastering new media. This is as true for small children learning to decode print as it is for computer experts tackling a new piece of software.

Playing as not working

Playing demands a consequence-reduced zone. Unlike work, play does not have an immediate practical outcome, nor do we expect any direct utility from our activity. In play, we can try things out and work through our feelings about an idea in an arena where the results are often unimportant. Naturally, this opens a zone where we can contemplate very important ideas indeed, simply because the risk is lowered. To say that it is not work does not imply that something is not difficult or that it is not significant. Play can be extremely challenging (Papert's 'hard fun' [Johnston 1999: 12] comes to mind), and its consequences can be profound and life-long.

I believe this element of not-work is highly important to the kind and quality of attention that we pay to such texts. We live in an economy of attention that provides many, many not-work calls on our time and energy, in a surplus of recreational options. It is not surprising that even the youngest of these students could draw on a sophisticated apparatus for marshalling forms of playful attention even in encounters with previously unfamiliar media.

Some implications of playfulness in the processing of texts

This chain of associations evoked by the verb *playing* is neither complete nor definitive. What it offers is a way of looking at the interpretive activities that cross a number of media boundaries.

The prismatic, multifaceted qualities of the concept of *playing* mean that we are already familiar with the idea of this verb shifting meanings as it acquires new subjects and objects and fits into new sentences. Such a protean verb meets the specialized needs of a study that sets out to explore what is common and what is distinctive about the ways in which we approach different kinds of text and media. In most cases, the word has a common usage and we are not stretching things too far by using it in this way: we regularly play music, play a video, play a game. Nevertheless, the phrase *playing the text* is not in ordinary use, and there is no common precedent for speaking of playing a story or playing a reading. Neologism for its own sake is very annoying, but I think there is some value in reconsidering our ideas of reading in light of this concept.

The need for a generic verb for text processing activities is well known. Any such verb carries its own baggage, and we need to think through the connotations of any selection. For example, Robert Yanal has made a different choice, one with its own repercussions:

> Given the various senses employed to engage ourselves with the narrative – we say we *saw* the play, *heard* the ballad, *viewed* the film – there will occasionally be a need for a genus word, and I'll then speak of an audience as *receiving* the narrative, and sometimes of an audience themselves as *receivers*.
>
> (Yanal 1999: 8)

Compared to the relatively passive activity of *receiving*, *playing* is a word that makes much more room for the agency and energy of performers. The idea of playing has a further virtue for this purpose, in that it calls for both internal and external accommodation to the activity: to play involves a commitment of the mind as well as appropriate behaviour of the body, a fruitful concept for considering the activities of text processing. Furthermore, the word *play* makes room for a kind of mental and dispositional 'on-switch' – an active commitment to the engagement – whose importance is sometimes overlooked in ordinary language about different kinds of text processing.

Theories of play and art

Many scholars, of course, have written about the subject of play, both in its free-form 'childish' incarnation and in the more deliberate forms of play that we describe as art. Two philosophers address issues that are particularly pertinent here.

Hans-Georg Gadamer draws an interesting common ingredient of the idea of *play* from such phrases as 'the play of light, the play of the waves, the play of gears or parts of machinery, the interplay of limbs, the play of forces, the play of gnats, even a play on words. In each case', says Gadamer, 'what is intended is to-and-fro movement that is not tied to any goal that would bring it to an end' (1989: 103). The meaning of *play* thus described is a medial one; it happens *between*.

Gadamer, however, is not talking about play happening between players; his focus is on what happens between the player and the game, an intense form of imagining into that is internal rather than social. 'All playing', he says, 'is a being-played. The attraction of a game, the fascination it exerts, consists precisely in the fact that the game masters the players' (1989: 106).

In terms of the medial qualities of play, it seems to me that Gadamer is referring, at least partially, to the elements I have described as present participles. The durational aspects of any narrative text processing involve what is *going on* as the reader/viewer/player moves through the story. The idea that the *going on* is the purpose of the activity is certainly one element of what we value as we process any kind of text; we do not do aesthetic (as opposed to efferent) text processing simply to be at the end (see Rosenblatt 1970).

However, Gadamer's approach to the idea of playing is rather more monolithic than the behaviours I observed among the students in this project. Ironically, he does not seem to make much room for a more playful kind of playing, where the exercise involves medial movement within the playful activity and also movement in and out of the play itself. 'Play fulfills its purpose only if the player loses himself in play', he says, and 'seriousness in playing is necessary to make the play wholly play. Someone who doesn't take the game seriously is a spoilsport' (1989: 102). Yet the variety of engagements demonstrated and/or described by these students involved many variations of non-'serious' playing in Gadamer's terms. I observed many elements of tinkering and toggling that are outside his description. Indeed, often the capacity not to take the play seriously was actually part of the appeal of the kind of play on offer. Madeleine's many reiterations of 'Oh, well, we'll just die and start again' are not exemplars of serious, all-consuming play, nor is the conversation by Tom and Jordan about watching for special effects versus watching for story.

It may be useful to return to Christopher Collins's fascinating description of words in print as 'nouns situated in a void' (1991: 151). Readers themselves, according to Collins, infill much of the background detail from their own experience. I refer to this phrase because I want to adapt it and raise the question of whether Gadamer, in certain ways, is talking about 'present participles situated in a void'. Without specific examples and particular contexts, he describes an idealized version of playing. Such an account is vitally useful, but it can perhaps be more useful if we recognize its schematic qualities. The quality and intensity of engagement during the play itself is important, but it is differently realized on particular occasions. Specific examples of situation and context will not only infill the background of what Gadamer is describing as pure and exclusive engagement, but may actually offer their own counter-examples of how real-life behaviour is not necessarily so pure. What seems more useful is an idea that may perhaps be best described as an ecologically inflected present participle. Some conditions of engagement are contingent even as some are undoubtedly constant.

Gadamer is also interesting on the topic of the comparison between play as in children's make-believe and play as it manifests itself in a work of art: 'All play is potentially a representation for someone. That this possibility is intended is the characteristic feature of art as play. The closed world of play lets down one of its walls, as it were' (1989: 108). In a footnote, Gadamer adds, 'It is precisely the fourth wall of the audience that closes the play world of the *work of art*' (1989: 108). '[O]penness toward the spectator', he continues, 'is part of the closedness of the play. The audience only completes what the play as such is' (1989: 109). The make-believer is essential to the make-belief, whether within the self-run world of a child's game or in the deliberately composed universe of a text-based make-believe where it is the audience who bring the essential make-believing agency to bear.

Mikhail Bakhtin also discusses the boundaries between make-believe and art, but takes a more plural perspective. Like Gadamer, he places the audience as spectator, part of the play but not inside it:

> While children are in the midst of a game, it is real experience for them, something innately experienced, imagined but not given as an image. But play may approach art when an 'actively contemplating' outside spectator begins to admire it. As long as such a spectator watches, we have the kernel of a dramatic aesthetic event. When the spectator leaves, or when he becomes so interested that he joins the game, what Bakhtin in later years would call 'footlights' disappears from the scenario and the aesthetic event returns to the status of play.
>
> (Morson and Emerson 1990: 189)

Bakhtin and Gadamer both posit the spectator as essential to play becoming art, but Bakhtin's spectator is livelier, moving in and out of different relationships with the text, an account that accords more closely with the behaviour of the students in this study, and an account that makes more theoretical room for oscillating behaviours.

A comparable (and highly important) distinction could operate between our regular understanding of *playing a game* (from the inside, with wholehearted commitment to the internal premises of the narrative) and my newer idea of *playing the text*. In this latter case, the element of spectatorship provides the crucial ingredient of outsidership, where not only the premises but also the form and shape of the text are part of what is played. Oscillation between surface and interior is an essential element of such a spectator role. *Receiving* a text, on the other hand, is confined to the outside.

Re-workings and re-playings

One striking phenomenon of our contemporary cultural ecology is the way that many texts are produced in simultaneous cross-media incarnations. Indeed, Frank Zingrone argues that the 'one-medium user is the new illiterate' (2001: 237). The implications for the reading/viewing/playing public are substantial.

In a postmodern ecology of attention, originality may not always be regarded as highly prized. Yet the students in this study were not oblivious to issues of 'which came first', and did not automatically find any re-working of interest simply because it opened a space between one version of a story and another. Many who thoroughly enjoyed the movie of *Men in Black* rejected the computer game. It was clear that the general enthusiasm for the video of *Anne of Green Gables* was based on its merits as a text in its own right; otherwise the students would have been equally enthusiastic about the CD-ROM of the same story, and they were not. At the same time, it is clear that they were open to the charms of the space between texts when the space itself was of interest. The dynamic between the television programme of *The Simpsons* and the CD-ROM of *Virtual Springfield* intrigued some (though not all) of the students and was clearly a factor in their judgement of the computer text. But the opening of such a space, all by itself, was not interesting enough to please them without any further qualification; they had to value the second text on its own terms to take an interest in the space between.

The word *replay* as it is commonly used today and as I have used it in my discussion of deictics involves an identical reproduction of a recorded moment. But I think there is room for a secondary meaning, perhaps signified by a hyphen. To treat an adaptation as a re-*play* of a story can be a useful antidote to a more earnest approach that values slavish fidelity to the original as the main criterion of judgement. Many of the young people I have spoken to in this and other studies treat adaptations in this more playful way, speaking of textual variations and discrepancies as interesting rather than annoying. But, to succeed, the re-played text has to offer its own play value (a common enough phrase but one whose literal meaning is useful in this context).

The production of a new version of a previously published text is commonplace in our culture, and it raises other interesting aesthetic and cultural questions. Some theorists argue that adaptations should be evaluated:

> not in terms of their fidelity, or even . . . in terms of how the cinematic adaptation functions as an autonomous work of art, but rather in terms of how the encounter with a literary source creates a commentary on the narrative process itself.
>
> (Mayne 1988: 6)

The students in this study, moving easily between versions, are quite sophisticated in terms of the 'narrative process itself', not a surprising turn of events if Mayne is right in her analysis. Peter Lunenfeld offers a different perspective on the plurality of versions which these students clearly take for granted. Talking about the potential of hypertext to create a story that is never finished, he goes on to address the issue of changes in the publishing industry and their impact on multiple versions:

> French literary theorist Gerard Genette refers to the 'paratext': the materials and discourses that surround the narrative object. Genette generated his theories from a study of literature and considers the paratext in terms of the publishing industry: cover design, book packaging, publicity materials, and

so on. I would say, however, that the transformation of the publishing industry in the past two decades – the melding of publishers with moviemakers, television producers, and comic book companies, and the development of media conglomerates like Time Warner, Disney/ABC, and Sony – has bloated the paratext to such a point that it is impossible to distinguish between it and the text.

(Lunenfeld 2000: 14)

Using the example of the 1995 film *Johnny Mnemonic*, Lunenfeld talks about the numerous incarnations of this single story (movie, soundtrack, CD-ROM game, merchandise, websites, etc.) that were released simultaneously. He addresses the implications for our cultural life in a world of unfinished works:

The result of such dubious corporate synergy is the blending of the text and the paratext, the pumping out of undifferentiated and unfinished product into the electronically interlinked mediasphere. Final closure of narrative can not occur in such an environment because there is an economic imperative to develop narrative brands: product that can be sold and resold.

(Lunenfeld 2000: 15)

Living in a world of such narrative flux and flexibility, it is not surprising that students played with narrative form in many ways, not simply in dealing with the adaptations. They crossed many kinds of diegetic boundaries with skill and ease. The media formats most unfamiliar to them (the e-book, the CD-ROM picture book, the DVD) caused them to articulate most explicitly how they alternated attention between looking through and looking at the surface presentation of the text, but such shifts (swift and reversible) happened in all of the texts. The narrative of 'Tunnel' became opaque as they failed to find their initial predictions fulfilled, and they paid more attention to the verbal surface in the latter stages of their reading. Their developing perception of *Shortcut* as a kind of game led them to adjust their seating and posture and to attend differently to details of information in print and graphic forms. Their confusion in the initial stages of the computer games led them to scan in an open-ended way for unspecified possibilities, but their demeanour shifted when they perceived a detail that could be processed purposefully within the parameters of a story. The movement back and forth between surface and depth was constant, and seemingly independent of medium.

These students moved back and forth between media, drawing on different experiences to support their text processing activities. Not surprisingly, it is possible to observe that even 'old' media are changing to take account of such an increase in sophistication. Eliza Dresang (1999), in her book *Radical Change: Books for Youth in a Digital Age*, discusses ways in which texts addressed to young people and produced in print on paper are altering. She supplies an enormous list of examples to support her argument that texts are changing as reading changes, and vice versa, the very epitome of an active ecology. Richard Lanham speaks more generally about changing rhetorics in the electronic age, and offers a new definition of rhetoric as 'the economics of human attention-structures' (1994: 227). We are, says Lanham, 'in the midst of a major expansion of the imaginative franchise' (1994: 231), and developing a 'new acculturation of attention' (1994: 235). The plasticity of attention which the students in this study brought to bear on the different texts supplied to them is a feature of a contemporary ecology where an alert flexibility is a hallmark of successful literacies.

An ecology of attention

Reading and viewing and playing are socially framed practices and these social frames are layered. At one level, all the students in this project met each text within the social framework of the project itself. This framing existed as a very specialized and distinctive subset of another set of social frames, those that marked and bounded their daily life in school over the two years of the study. The participants also engaged with the texts within the context of their own social, cultural, economic and political histories, and their own roles as late-twentieth-century Western consumers. At another level, their encounters with the texts varied according to the nature of the engagement established by the nature of the text itself. The ways in which the participants' attention was attracted, directed and sustained were affected by these elements, and undoubtedly by many others.

'Their attention was attracted, directed and sustained' – I hesitated as I wrote this phrase, and of course my grammar checker is not at all happy with that passive rendition of the verbs. I tried to recast the words in a more active mode, but it is not possible to say 'They attracted, directed and sustained their own attention.' The agency of the participants is necessary but not sufficient when it comes to reading or other forms of text processing; the text must, in some way, attract the attention of the reader. Psychologists speak of attention being captured, a word that has an involuntary ring to it, even if subjects subsequently choose to reject or resist the object that has, as we say, caught their eye. The word *stimulus* makes many people uneasy, for good historical reasons, but, no matter how much the response to a text is created by a reader, there is still an essential element of any text being *outside* the reader and having to draw the reader in. As Gadamer says, the playing is a being-played (1989: 106).

There are consequences to this inevitable 'outsideness' of a text. When you look at the mysterious empty dock of *Myst*, for example, there are some conclusions you may not draw: you are not looking at a simulation of a crowded football game, for example. And you may choose not to take an interest in the opening scene, but you probably cannot refuse to hear the waves lapping on the dock. You may (you probably must) set up the warp of your own interpretive concerns, priorities and expectations, but some of the weft you incorporate into your textual fabric comes from the conditions of the text – not simply the content but also the nature of its invitation to your participation.

Other readers or players are also 'outside', and their contributions to the playing of the text come in many ways. Obviously, all text processing is socially governed in the large sense in which conventions are worked out by a kind of implied collective. On a more local and detailed level in this project, it was possible to see social influences at work in more contingent ways. Furthermore, there were examples of social impact at many different stages: before engagement (Jack's friends pressing him to read *The Golden Compass*), during engagement (Madeleine calling on her brother for help when a computer game proved too complicated for her to keep playing on her own) and after engagement as part of the process of establishing coherence (Kyle's quick exchanges with his friends, on the day after a programme aired, to establish the point of obscure *Simpsons* jokes).

The close-up conditions of this study mean that it provides examples of that point of encounter between a specific individual and a particular text. The singularity of any one of these encounters is irrefutable and irreducible. Yet there are generic elements also at work. In a similar way, the deictic shifters 'I' or 'today' can only ever have a complete meaning in each singular interpretation, yet we compose and comprehend sentences containing such words in normal, socially governed, rule-bound ways.

Does the idea of playing the text alter how we view this complex ecology? I believe it may affect certain implicit assumptions.

For example, in terms of play as not-work, one obvious place to consider the idea of playing the text is the English classroom. 'Now we're going to play this new book' is a small change in vocabulary, yet, taken seriously, one with radical potential for altering the framework of many classroom discussions. There are plenty of teachers who already think of reading as a form of deep play ('hard fun', perhaps), yet the notion of reading only as work often triumphs, and many students are the losers as a consequence.

Emphasizing the performance elements of silent reading or movie viewing is another useful bonus of this approach. It is too easy to think of such activity as routine and invisible, with one instance simply reproducing another. A performance involves a singular incarnation that is never identical to a predecessor.

Making allowance for the bodily requirements of playing the text is another helpful fall-out from this discussion. It is possible for people – students seated at their classroom desks, for example – to do a variety of text processing activities all in a condition of identical posture. You can read a printed text, watch a video, check items on a graph, all while stationary in a hard and probably uncomfortable chair with your desk a fixed distance from your eyes. The idea of play, however, does raise serious questions about posture and attention. The concept of *playing* does imply a certain autonomy for the player, even in physical details. In play, conditions of attention are determined by the requirements of whatever is being played and by the decisions of the player. I think we can usefully ask about conditions of attention in many classrooms. Real attention also involves at least a minimal amount of autonomy and cannot be commanded simply through an enforcement of certain postures and physical attitudes.

Perhaps even more importantly, the idea of playing offers a connotation of relative freedom, of not being confined to the tramlines, of negotiating at least some of the terms of engagement. With regard to how we approach texts, this implication has particular importance for teachers, who often imply, whether they mean to or not, that there is a single meaning to a text that is more correct than all the others. Robert Morgan, talking about media education, refers to it as 'a kind of disciplinary unconscious, which posits meanings as simply *there*, immanent in the object of attention, waiting to be "discovered"' (1996: 16). If we say that a text has a certain amount of *play* in how it is interpreted, we are describing exactly the kind of flexibility (constrained but real) that Morgan says is all too often missing in the 'disciplinary unconscious'.

Conditions and constraints of the study

A summary of the findings of this project may realistically deal only with the social and conventional elements of the students' encounters with many different forms of text. While a re-listing of individual experiences might be more truthful to the inexorable plurality of the study, it would hardly be useful at this stage.

Although the students explored texts in a variety of media, there was one element that all the titles had in common: in the final analysis, they were all texts that had already been crafted and closed. Students experienced them differently but in all cases they were aware that somebody else had organized the potentialities and possibilities of their encounters long before they had begun. I stress this point because it is important to recognize that not all the texts these students will be meeting, either today or in the future, fall into this category of being completed by somebody else before the engagement begins. The development of more interactive and open-ended forms of text may represent a major ecological change of our era (for example, see Murray 1997).

Be that as it may, this study did not explore the kinds of open-ended texts where readers are contributors to the ongoing development of the text itself. The students in this project were using their understandings of conventions and protocols to explore texts that were essentially closed before the readers came anywhere near them. All the students were exceedingly familiar with the nature of this kind of text, and clearly drew on a broad range of understandings in order to make sense of new materials and formats as they were presented to them.

Similarly, it is worth noting that I made no attempt to engage the students with texts outside the Western, the familiar or the contemporary. It was a deliberately applied constraint; I was trying to work within the students' likely comfort zone of experience and expertise.

Yet even with this deliberate restriction of the study to materials likely to be similar to texts already known to the students, there were moments when the intuitive leap had to happen for interpretive progress to be made – and sometimes that leap was missing. The role of that *zap* moment when the strands come together and the text begins to take shape is often overlooked, but its absence is crippling.

And more readers and players than we may sometimes acknowledge are wary of being unable to make some necessary connection and of 'failing' in understanding and even in enjoyment.

A Ph.D. student once highlighted this concern to me:

> I know I have, before I start reading a book, in any context . . . some anxiety about being interested in this book. And I always think about that when I start. Okay, when's it going to be that I get it, that I catch on to what's going on? When's it going to be?
>
> (Mackey 1995: 216)

Willingness to take on a new text, familiarity with conventional approaches, an inclination to experiment and/or wait for the text to make itself clearer – all of these textual approaches are necessary but in the final count not sufficient. The reader or viewer or player has to 'get it' – to make the text work as a whole. And I suspect that no amount of outside observation and analysis is ever going to completely disentangle the mystery of that moment.

Conclusions

A recapitulation of the strands that have woven through this book leads to a description of some general patterns of text processing behaviour. In meeting a text for the first time, the students appeared to apply a measure that explored the balance between issues of personal salience and questions of fluency of access. In all of their engagements with different texts, they oscillated readily between 'looking through' the text to get into the meat of the story and 'looking at' the text to explore the way it worked. Furthermore, they moved easily among diegetic levels, including an extradiegetic zone where they could discuss questions of strategy, or investigate elements involved in the making of the story. They drew on conventions of one medium to make sense of another and, where they could not find an easy way to do so, they fell back on a default position of being maximally observant of details in the text while seeking possible categories with some narrative potential. They responded to puzzles and enigmas with as full a strategic arsenal as they could readily muster, yet they also maintained a certain attitude which I can best describe as a necessary readerly passivity in the face of the givens of the text.

Perhaps it is appropriate that the clearest way of summarizing how such activities fit into the broader textual ecology is by means of a metaphor that, while now rather shopworn, is possible only because of our experience with media, in this case film. If we think of a camera focused in close-up on an activity and then gradually panning backwards, it becomes relatively straightforward to picture a complex encounter. In the case of this study, we have the added ingredient that there literally was a camera focused in close-up on at least some of the textual activities, and the question of what that camera did and did not see is a fascinating one.

In extreme close-up then, we are perhaps closest to Gadamer's pure present participle of playing, though elements of that engagement are beyond the purview of any external camera. Extrapolating from the students' words and actions concerning the text in hand, we may consider their decisions about salience and fluency. Salience is in many ways at the heart of any textual encounter; it is probably a deeply personal sense of salience that activates the on-switch of the performance, so to speak.

What the real camera does record in this close-up perspective is an associated materiality of the text. Students engage with the text, in whatever medium, with hands and bodies as well as minds.

Still in the close-up perspective, we can observe many elements of oscillation between 'looking through' and 'looking at' the surface of the text. As we pan our metaphorical camera back to a mid-shot, we can see this oscillation working both between diegetic layers of the text on hand and between alternative forms of the text in different media. In addition, the boundary crossing at work in many of the encounters recorded in this study sometimes operated between the story world and an outer but associated 'zone of influence', often involving strategic considerations or ways of thinking of the text as a construction. On other occasions, the boundary crossing drew in external but related texts. The setup of the study itself did not make a lot of room for more generic intertextual connections, but these were undoubtedly part of the picture as well.

Panning our camera further back again, we can see that such connections among layers of text and among assorted related texts is a strong feature of the contemporary popular culture in which these young people were learning about texts and interpretation. The students developed expertise in particular elements of this culture and shared their knowledge with their friends as part of their normal daily conversations. Yet, as Victor Watson reminds us, this environment is not neutral. He says we:

> need to accept the fact that all meetings between texts and children – whether they take place in quiet libraries, in crowded classrooms, in drama studios, or at screens of one kind or another – in a very real sense take place in a marketplace, within the apparently implacable realities of publishing and marketing economics.
>
> (Watson 2000: 5)

The camera metaphor implies that it is possible to enlarge our perspectives steadily and in a rather linear fashion. But in fact, the market factor feeds back into some of the close-up perspective: part of how the text is addressed to the readers, part of the deictic connection, is often related to the economics of the production of the text itself. Cross-references between different versions of the same story, for example, have an aesthetic impact within the textual encounter itself but they are also driven by a particular market imperative, and many of the conversations recorded in this study demonstrate that the students are aware of both layers.

The cultural and financial materiality of textual engagements is as important an issue as the tactile materiality. It is perhaps easier to see this element at work in those texts we conventionally see as emanating from a commercially motivated apparatus: *Friends*, *The Phantom Menace*, *The Young and the Restless*. But the fact that these students could read a contemporary Canadian short story is also the consequence of a history of deliberate commercial decisions; thirty years ago there was virtually no Canadian publishing for young people.

Aesthetic, commercial and technological issues intertwine in many ways. *Shortcut* is a genuinely successful exploitation of the technological qualities of the bound picture book on paper: the quality of printed images, the aesthetic and intellectual implications of the limits of the page and the binding, the conventions that ensure readers will assume connections between disparate plot elements, a long history that makes many such texts affordably available thus enabling readers to learn how to read them – all these ingredients mesh together. By contrast, *Lulu's Enchanted Book* suffers in some respects by its sheer novelty. The technology of the still and moving image in this particular CD-ROM is cumbersome and clumsy. Commercial distribution of CD-ROMs has never been completely successful, so the texts are more expensive than they should be and correspondingly rarer; thus readers' comfort with their conventions is lower. Such difficulties also ensure that there are fewer examples of success, as even breaking into the market is difficult.

Another vital issue, and one addressed in this study only through the interviews, is the question of agency. These young people make use of texts to foster and present an idea of themselves. The close-up focus on their interpretive efforts could be said to provide access to a rather schematic version of text processing. They were willing to cooperate with me, and in many cases they genuinely enjoyed the texts, but the elements of selection and self-presentation, which are heavily implicated in our private and independent text choices, were severely constrained for them in the context of this study. Their conversation about their own choices of movie, TV programme, book and computer game occupied a different psychological and social framework, one where they are involved in creating a sense of self along with an understanding of genre, skill with convention and so forth.

Tia DeNora talks about the importance of such self-definition in terms of music:

> music is an active ingredient in the organization of self, the shifting of mood, energy level, conduct style, mode of attention and engagement with the world. In none of these examples, however, does music simply *act upon* individuals, like a stimulus. Rather, music's 'effects' come from the ways in which individuals orient to it, how they interpret it and how they place it within their personal musical maps, within the semiotic web of music and extra-musical associations.
>
> (DeNora 2000: 61)

Particularly in the interviews that concluded this study, it is possible to see the Grade 9 students working on terms of orientation, interpretation and personal agency in connection with particular texts; thus we see the *Star Wars* expert or the bashful viewer of a daily soap opera drawing on their understanding of particular texts to create elements of their social identity.

All these issues do not fit comfortably into the image of our camera steadily panning backwards. Nevertheless, if we can return to that metaphor for a moment, I think it still has a few insights to offer. As our camera takes in an ever-widening angle on the encounters with these texts, we can see other elements at work. Students' domestic lives impinged in many ways on how they processed the texts I offered. What kinds of texts and technologies they had domestic opportunities to master certainly affected how they dealt with my selections. What they could do at home, at their friends' houses and at school all mattered. What other kinds of support were on offer at home was also an issue of great significance. Leonard's mother faithfully taping *The Young and the Restless*, Jack's parents in two different cities turning up Jeffrey Archer books for him to read, Janice's family making regular outings to National Hockey League games and Angela's family tracking their hockey-playing cousin on the Internet, Madeleine's little brother sharing his 10-year-old perspective on computer games, the Grade 5 girls all being knowledgeable about *Where in the World is Carmen Sandiego?* because just one of them owned it – this list could go on indefinitely. The conversations emphasized the degree to which Gadamer's pure present participle can actually be observed *only* in extreme close-up, at least when it comes to text. Undiluted make-believe is possible in what we normally understand as children's play; it is possible to play a game with no props apart from the imagination of the participants. Textual play, however, involves the materiality of the text (whether that be book, Internet site, stage play or ballet, television programme, whatever) and therefore some elements of outside agency necessarily impinge on the purity of the engagement. In the case of these young people, many of the material conditions of access to texts depended on their families and friends.

Other background scenarios impinge on textual encounters, depending on where we direct the focus of the camera. The local Alberta curriculum undoubtedly had an impact on these young people and what they understood about the world; so did the textual practices of their school environments (the Young Readers' Choice Award promotion in the elementary school, the daily reading break in the junior high, for example). Friends offered crucial access to alternative tastes as well as particular technologies and texts.

The domestic, economic and ethnic backgrounds of these students are not identical. Nevertheless, they are all accustomed to moving fluently through standard Western texts. I do not think I am stretching things to say that they regard themselves as the implied audience for many of the kinds of texts I gave them, a self-image that incorporates a variety of political and commercial assumptions. Whatever the local details, in general terms they are all part of a North American mainstream audience and regard themselves as full participants in that particular culture, with repertoires that strike them as appropriate to the kinds of tasks I offered. Yet despite this generic 'goodness of fit' between the items of contemporary culture that I offered and these young readers, the details of each individual case also remain singular.

In short, the ecology revealed by the recorded encounters with texts, the diaries and the conversations of the young people that combined to form this study is complex, mobile and determined by innumerable interacting factors. Yet despite its complexity, these students move through it with ease and assurance. They know how to process some kinds of text and they fully understand that literacy in their lifetime also involves developing strategies to deal with completely new forms of text, as well as strategies for directing the scarce resource of their attention.

I said goodbye to these students with great regret. Returning to the transcripts meant reactivating the present participles of our encounters, a fascinating and satisfying activity with its own potential for surprises. Yet even as I work through the records of our meetings, I know these students have already moved on, learned more, enjoyed more, been frustrated by more. The textual ecology within which they function is fluid; so are they.

Afterword: new literacy ecologies of the twenty-first century

It is 2006, and the participants in this study are now aged from 18 to 21. I have not spoken with any of them since 1999, and for the most part in the afterwords that conclude these chapters I have represented their potential development through statistics of their demographic. For this final chapter, I turn instead to a contemporary and local example of play that offers an oblique lens on their generation of media users.

In the spring of 2006, the city of Edmonton collectively engaged in a serious form of play in relation to a major sporting event. Edmonton has an ice hockey team, the Oilers, who compete in the premier North American league, misleadingly named the National Hockey League. During the 1980s, the Oilers were a great team, but since 1990 their championship performance has been very poor. In 2006, however, the Oilers unexpectedly made a terrific showing in the playoffs and came within one game of winning the championship and its coveted trophy, the Stanley Cup. The city of Edmonton was heavily engaged with the team's fortunes in ways that demonstrate many forms of new media at work. Using this example, I will explore the implications of such play, in both its mediated and its unmediated forms, for the young adults that the participants in this study have become in the years since my study ended.

The National Hockey League playoffs involve four best-of-seven series, so that the final winner must take a total of sixteen games over a two-month period between April and June. During that time, as the Oilers progressed much further than anybody had expected into the final round (they played a total of twenty-four playoff games), the city of Edmonton found many ways to spectate, participate and celebrate.

Major sporting events offer a temporary fulcrum for personal and mediated participation in a common playful cause. Indeed, sport regularly plays a significant role in accelerating media change and development (Potter 2005: 328). I am choosing the local example of the Oilers to explore how the generation described in this book has evolved into different kinds of media users, but I could have as easily chosen the World Cup football championship (also played over an extended period during the spring of 2006) as my exemplar, based in any number of international cities. There were many similarities, though the success of the Oilers was unexpected and did not make room for the kinds of serious commercial investment in supporting a team that now attends World Cup participation. The most intense support was local rather than national (though, as other Canadian teams were knocked out of the competition, national interest in Edmonton's fortunes increased). I was in England for part of the World Cup run and saw many substantial and elaborate advertising campaigns focused on the games; such commercial participation was present in Edmonton but in much more local and limited terms.

In using this afterword to explore ways in which mediated play is developing, I will therefore investigate the local example of the Oilers. This tiny case study, drawing on considerable anecdotal evidence, enables me to explore the local literacy ecology in which my participants are growing up; in this section I will discuss how old and new media are implicated in the extended community play of these two months in Edmonton.

At a basic level, of course, it was the team members of the Oilers who actually played; everyone else was a spectator (although both hockey players and fans spoke of the importance of the home crowd as a factor in the games). But the ways in which fans found possibilities for inserting themselves into the ongoing story of team success were interesting comments on the potential of new media to enable outsiders to exert forms of narrative control. Rob Cover, describing new forms of interactivity, presents some of the potential for re-working a given story:

> The interactive and digital nature of computer-mediated communication results in several new tensions in the author–text–audience relationship, predominantly through blurring the line between author and audience, and eroding older technological, policy and conventional models for the 'control' of the text, its narrative sequencing and its distribution.
>
> (Cover 2006: 140)

At one level, the story of the Oilers in 2006 was a very linear one. They progressed from game to game, winning one series after another until they lost Game 7 of the finals. The nature of the conventions of the sport meant that no other procedure was possible. The outcome of every game was unclear until it happened; there was no possibility of sneaking a peek at the end of the story. But fans inserted themselves into this story in a variety of interesting and illuminating ways, subverting and/or playing with some of the 'official' narrative provided by newspapers and television.

The ways in which Edmontonians participated in 'old media' engagement with the hockey were not surprising except in their ubiquity. Even normally uninvolved Edmontonians watched the games, either in person or on television, listening to car radios when forced to go out during game time (honking at each other when the Oilers scored a goal), reading sports commentaries, and responding with alacrity to any casual question along the lines of 'How about those Oilers?' One local newspaper produced a flyer saying 'Go Oilers Go!' and this poster appeared in the windows of shops, homes and cars all over the city. In Edmonton, buses display their route numbers and destinations in moving lights on a front panel of the vehicle; during the playoff that information alternated with the slogan 'Go Oilers go', and similarly the printed receipts at the supermarket exhorted 'Go Oilers' across the bottom. Large numbers of vehicles sported an Oilers flag, and very unlikely-looking people wore Oilers jerseys to work and school, participating in a kind of wearable play (indeed, as the series progressed, the Mayor recommended that civic workers wear their jerseys on the job). Little children set up lemonade stands decked with team flags and signs saying 'Honk for the Oilers!'

So far, it all sounds relatively traditional in terms of the sporting hysteria that occasionally sweeps otherwise rational places. It was, however, intriguing to observe the mediated activities that simply could not have happened the last time the Oilers made any progress in the Stanley Cup playoffs, early in the 1990s; some of them would still have been impossible at the time of my study at the end of the 1990s.

In 2006, even the live action of the home games, played at Rexall Place in Edmonton, was mediated in increasingly sophisticated ways, with the Jumbotron screens used to direct crowd attention, and music selected to appeal to a particular demographic (Duhatschek 2006: R7 – and see Auslander 1999 for interesting observations on the increasingly porous connections between live performance and mediation). For the final series, games played away from home were telecast on the giant screens of the Jumbotron and Rexall Place was packed with fans, in an interesting merger of a live and a mediated experience.

The events of the games and the activities of spectating and celebrating blurred the boundaries between public and private in various interesting ways. For example, the first home game of the third, semi-final series involved a wildly excited Edmonton crowd. Full-throated singing is commonplace in many European sporting events but very rare in Canada, so it was an unusual event when the crowd sang the national anthem so vigorously that the official soloist held his microphone up to the audience after the second line and let them finish it, unaccompanied and with great fervour. The Canadian Broadcasting Corporation telecast the event, and the next day there was much enthusiastic comment in all the regular media outlets. An unidentified Edmonton resident ('Northlands') went further, posting a digital video clip of the CBC coverage to YouTube.com, a web repository for privately submitted videos (http://www.youtube.com/watch?v=meLpuF9UMvk, accessed 26 May 2006). By the end of that week the clip stood at number ten in YouTube's most viewed video list. Between the Tuesday evening when the event occurred and 4 p.m. on the subsequent Friday, 74,219 people watched it, according to the *Edmonton Journal*, where the story made page 3 of the Saturday paper ('Anthem-singing' 2006: A3). As a news item, this incident is of fairly parochial interest, but the complex route by which the parochial became public deserves some attention: the CBC provided licensed coverage, which was then taped and clipped and re-posted elsewhere by a private (probably law-breaking) individual; from the Internet site, it was viewed, downloaded, forwarded by e-mail, and linked into by blogs; and in short order, the press of attention for this posting became a news item in its own right. Furthermore, this mediated event fed back into live behaviour; it became the norm for fans watching the game in sports bars to rise and sing the national anthem along with the televised fans in the stadium, and in the warm spring nights it was possible to hear the singing emanating from many bars at once.

The *Edmonton Journal* probed another public–private boundary in its call to fans:

> Send us pictures of you and your friends cheering on the Oilers – in Rexall Place, in your basements, or wherever you celebrate. We'll run them on our website. The pictures should be in medium-resolution jpeg format or from a cell phone.
>
> (Photo Gallery 2006: C2)

The smoothness of digital transmission blurs many boundaries; a different public venue for private images contributes to the *Journal*'s record of Edmonton events, and fans, in a small-scale, personal way, become part of the story. The technical specifications are assumed to require no further explication, which suggests that the implied reader is comfortable with digital images and their transportation.

At the same time, away from public view, different forms of digital celebration sprang up all over the city. Normal computer use, for example, was rendered playful in a variety of ways: from Oilers screen-savers to messaging exchanges (a relative of mine in a different city said she could no longer identify who was online to chat from Edmonton since they all changed their names to screen monikers such as 'Woo-hoo!', 'Go Oil' and the like). List-serv participation, e-mail commentary, discussion board postings, all took a distinct turn towards analysing the games, the coaching decisions and many other hockey-related topics. Many keen fans read both the local papers (often online) and their favourite hockey blogs and discussion sites with equal attention – and then wrote their own opinions for others to consider and respond to.

Mobile phones were also hauled into the service of playfulness in a variety of ways. Each stage of success was celebrated in street parties on Whyte Avenue in Edmonton, and those physically in attendance, both at the games themselves and at these parties, used their cellphones to communicate the atmosphere to those elsewhere through audio and photo connections. Commentaries, still photos and videos of both the games and the street parties were posted on discussion boards, blogs, and sites such as flickr.com, YouTube.com and MySpace.com. In a variety of venues, spectators became participants and analysts who commented on and sometimes contested team strategy and performance, media coverage, police strategies for the street parties, and other fans.

The computer also expanded forms of access to the games. Online radio supplied live commentary to a much broader audience than is reached by the local radio stations, and team websites supplied live shift-by-shift updates to ongoing written game descriptions. Some fans subscribed to a commercial game update service direct to their cellphone. Others did it the 'home-spun' way if they were obliged to be at work or in class during game time: I heard several accounts of people in such circumstances who had friends text them updates, with the phone ring set to vibrate silently when something significant happened. The most extreme case of redirecting game data that I am aware of involved a group of people in their 20s, several of whom lived out of town and did not have television access to one of the games. In this example, a sympathetic relative set up a web-cam in front of the television screen in Edmonton and streamed the game through Messenger to the recipient's computer; a VoIP telephone connection supplied the audio commentary.

Clearly, at one level, all this exaggerated response represented preposterous overkill and a waste of time, energy and some money in a phenomenon of modest historical importance. But there was a broadspread collective agreement in Edmonton to behave 'as if' the Stanley Cup championship really mattered, and this social accord meant that in many significant ways it did. The new immigrant to Edmonton who told me how much it meant to him to participate on equal terms as a 'local' in such a civic event would probably argue that the consequences were substantive if intangible. Yet the 'as if' quality was an important part of the whole event; it was clearly a *game* that the city took part in. Given the short-term pressure cooker effect of the playoff arrangements, the people of Edmonton collectively agreed to abandon some components of reasonable life for a short period of time. This collective decision was not completely tacit; there was much explicit discussion of 'rules of the game' involving questions such as the following: With what degree of force should the police maintain social order at the post-game street parties? What were the rights of the residents and businesses on Whyte Avenue, where the most intense partying took place? Should limits be set on the selling of alcohol, both at the game and elsewhere? (Such explicit setting of limits was also part of the conversation surrounding World Cup activities in England, where an arrangement to show game coverage on giant screens in city squares ran into problems with crowd violence and police crackdowns [Morris and Gibson 2006: 3]; civic forms of play do invite articulation of agreed boundaries.)

As an example of intensely situated and mediated play, the Edmonton celebrations offer many instructive glimpses of how broadcast and digital features may change and broaden the way we engage with what Bruner calls the 'subjunctive' (1986: 26). They also serve as a reminder that real life differs from mediated life in unpredictable and messy ways. The street parties were always at risk of being taken over by drunkards whose silly and occasionally dangerous antics were not always containable by unspoken social agreements. Such threats, of course, provided an edge to the party that is communicated in some of the amateur videos, and offered thrills to some participants, fear and annoyance to others.

The playoffs represented a short time frame of live action and genuine suspense. Those who were otherwise occupied during the games had the option of video-taping the game and watching it later, but knowing the outcome at the same time as everybody else seemed to be an important feature of taking part for many people. The social and technological arrangements made to facilitate live updating from the games and from the parties were a marker of a generation confident that digital facilities are there to serve them, in their play as well as in their more serious endeavours.

Such short-term, intense, broadly shared playfulness offers a useful measure of potential changes in how we agree to play together, even in the short interval since the end of the 1990s. One significant development was the portability of media content and the resulting impact on spectators' agency. People watching the game were not confined exclusively to a role of reception; those in actual attendance sent images and sounds and texted words out of the arena; those in front of the television set or the multimedia computer recorded the game in a variety of ways and forwarded their recordings to a variety of destinations (even if some methodologies were less legal than others).

The portability of media is not new – the car radio undoubtedly played an important role in the civic 'game' of following the Oilers in the glory days of the 1980s, and the Oilers jersey has been a portable prompt to the imagination for decades. But the current context offered many more ways for online and offline life to permeate each other (see Leander and McKim 2003 for a discussion of the implications of such permeation) and made it possible both for participation in the 'live action' component of the games to be widespread and for spectators to mutate into producers.

The potential for play in being an Oilers fan who lives elsewhere than Edmonton should now logically be unlimited – and, indeed, our local paper featured a story about fans in Grise Fiord, Canada's northernmost community: 'Hockey is still so popular that hunters on the sea ice 100 kilometres from town keep track of the games' (Vanderklippe 2006: A20). And yet, in this virtual space of games ascribed with an arbitrarily imposed significance, the quality of physically being in Edmonton still held sway. It was the physical sense of being present at the games that was flashed out from the mobile phones in attendance; similarly, the sights and sounds of the street parties were recorded and transmitted as evidence of authentic bodily presence at an important event. The portability of the newest media allowed for different kinds of portal to the specific experiences of Edmonton in 2006 (see Ito et al. 2005 for further perspectives on the significance of porta-bility).

In a similar way, many people travelled to Germany for the World Cup, even though they had no prospect of obtaining tickets for even a single game. In Canada, in fact, we were constantly reminded throughout the Stanley Cup playoffs of the excitement of this version of virtual participation, through an advertisement that incessantly touted the thrill of going to Germany with your friends in order to watch the football on your cellphone feeds. This playful combination of physical presence at the *event* yet mediated attendance at the actual *game* is a complex phenomenon, which deserves more attention than I can pay it in these pages.

A protracted sporting event such as the one I describe here undoubtedly exaggerates the usual level of social commitment to playfulness, and it therefore supplies a larger-than-daily-life perspective on ways in which members of our society are registering physical presence and mediated presence. The porousness of the numerous different ways in which we now may be 'present to play' was demonstrated in close-up in this single example, and it is rare for so many of a community to participate simultaneously in such a large-scale and ongoing game. But as a hint of where our sense of play may be taking us, this scenario offers some instructive insights.

We have always been able to choose to play; now we can choose to include many more players, at least vicariously. For decades, via our broadcast media, we have more often been at the reception end of other people's play; the protean nature of digital engagement means we can now participate with a greater sense of personal connection in productive as well as receptive forms of mediated play. The consequences of these technological changes include an altered sense of agency, and differential portals for personal connection to playful events. The television picture is probably more informative, and is available for repurposing after the event in new ways, but the image from the cellphone of a friend actually present in the stadium offers a different kind of immediacy – and it is no coincidence that YouTube displayed amateur as well as professional video of that crowd at Rexall Place singing the national anthem in Game 3 of the third series (http://www.youtube.com/watch?v=WF0f4vts7s0&search=national%20anthem%20edmonton%20anaheim, accessed 30 May 2006). It is probably not even surprising that YouTube also posted video images of patrons at a Whyte Avenue bar singing the national anthem along with the televised crowd at the stadium (http://youtube.com/watch?v=94SP_H4ScoE&search=national%20anthem%20whyte%20avenue, accessed 29 June 2006). In this amateur video, the CBC images on the giant screens of the bar are visible over the shoulders of the patrons as they stand to sing; the sense of *mise en abyme* is overwhelming.

The street parties that followed the biggest games represented another kind of play. Those celebrating on Whyte Avenue in Edmonton were conscious that their parties were one component of the media coverage. Young women flashed their breasts in imitation of similar celebrations in the neighbouring city of Calgary two years ago, which in their turn may well have been modelled on television versions of carnival licence. A large and good-humoured game of street hockey, which was played up and down Whyte Avenue as part of the celebrations one night, may or may not have been a re-working of a very well-known and popular Canadian beer commercial – and, of course, the advertisement itself was a remediated version of a genuine phenomenon. The pick-up street hockey game is part of Canada's social fabric (though even such a low-key and amateur event may be mutating in subtle and mediated ways; during May 2006, I passed one such street game in which a pre-teen player listened to his iPod headphones as he played).

The two months of the playoff season in Edmonton had a surreal quality to them. To talk of civic bonding seems pretentious but there was certainly a joyous and playful feeling in the city. Complete strangers talked and laughed together. The car banners and bus signs signalled a kind of ongoing party. A whole community, inclusive of the very old and the very young, focused on a set of playful events with an uncertain outcome. John T. Caldwell offers a description that sums up many of the qualities of this unusual period in Edmonton, talking about:

> liminal spaces and ceremonial rituals intended to exist outside of everyday time, to suspend normal expectations of cause and effect, and to exist between past and future. This subjunctive rather than indicative temporal register allows communities extended, ritualistic opportunities for cooperative what-if reflections on change and identity.
>
> (Caldwell 2006: 106–7)

Rather than talking about an event imbued with at least some social spontaneity, however, Caldwell here is actually describing the rituals of a television 'pitch session', in which potential producers attempt to sell networks and advertisers on the virtues of their proposed programming. The exact fit of his description raises interesting questions about the degree to which Edmonton's delighted young people were partying spontaneously and the degree to which they were manifesting an internalized understanding of the media conventions for such celebrating. The unclear origins of the giant street hockey game marked one such zone of ontological ambiguity. The idea that the street parties also involved certain kinds of performance was reinforced by local anecdotes of young men who yelled 'Show us yer tits!' to the young women in the street but stopped and apologized punctiliously if they actually jostled one of them.

It is possible that every one of the participants in this study was present at an Oilers event during the two months between April and June of 2006; equally it is possible that they all ignored every bit of it. There is no way for me to know. What is clear is that this temporary phenomenon offers one window on the kinds of media users that they and their contemporaries are becoming. We saw fluid forms of oscillation between live actions and the mediated recording and transmitting of those actions to a broader public – by means of various digital recording devices, through personal cellphone communication and via websites dedicated to social broadcasting. This movement between responding and producing is one marker of the kinds of change that will become ever more commonplace as access becomes faster and equipment becomes more portable. The collective experience of the Oilers' 2006 championship run had their twenty-four playoff games at its core, but the power to shape mediated versions of that experience was far more broadly distributed than ever before.

As years pass and the physical apparatus of technology shrinks, a number of borders will continue to mutate: the line between physical and virtual presence, the distinction between synchronous and asynchronous participation, the categories of reception and production, the characteristics of being at work (with live game results vibrating in your pocket) and being off duty, the idea of being in control as an active agent and being a passive recipient. The border between being swept up in the event and developing some sense of critical proportion remains an important line of demarcation, but not one that was much discussed by hockey lovers new and old during the heat of the moment.

The participants in this study demonstrated attitudes of great flexibility in coming to terms with old and new media. Their peers, seen under the microscope of the Oilers' playoff run a few years later, manifested their comfort with different levels of technological flexibility in many ways. Such adaptability will stand them all in good stead as they move through a world where boundaries are in constant fluctuation and where the concept of play takes many shapes. Finding ways to develop critical perspectives in the heart of such play remains the challenge for us all.

References

'Anthem-singing Fans a Hit on the Web' (2006) *Edmonton Journal*, 27 May, A3.

Auslander, P. (1999) *Liveness: Performance in a Mediatized Culture*, London: Routledge.

Bakhtin, M.M. (1988) *The Dialogic Imagination: Four Essays*, trans. M. Holquist, ed. C. Emerson and M. Holquist, University of Texas Press Slavic Series, Austin, TX: University of Texas Press.

Baldick, C. (1990) *The Concise Oxford Dictionary of Literary Terms*, Oxford: Oxford University Press.

Barton, D. and Hamilton, M. (1998) *Local Literacies: Reading and Writing in One Community*, London: Routledge.

Beller, J.L. (1994) 'Cinema, Capital of the Twentieth Century', *Postmodern Culture*, 4(3), http://muse.jhu.edu/journals/postmodern_culture/v0004/4.3beller.html.

Blodgett, E.D. (1997) *Apostrophes II: Through You I*, Edmonton, AB: University of Alberta Press.

Bloom, R. (2004) 'Hooked on Your Cell? You Must Be Canadian', *Globe and Mail*, 23 November, B9.

Bolter, J.D. and Grusin, R. (1999) *Remediation: Understanding New Media*, Cambridge, MA: MIT Press.

Booth, W.C. (1988) *The Company We Keep: An Ethics of Fiction*, Berkeley, CA: University of California Press.

Boynton, S. (2002) *Philadelphia Chickens*, lyrics and drawings by Sandra Boynton, music by Sandra Boynton and Michael Ford, New York: Workman Publishing.

Bresnick, A. (1999) 'Surprises of the Soul', review of P. Fisher, *Wonder, the Rainbow, and the Aesthetics of Rare Experiences*, *Times Literary Supplement*, 24 December, 9.

Brody, F. (2000) 'The Medium is the Memory', in P. Lunenfeld (ed.), *The Digital Dialectic: New Essays on New Media*, Cambridge, MA: MIT Press.

Bruner, J. (1986) *Actual Minds, Possible Worlds*, Cambridge, MA: Harvard University Press.

—— (1990) *Acts of Meaning*, Cambridge, MA: Harvard University Press.

Caldwell, J.T. (2006) 'Critical Industrial Practice: Branding, Repurposing, and the Migratory Patterns of Industrial Texts', *Television and New Media*, 7(2), May, 99–134.

Coleman, M. (2003) *Playback: From the Victrola to MP3, 100 Years of Music, Machines, and Money*, Cambridge, MA: Da Capo.

Collins, C. (1991) *The Poetics of the Mind's Eye: Literature and the Psychology of Imagination*, Philadelphia, PA: University of Pennsylvania Press.

Cover, R. (2006) 'Audience Inter/active', *New Media and Society*, 18(1), 139–58.

Crago, H. (1982) 'The Readers in the Reader: An Experiment in Personal Response and Literary Criticism', *Signal*, 39, 172–82.

Damasio, A. (1999) *The Feeling of What Happens: Body and Emotion in the Making of Consciousness*, New York: Harcourt Brace.

Damsell, K. (2003) 'DVDs a Hit in Canada, especially among Gen Y', *Globe and Mail*, 9 April, B4.

de Kerckhove, D. (1997) *Connected Intelligence: The Arrival of the Web Society*, Toronto: Somerville House.

DeNora, T. (2000) *Music in Everyday Life*, Cambridge: Cambridge University Press.

'Did You Know?' (2000) *Edmonton Journal*, 30 May, B1.

Dobson, T. (2001) 'Reading Literary Hypertext', Ph.D. thesis, University of Alberta.

Dobson, T., Johnston, I. and Mackey, M. (1999) 'Mocking up Moulthrop: Reading/ Performing Literary Hypertext', paper presented at the American Educational Research Association, Montreal, Quebec, April.

Douglas, S.J. (1999) *Listening In: Radio and the American Imagination from Amos 'n' Andy and Edward R. Murrow to Wolfman Jack and Howard Stern*, New York: Times Books/Random House.

Downes, L. (1998) *Unleashing the Killer App*, Cambridge, MA: Harvard Business Review.

Dresang, E.T. (1999) *Radical Change: Books for Youth in a Digital Age*, New York: H.W. Wilson.

Duhatschek, E. (2006) 'Oilers Reaching Out to New Generations of Fans', *Globe and Mail*, 25 May, R7.

Ellis, S. (1996) *Back of Beyond*, Toronto: Groundwood-Douglas and McIntyre.

Ferguson, S. (2000) 'The Wired Teen', *Maclean's*, 29 May, 38–40.

Fiske, J. (1994) *Media Matters: Everyday Culture and Political Change*, Minneapolis, MN: University of Minnesota Press.

Gadamer, H.-G. (1989) *Truth and Method*, 2nd edn, trans. J. Weinsheimer and D. Marshall, London: Sheed & Ward.

Geirland, J. and Sonesh-Kedar, E. (1999) *Digital Babylon: How the Geeks, the Suits and the Ponytails Fought to Bring Hollywood to the Internet*, New York: Arcade Publishing.

Gelernter, D. (1994) *The Muse in the Machine: Computers and Creative Thought*, London: Fourth Estate.

Genette, G. (1986) *Narrative Discourse*, trans. J.E. Lewin, Oxford: Basil Blackwell.

Gerrig, R.J. (1993) *Experiencing Narrative Worlds: On the Psychological Activities of Reading*, New Haven, CT: Westview Press.

Gibson, O. and Day, J. (2006) 'Radio Gaga', *MediaGuardian*, 12 June, 1–2.

Goldman, L.R. (1998) 'Child's Play: Myth, Mimesis and Make-believe', in B. Bendern, J. Gledhill and B. Kapferer (eds), *Explorations in Anthropology*, Oxford: Berg.

Grodal, T. (1999) *Moving Pictures: A New Theory of Film Genres, Feelings, and Cognition*, Oxford: Clarendon and Oxford University Press.

Harding, J. (2000) 'The Net's No Threat to Radio', *Marketing*, 10 July, 11.

Hayles, N.K. (2000) 'The Condition of Virtuality', in P. Lunenfeld (ed.), *The Digital Divide: New Essays on New Media*, Cambridge, MA: MIT Press.

Heath, S.B. (2000) 'Seeing Our Way into Learning', *Cambridge Journal of Education*, 30, 121–32.

Henighan, T. (1999) 'Slow Down for a While to Read This', review of J. Gleick, *Faster: The Acceleration of Just About Everything*, *Edmonton Journal*, 26 December, E15.

Hoban, R. (1974) *How Tom Beat Captain Najork and his Hired Sportsmen*, London: Jonathan Cape.

Iser, W. (1978) *The Act of Reading: A Theory of Aesthetic Response*, Baltimore, MD: Johns Hopkins University Press.

Ito, M. (in press) 'Technologies of the Childhood Imagination: Yugioh, Media Mixes, and Everyday Cultural Production', in J. Karaganix and N. Jeremijenko (eds), *Structures of Participation in Digital Culture*, Durham, NC: Duke University Press.

Ito, M., Okabe, D. and Matsuda, M. (eds) (2005) *Personal, Portable, Pedestrian: Mobile Phones in Japanese Life*, Cambridge, MA: MIT Press.

James, R. (1999) 'Navigating CD-ROMs: An Exploration of Children Reading Interactive Narratives', *Children's Literature in Education*, 30, March, 47–63.

Johnston, C. (1999) 'Children Need to Have Hard Fun', *Times Educational Supplement*, 3 September, 12.

LaBerge, D. and Samuels, S.J. (1985) 'Toward a Theory of Automatic Information Processing in Reading', in H. Singer and R.B. Ruddell (eds), *Theoretical Models and Processes of Reading*, 3rd edn, Newark, DE: International Reading Association.

Lanham, R.A. (1994) *The Electronic Word: Democracy, Technology, and the Arts*, Chicago: University of Chicago Press.

Leander, K.M. and McKim, K.K. (2003) 'Tracing the Everyday "Sitings" of Adolescents on the Internet: A Strategic Adaptation of Ethnography across Online and Offline Spaces', *Education, Communication and Information*, 3(2), July, 211–40.

Lee, D. (1998) *Body Music*, Toronto: Anansi.

Lenhart, A., Madden, M. and Hitlin, P. (2005) *Teens and Technology*, Washington, DC: Pew Internet and American Life Project.

Liu, J.S. (2002) *Yellow Umbrella*, music by Dong Il Sheen, La Jolla, CA: Kane/Miller.

Livingstone, S. (1998) *Making Sense of Television: The Psychology of Audience Interpretation*, 2nd edn, London: Routledge.

Livingstone, S. and Bober, M. (2005) *UK Children Go Online: Final Report of Key Project Findings*, London: Economic and Social Research Council.

Logan, G.D. and Compton, B.J. (1998) 'Attention and Automaticity', in R.D. Wright (ed.), *Visual Attention*, New York: Oxford University Press.

Luke, C. (1998) 'Pedagogy and Authority: Lessons from Feminist and Cultural Studies, Postmodernism and Feminist Pedagogy', in D. Buckingham (ed.), *Teaching Popular Culture: Beyond Radical Pedagogy*, London: UCL Press.

Lunenfeld, P. (2000) 'Unfinished Business', in P. Lunenfeld (ed.), *The Digital Dialectic: New Essays on New Media*, Cambridge, MA: MIT Press.

McCourt, T. and Burkart, P. (2003) 'When Creators, Corporations and Consumers Collide: Napster and the Development of On-line Music Distribution', *Media, Culture and Society*, 25, 333–50.

McCoy, H. (2006) 'Canadians Lead the Way with Unauthorized Downloads of Music', *Edmonton Journal*, 5 January, C4.

McHardie, D. (2000) 'Web-surfing Teens Turn off the TV', *Globe and Mail*, 24 May, A1, A5.

McKeen, S. (1999) 'Beyond the Pages', *Edmonton Journal*, 24 September, C1.

Mackey, M. (1995) 'Imagining with Words: The Temporal Processes of Reading Fiction', Ph.D. thesis, University of Alberta.

—— (1997) 'Good-enough Reading: Momentum and Accuracy in the Reading of Complex Fiction', *Research in the Teaching of English*, 31, 428–58.

—— (2006) 'Serial Monogamy: Extended Fictions and the Television Revolution', *Children's Literature in Education: An International Quarterly*, 37(2), Online First: http://www.springerlink.com/(nawd0d45j1jjai45reqvz5iq)/app/home/contribution.asp?re ferrer=parent&backto=issue,5,5;journal,1,139;linkingpublicationresults,1:104754,1.

Mackey, M. and McClay, J.K. (2000) 'Graphic Routes to Electronic Literacy: Polysemy and Picture Books', *Changing English*, 7, 191–201.

Mandel, C. (1998) 'Taking a Reading on Paperless Books', *Globe and Mail*, 8 August, C1, C10.

Manguel, A. (1996) *A History of Reading*, Toronto: Alfred A. Knopf.

Mann, C.C. (2000) 'The Joy of Text', *Yahoo Internet Life*, June, 115–20.

Mayne, J. (1988) *Private Novels, Public Films*, Athens, GA: University of Georgia Press.

Mechner, J. (2006) 'The Hollywood Trap', *Wired*, 14(04), April, 145.

Media Awareness Network (2005) *Young Canadians in a Wired World, Phase II: Student Survey*, November, Ottawa: Industry Canada.

Meek, M. (1988) *How Texts Teach What Readers Learn*, Stroud: Thimble Press.

Morgan, R. (1996) 'PanTextualism, Everyday Life and Media Education', *Continuum*, 9, 14–34.

Morris, S. and Gibson, O. (2006) 'Blow to BBC Image as Liverpool and London Pull the Plug on Big Screens', *Guardian*, 13 June, 3.

Morson, G.S. and Emerson, C. (1990) *Mikhail Bakhtin: Creation of a Prosaics*, Stanford, CA: Stanford University Press.

Murray, J.H. (1997) *Hamlet on the Holodeck: The Future of Narrative in Cyberspace*, New York: Free Press.

—— (2005) 'The Last Word on Ludology v Narratology in Game Studies', Preface to Keynote Address, Digital Games Research Association, Vancouver, BC.

Nardi, B.A. and O'Day, V.L. (1999) *Information Ecologies: Using Technology with Heart*, Cambridge, MA: MIT Press.

New London Group (1996) 'A Pedagogy of Multiliteracies: Designing Social Futures', *Harvard Educational Review*, 66, 60–91.

O'Brien, G. (1999) 'Rock of Ages', review of J. Miller, *Flowers in the Dustbin: The Rise of Rock and Roll, 1947–1977*, *New York Review of Books*, XLVI(20), 16 December, 40–6.

Oxford Guide to the English Language (1984) London: Guild Publishing.

Palmer, J. (1991) *Potboilers: Methods, Concepts and Case Studies in Popular Fiction*, London: Routledge.

Partridge, J. (2005) 'Canada Greatly Lags U.S. in Wireless Penetration', *Globe and Mail*, 5 October, B3.

'Photo Gallery' (2006) *Edmonton Journal*, 27 May, C2.

Plowman, L. (1996a) 'Narrative, Interactivity and the Secret World of Multimedia', *English and Media Magazine*, 35, 44–8.

—— (1996b) 'Narrative, Linearity and Interactivity: Making Sense of Interactive Multimedia', *British Journal of Educational Technology*, 27, 92–105.

Poole, S. (2000) *Trigger Happy: The Inner Life of Videogames*, London: Fourth Estate.

Poplak, C. (2006) 'Fiction Publishing in the 21st Century', *Books for Keeps*, 158, May, 6–7.

Potter, W.J. (2005) *Media Literacy*, 3rd edn, Thousand Oaks, CA: Sage.

Powers, A. (1999) *Living with Books*, San Francisco: Soma.

Pullman, P. (2000) *A Look at the Kids Book Market*, http://www.independent.co.uk/Boyd_Tonkin/weekinkidsbooks150400.shtm (accessed 15 April 2000).

Rabinowitz, P.J. (1987) *Before Reading: Narrative Conventions and the Politics of Interpretation*, Ithaca, NY: Cornell University Press.

Radway, J. (1994) 'Beyond Mary Bailey and Old Maid Librarians: Reimagining Readers and Rethinking Reading', *Journal of Education for Library and Information Sciences*, Fall, 275–96.

Renzetti, E. (1998) 'Literary Publishing Gets Caught Up in the Net', *Globe and Mail*, 14 February, C8.

Robeck, M.C. and Wallace, R.R. (1990) *The Psychology of Reading: An Interdisciplinary Approach*, 2nd edn, Hillsdale, NJ: Lawrence Erlbaum Associates.

Rosenblatt, L.M. (1970 [1938]) *Literature as Exploration*, London: Heinemann.

—— (1994) *The Reader, the Text, the Poem: The Transactional Theory of the Literary Work*, Carbondale, IL: Southern Illinois University Press.

Rushkoff, D. (1996) *Media Virus!: Hidden Agendas in Popular Culture*, New York: Ballantine Books.

Sainsbury, L. (2000) 'Tales from The Mouse House: Playing with Reading on CD-ROM', in E. Bearne and V. Watson (eds), *Where Texts and Children Meet*, London: Routledge.

Savan, L. (1994) *The Sponsored Life: Ads, TV, and American Culture*, Philadelphia, PA: Temple University Press.

Scarry, E. (1999) *Dreaming by the Book*, New York: Farrar, Straus & Giroux.

Seiter, E. (1999) *Television and New Media Audiences*, Oxford Television Studies, Oxford: Clarendon Press.

—— (2004) 'The Internet Playground', in J. Goldstein, D. Buckingham and G. Brougere (eds), *Toys, Games, and Media*, Mahwah, NJ: Lawrence Erlbaum Associates.

Silberman, S. (1998) 'Ex Libris: The Joys of Curling Up with a Good Digital Reading Device', *Wired*, 6, 98–104.

Sipe, L.R. (1998) 'Individual Literary Response Styles of First and Second Graders', *National Reading Conference Yearbook*, 47, 76–89.

Smith, R. (2000) 'Russell Smith', *Globe and Mail*, 8 January, R4.

—— (2005) 'Stern's Shirt Signals Radio's Decline', *Globe and Mail*, 8 December, R1, R4.

Statistics Canada (2005) 'Radio Listening', 8 July, http://www.statcan.ca/Daily/English/050708/d050708b.htm.

Tellegen, S. and Frankhuisen, J. (1999) 'Lost in a Book or Absorbed by Computer Games: Some Results from an Empirical Exploration', paper presented at the Children's Literature Association, Calgary, Alberta, July.

Tschichold, J. (1991) *The Form of the Book: Essays on the Morality of Good Design*, trans. H. Hadeler, ed. R. Bringhurst, Washington, DC: Hartley and Marks.

Turkle, S. (1995) *Life on the Screen: Identity in the Age of the Internet*, New York: Simon & Schuster.

Tyner, K. (1998) *Literacy in a Digital World: Teaching and Learning in the Age of Information*, Mahwah, NJ: Lawrence Erlbaum Associates.

Vanderbilt, T. (1997) 'The Advertised Life', in T. Frank and M. Weiland (eds), *Commodify your Dissent: Salvos from* The Baffler, New York: W.W. Norton.

Vanderklippe, N. (2006) 'Oilers Mania Grips North', *Edmonton Journal*, 19 May, A1, A20.

Watson, V. (2000) 'Introduction: Children's Literature is Dead: Long Live Children's Reading', in E. Bearne and V. Watson (eds), *Where Texts and Children Meet*, London: Routledge.

Williams, R. (1983) *Writing in Society*, London: Verso.

Wilson, F.R. (1998) *The Hand: How Its Use Shapes the Brain, Language, and Human Culture*, New York: Pantheon Books.

Wilson, P. (2005) 'Growing Number of Cellphone Users are Letting their Fingers Do the Talking', *Edmonton Journal*, 26 March, B1.

Yanal, R.J. (1999) *Paradoxes of Emotion and Fiction*, University Park, PA: Pennsylvania State University Press.

Zingrone, F. (2001) *The Media Symplex: At the Edge of Meaning in the Age of Chaos*, Toronto: Stoddart.

Index